Education in Political Sci

This pioneering volume is devoted to the analysis of education from the perspective of political science, applying the full range of the discipline's analytical perspectives and methodological tools.

The contributions demonstrate how education policy can be explored systematically from a variety of political science perspectives: comparative politics, public policy analysis and public administration, international relations, and political theory. By applying a governance perspective on education policy, the authors explore the changing institutional settings, new actors' constellations, horizontal modes of interaction and public–private regulatory mechanisms with respect to the role of the state in this policy field. The volume deals with questions that are not merely concerned with the content or outcomes of education, but it explicitly takes a political science view on how education politics work. Including country case studies from the Americas and across Europe, institutional analyses of education policy in the EU and the WTO/GATS as well as normative reflections on the topic, the volume provides a grand overview on the diversity of issues in education policy. Dealing with a so far neglected field of policy, this book provides a comprehensive and accessible analysis of a rapidly changing topic.

Education in Political Science will be of interest to scholars and students of political science, education, sociology and economics.

Anja P. Jakobi is a Senior Researcher at the University of Bremen, Germany. **Kerstin Martens** is an Assistant Professor of International Relations at the University of Bremen, Germany. **Klaus Dieter Wolf** is a Professor of Political Science, Darmstadt University of Technology, Germany.

Routledge/ECPR studies in European political science
Edited by Thomas Poguntke
Ruhr University Bochum, Germany, on behalf of the European Consortium for Political Research

ecpr

The Routledge/ECPR studies in European political science series is published in association with the European Consortium for Political Research – the leading organization concerned with the growth and development of political science in Europe. The series presents high-quality edited volumes on topics at the leading edge of current interest in political science and related fields, with contributions from European scholars and others who have presented work at ECPR workshops or research groups.

1 **Regionalist Parties in Western Europe**
Edited by Lieven de Winter and Huri Türsan

2 **Comparing Party System Change**
Edited by Jan-Erik Lane and Paul Pennings

3 **Political Theory and European Union**
Edited by Albert Weale and Michael Nentwich

4 **Politics of Sexuality**
Edited by Terrell Carver and Véronique Mottier

5 **Autonomous Policy Making by International Organizations**
Edited by Bob Reinalda and Bertjan Verbeek

6 **Social Capital and European Democracy**
Edited by Jan van Deth, Marco Maraffi, Ken Newton and Paul Whiteley

7 **Party Elites in Divided Societies**
Edited by Kurt Richard Luther and Kris Deschouwer

8 **Citizenship and Welfare State Reform in Europe**
Edited by Jet Bussemaker

9 **Democratic Governance and New Technology**
Technologically mediated innovations in political practice in Western Europe
Edited by Ivan Horrocks, Jens Hoff and Pieter Tops

10 **Democracy without Borders**
Transnationalisation and conditionality in new democracies
Edited by Jean Grugel

Also available from Routledge in association with the ECPR:

Education in Political Science

Science

Discovering a neglected field

Edited by Anja P. Jakobi,
Kerstin Martens and
Klaus Dieter Wolf

Routledge
Taylor & Francis Group

LONDON AND NEW YORK

ecpr

First published 2010
by Routledge
2 Park Square, Milton Park, Abingdon, Oxon OX14 4RN

Simultaneously published in the USA and Canada
by Routledge
711 Third Ave, New York, NY 10017

Routledge is an imprint of the Taylor & Francis Group, an informa business

© 2010 Selection and editorial matter, Anja P. Jakobi, Kerstin Martens
and Klaus Dieter Wolf; individual contributors, their contributions

Typeset in Times by Wearset Ltd, Boldon, Tyne and Wear

First issued in paperback 2013

British Library Cataloguing in Publication Data
A catalogue record for this book is available from the British Library

Library of Congress Cataloging in Publication Data
A catalog record for this book has been requested

ISBN13: 978-0-415-49477-9 (hbk)
ISBN13: 978-0-203-87331-1 (ebk)
ISBN13: 978-0-415-84842-8 (pbk)

Contents

Illustrations

Figures

Tables

1   Introduction

A governance perspective on education policy

Anja P. Jakobi, Kerstin Martens and Klaus Dieter Wolf

Devoting an edited volume to the analysis of education from the perspective of political science is not as self-evident as it might seem. Although the Bologna Process and the 'Programme for International Student Assessment' (PISA) have by now established themselves as prominent political issues with a substantial impact on many political agendas, political scientists have been more than reluctant to pay particular attention to this field. In the discipline, education has remained a 'homeless' and widely underestimated topic during the last decades. Although education policy made some guest appearances in policy analysis, it remained a subordinated issue and, compared to environmental policy, social policy or foreign policy, it has not become an original, autonomous policy field in its own right. In contrast to sociology or education science, political science traditionally has only played a minor role when it came to applying the full range of its analytical perspectives and methodological tools to education as a field of study. Against this background, this book is pioneering work, and we hope that it paves the way to further explorations in the discipline. The volume demonstrates how education policy can be explored systematically from the perspectives of all major sub-disciplines of political science: comparative politics, public policy and administration, international relations (IR) and political theory.

The current discovery of education may well have been triggered by the fact that this policy field has become a particularly hot topic on the political agenda; but this growing importance is only one, namely external, reason for its immense attractiveness. The other one originates from recent developments within political science itself: the emergence of the governance concept as a new analytical perspective with a broad range of innovative research questions and with a high integrating potential across the different sub-disciplines. While the term government refers to a very specific, state-centred mode of social and political organization, governance is defined as a multitude of formal or informal steering and coordination mechanisms, 'to make demands, frame goals, issue directives, pursue policies and generate compliance', whether by public or private actors (Rosenau 2004: 31, compare also Benz *et al.* 2007: 13–20). The perspective of governance brings several changes in the field of education right into the centre of political science: the rise of new actors; the growing shift to multilevel political processes; and the new and complex interplay between the private and the public sector. But a governance perspective not only smoothes the way for linking education policy with the discipline's mainstream research; it is also particularly productive in offering new insights into recent educational reforms, because it expands the attention from the dimension of policy to politics and polity. The perspective thus underlines questions that deal not merely with the outcomes of education, but with the way education politics work.

The search of the state for a new role in education, the consequences and the limits of de-nationalization – these and related trends of change raise new questions which can be easily addressed and subsumed under the umbrella of 'new modes of governance', a shift from a hierarchical mode of steering to various loci and ways of governance. In fact, once seriously examined, education turns out to be a particularly enlightening field of observation, in which many general patterns of policy changes, the conditions under which they take place, and the problems raised by them, can be analysed. In many ways, the field is predestined to make significant contributions to the more general research agenda about the causes and consequences of statehood in transition: while the political goals to enable or pursue the education of citizens are still inherent in countries all over the world, and all the more in times of worldwide debates on lifelong learning (Jakobi 2007b, 2009), the provision of education increasingly differs, standards of education might be ensured by semi-private or private bodies, or the funding of educational institutions relies on private investments. We can observe business models built on educational provision, international processes that enhance convergence of national education policy systems, such as the Bologna Process, or the definition of education as a service sector.

In this volume, we are particularly interested in two directions of these processes of change, namely the privatization and internationalization of education. We apply both terms broadly: privatization refers to the process of shifting responsibility, regulations from public to private or non-governmental actors. It also includes the introduction of market mechanisms or other modes of self-regulation in formerly state-governed realms, or the growth of education industries. Internationalization refers to the process of shifting elements of the policy-making process to the international level, such as regulation and evaluation, but also the identification of policy goals. It includes international organizations as new actors in education policy-making. However, there are also trends visible that include a growing regionalization or increased local governance of education, decentralizing formerly centralized national policy processes. In sum these developments create a new order in education policy, and this volume is part of the ambition to grasp these empirically as well as theoretically. Thus, the book is consequently built around research questions dealing with new actors' constellations, the interplay of public and private activities and preferences, and the changing importance of traditional and future modes of governance in terms of the effectiveness and legitimacy of political decision-making processes.

By applying conceptual and theoretical tools of different sub-disciplines of political science, this book informs a political science and education audience at the same time. On the one hand, as an observation field for political scientists, education policy is used as a laboratory from which new, and probably generalizable, insights can be gained about one of the basic research questions of political science: the controversial debate on the future of the state. On the other hand, the theoretical and analytical toolbox of political science, in particular when applied within the conceptual framework of the governance perspective, can help those with a specific interest in education to learn more about patterns of change in this field which had either not been systematically observed before or have developed only recently. In this sense, our volume aims at a mutual learning process: it demonstrates to 'educationists' from other disciplines as well as to political practitioners what political science can contribute to the body of knowledge in 'their' field, and at the same time it can provide political science with crucial, but so far untapped empirical evidence about the changing role of the state in one of the core areas of its responsibility.

In the light of these general objectives and in order to provide a common background to the different case studies presented in this volume, we first give a brief account of the state of the art in this introductory chapter. What role has the study of education so far played in political science? It will come as no surprise that this account will be one of a comparatively poor record and will identify the relationship between political science and education as a largely neglected one, despite the fact that education policy is generally considered a classic prerogative of the modern nation state. We will then proceed to introduce the governance perspective as the conceptual framework which serves as a common ground for the different chapters of this volume. A short account of the 'government era' of education policy illustrates that such a perspective on political change offers a new and promising key to observing basic patterns of change in education policy-making as well as putting these observed changes in the broader comparative perspective of changing modes of governance in general. Finally, this introduction will give a brief description of how the following chapters apply the analytical and theoretical toolbox of political science to the field of education and, seen as a whole, provide a selective, yet representative view which cuts across the different sub-disciplines of political science.

Education policy-making: a neglected research field

The need for a volume on education is rooted in the stunning discrepancy between the important position of education on the current political agenda and the reluctant attitude of political scientists towards this phenomenon (see McGuinn 2006: 2–3). In current education science, both privatization as well as internationalization processes have been an issue (e.g. Dale 1999, 2005; Dale and Robertson 2002; Robertson *et al.* 2002). In particular the emergence of market-based governance instruments, the rise of private education institutions, the creation of global education markets or the growing importance of international organizations have been triggers for research efforts in this field.

In the context of social policy, education has partly been considered (Heidenheimer 1981; Mok 2001; Allmendinger and Leibfried 2003), but not often included systematically (Hill 2006: 157–158). It also depends on national traditions how close education has been linked to welfare policies: while this link has been strong in Anglo-Saxon traditions, it has been rather weak in Germany (Opielka 2006: 7). Education policy-making was part of political science's classics, such as Dahl's *Who Governs?* (Dahl 2005). It has also been part of earlier discussions on federalism, as in the German case (Mäding 1989) or in current research on the United States (Manna 2006). In recent years, financing of education and the link of education to political economy have become more prominent (Schmidt 2003; Busemeyer 2007), and international activities have been examined (Walkenhorst 2008).

Basically, education policy has been examined from three main perspectives. Although not necessarily mutually exclusive, they differ in their focus and also in the extent to which the questions they ask are also covered by other disciplines. First, we find some policy studies in education, in which education policy is evaluated and whose level of intended generalization across cases or policy fields is rather low. Research from this perspective mainly overlaps with sociology, economy or education science, in particular when linked to social policy problems (Jary 2005; Allmendinger and Leibfried 2003; Alexander *et al.* 1997).

The second strand of research links education to issues of democracy and government. Studies argue for the right to education of specific groups, assess the role of education for political order, deal with the need for minority education, or analyse the role of education in specific political systems. They are often based on an implicit or explicit normative orientation, but do not necessarily claim to have explanatory value. Research contributions from this perspective frequently overlap with disciplines such as political philosophy, law, history and, again, education science (e.g. Callan 2005; Patterson 2001).

A third and more recent trend in research on education focuses on politics. Empirical observations in the field of education are used to gain general insights into the political process. A prominent example is Mintrom's study (2000) on policy entrepreneurs, in which he analyses the diffusion of school choice in the United States to develop a theory of the policy entrepreneur. Further, Manna has derived the concept of 'borrowing strength' concerning federal agendas from the example of US federal education policy (Manna 2006). It is not necessarily a coincidence that these studies have been developed in a US context: this country has witnessed an enormous shift in responsibility for education in recent decades, and an explanation for this fact was obviously needed. Research on education by European political scientists is also gradually developing an interest in the politics of education (see also, for example, Andersen 2007; Walkenhorst 2008; also Rigby 2007 on the United States), but most often with slightly different prefixes: the Traditionally strong role of government seemingly giving way to privatization and internationalization, the reform of education systems has become a particularly interesting field of research, reifying the general trend towards new modes of governance.

Even when considering the above-mentioned research, education is still in its infancy in terms of becoming a 'policy field in its own right'. The usual neglect of education is already obvious in sheer numbers: analysing the number of political-science publications in the Social Science Citation Index (SSCI) over time shows the comparatively low number of education policy articles. While from 1970 to 2007 political scientists published only 31 articles with 'education policy' in their title, the comparable figures for 'social policy' (158) or 'environmental policy' (119), to name two other research fields, have constantly been higher.[1] Figure 1.1 illustrates the development from 1970 to 2007. Annually, research on education policy does not exceed three articles, while peaks in social or environmental policy publications are clearly higher. Looking at the annual baseline, we can see that from 1970 to 2007 there have been 17 years in which not a single article with education policy in its title was published; environmental policy in comparison has not reached this low since the mid-1980s and social policy never reached it. Standard reference works on the state of the art of the discipline do not even mention education policy (Katznelson and Milner 2002; Goodin and Klingemann 1998).

This seeming lack of interest is all the more striking since education has always been linked very closely to citizens, politics and the state: Educational institutions exert a major impact on the life of citizens. Nearly all countries have introduced compulsory education, which requires citizens to spend a substantial amount of their lifetime learning either in school or at home (Meyer and Ramirez 2003). As a precondition of national economic growth, education receives much attention, as the PISA tests of the Organization for Economic Cooperation and Development (OECD) have shown (Jakobi and Martens 2007). It is further

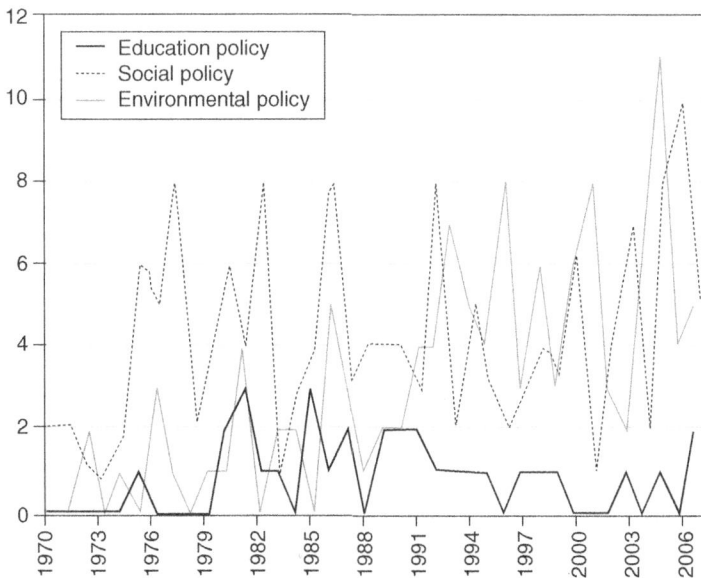

Figure 1.1 Number of articles per year on education policy, social policy and environmental policy (source: SSCI, own calculations).

assumed to be a major prerequisite for democracy. Schools are not only concerned with teaching the different disciplines, but also with educating responsible citizens. Moreover, education is increasingly seen as a lever to enhance the cohesion of societies. Through upgrading the skills of the population it is possible to allow people – immigrants and non-immigrants alike – to take active part in the labour market and in the democratic process. Especially the role of education in the integration of migrants in western societies is high on the political agenda throughout Europe.

Moreover, the significance of education is even mirrored in practical activities of political scientists: There have been recent examples of political-science associations engaging in educating the political minds of citizens, such as the Task Force on Political Violence and Terrorism, initiated by the American Political Science Association, which distributes syllabi for secondary school and college levels, or the proposals of the German Political Science Association concerning the core curriculum for educating future teachers of politics and economics (APSA 2007; DVPW 2007).

In sum, an updated research agenda for the study of education is indeed needed to explore the recent trends in education policy, but also in order to catch up with the strong interest and record of some neighboring academic disciplines, notably education science, as well as sociology or economics. However, they rarely look at the political processes and preconditions, and rather focus on specific questions that are strongly related to the core of the respective discipline, and in fact leave much room for inquiries by political scientists. This is not to say that research so far did not produce valuable outcomes, but that congruencies with disciplines such as education, sociology or economics cannot replace research within political science.

Education science has dealt with education policy prominently, including important specialized journals, such as the *Journal of Education Policy*. Such contributions often deal with the content of educational reform programmes and evaluate their outcomes. Systematic comparisons with other policy fields are highly unusual, and although trends towards privatization, internationalization and changing governance forms in general are also analysed (see, for example, Henry *et al.* 2001; Dale 1999; Schuetze 2006; Kallo and Rinne 2006). From a political-science perspective, they are not theory oriented and remain idiographic rather than being nomothetic. In a similar way, the related, often multidisciplinary higher education research has a strong link to administrative issues and focuses on policy development in this specific sub-sector (for example Witte 2006). It is also characterized by a strong focus on output and implementation.

Unlike political science, sociology is an academic discipline with a strong tradition in research on education. Indeed, a number of sociologists have dealt with the societal conditions and consequences of education systems, often with a focus on questions of social inequalities and how they may be overcome. For example, they explore the spread of education as a central institution (Meyer and Ramirez 2003), the impact of education on the individuals, their life and social equality (for a recent example see Alexander *et al.* 2007), or they critically examine the role of education in society, also in relation to the state (Collins 1979; Dale 1989). The sociology of education constitutes a highly acknowledged sub-discipline, and it applies a whole range of theoretical and methodological approaches, but political institutions and actors usually play only a minor role in its agenda.

Studies in economics, a further relevant discipline in the field of education, have dealt with the individual or collective revenue generated by education (path-breaking: Becker 1964), and findings often constitute a basis for political decision-making (for example McMahon 2003). Their emphasis, however, is usually reduced to the economic gains and returns that an education system should produce, while additional functions of education, as well as political or social conditions, remain underdeveloped.

The common conceptual framework: a governance perspective

In order to close the 'education gap' in our discipline and by approaching policy-making in the field of education from a governance perspective, this volume intends to move research on education closer to the centre of political science. It gives an account of the specific contributions our discipline can make to the study of this policy field, and it links the field of education to governance studies common in other policy areas. Education policy is an important field of study for political science, since the value of education for individual and collective progress is mostly uncontested, the political aim of ensuring education is common to many of today's countries and political actors. Thus, the question is less whether to promote education, but rather how to govern it, linking the subject directly to questions of political action and state activity.

Much research has been dedicated to the question of how the state will behave under the current wave of internationalization in terms of decreasing public budgets compared to ever-growing agendas (Zürn 1998; see also Hurrelmann *et al.* 2007). The state, as some research has proposed, is about to change in that it is delegating more tasks to the private and the international level. However, the state is still held accountable and responsible for ensuring collective goods or is the addressee of needs, even if tasks are delegated to other actors (Genschel and Zangl 2007). Thus, the question of governance moves centre stage: How do states actually govern specific fields, if not exclusively by government, but also in interplay with or by delegation to other bodies? The central role of education as part of the modern state makes education policy particularly attractive to assess such changes. The aim of ensuring an educated society is rather uniform across countries, but ways to reach this goal – its governance – can differ widely.

Basically, the term 'governance' goes beyond the traditional notion of political steering as hierarchical state regulation by command and control, which is generally associated with government. In response to the changing nature of real world politics, the debate on governance mirrors the emergence of an enriched set of actors and policy-making levels which are involved in the political process. As an analytical concept it thus refers to processes of de-nationalization along two different axes of change: from public to private on the one hand, and from national to multilevel governing on the other (see Leibfried and Zürn 2005). In the public–private dimension of change – also described by some as a shift from govern*ment* to govern*ance* – it involves regulatory agencies with new constellations of actors. The interplay among these often implies a delegation of functions formerly executed by the state to non-state providers or semi-private bodies (see for example Kooiman 2003; Benz and Papadopoulos 2006; Schuppert 2006). The new 'cooperative' or 'enabling' role of the state along this public–private axis of change has been referred to as a 'de-hierarchization' of the relations between state and society (Scharpf 1991). The territorial dimension of change, i.e. the emergence of multilevel governance, has become most prominent in the context of European politics in the shift of competencies from the national to the European or sub-national levels (Bache and Flinders 2005).

There are three basic questions which occupy the governance research agenda: First, in terms of systematic description, this debate deals with nothing less than the future political role of the nation state. The descriptive categories which have been developed to capture the process of political reorganization still have to be filled with more and broader empirical evidence in order to make strong and generalizable statements about the future shape and role of the state in the context of governance by, with or without government. Does the emergence of new modes of governance mean a general weakening of the state? Is it indicative of a retreat or even the end of the nation state (Strange 1996; Ohmae 1995)? Or, as another strand of literature suggests, are the current trends towards de-nationalization only indicative of a transformation rather than a weakening of statehood (Leibfried and Zürn 2005; Hurrelmann *et al.* 2007)?

Second, the causal relationships which trigger the emergence of new modes of governance and the transformation of the state are of interest. In this context, competing theoretical approaches offer different explanations (see Graz and Nölke 2008). Is there an underlying functional logic at work, triggered by the conditions of economic and political globalization? Or can the analysis of the strategic interests of powerful actors provide a more adequate account? From a benevolent point of view, the emerging new modes of governance, characterized by the inclusion of new actors, by institutional reforms, and new interaction patterns, may be assessed as some kind of state strategy to react more effectively amid the surrounding changes. Eventually, both perspectives may be usefully applied, or may even have to be supplemented by a view which highlights the incremental nature of individual processes of change and transition without exhibiting such a thing as a 'masterplan' or any general patterns of change.

Finally, from a normative perspective, the effects of the newly emerging modes of governance are investigated and evaluated. Unlike its previous preoccupation with evaluative standards which focus on the effectiveness dimension of governance, normative questions address the legitimacy of new modes of gov-

ernance and progressively gain more attention in the governance research agenda
(see Wolf 2006; Benz and Papadopoulos 2006).

The contributions to this volume are essentially embedded in this general discourse in political science about changing statehood, the emergence of new
forms of governance and the diffusion and decentralization of political authority.
The new modes of governance, the causes, limits and effects of de-
nationalization are visible with particular clarity in the field of education: The
globalization of labour markets, the growing importance of human capital as part
of the knowledge society and limited financial capacities have made education
policy a field of major reform processes. National curricula are being revised and
education systems are increasingly being restructured according to international
standards. New actors are taking part in domestic education policy-making or as
providers of education services. Linking such changes to the governance paradigm illustrates that exploring education politics is not an aim in itself, but
allows generalizing conclusions with some significance for other policy fields as
well. Compared to most other academic contributions on education policy, the
main advantage of the new 'governance paradigm' lies in transcending the
narrow focus on how 'optimal' outcomes in education policy should look or how
they should be brought about. Instead, the new perspective offers an integrating
conceptual framework for widening the scope of research questions to the politics and polity dimensions of how and why educational reforms evolve.

By making full use of the richness of the discipline, the individual chapters
apply a wide range of political-science tools to the field of education, indicating
the potential and significance of this field of research for learning more about the
general nature, causes and impact of political change. As a consequence, readers
will recognize analytical concepts that they usually find being applied to other
policy fields and research areas in political science, such as theories about veto
players, bounded rationality or network analysis.

Moving from government to governance in education

The authors represented in this volume share the assumption that the privatization and internationalization of political processes are the two most distinct
trends of de-nationalization. Privatization is the overarching term for the trend to
outsource specific state activities to private providers, to commodify formerly
public goods or to introduce market-based or other self-regulatory governance
instruments. As one consequence of this trend, public policy has witnessed the
rise of private providers in education, the introduction of new ways of budgeting
schools or higher education institutions, or changed mechanisms of quality
assurance (see Chapters 2, 4 and 7, this volume). Internationalization refers to
the rise of international actors as part of the education policy-making process or
the fact that education has increasingly been part of international cooperation.
As a consequence of this trend, education policy has become part of the
European Union's activities, or international assessments such as PISA have
become important for national policy-making (see Chapters 5 and 9, this volume;

Walkenhorst 2008; Martens and Wolf 2006). Both internationalization and privatization have been particularly obvious in the field of education (see Martens *et al.* 2007). Moreover, privatization and internationalization go together well: international organizations, such as the World Trade Organizations' General Agreement on Trade in Services (GATS) or the World Bank, conceive education as a service or promote primarily private investment in post-basic education (Chapter 8, this volume; Jakobi 2007a).

It is generally taken for granted that education services have always been performed by the state – often even almost exclusively as regards their provision, financing and standard-setting. Although we consider education policy a classic prerogative of the modern nation state, this is a recent phenomenon only. In ancient times, instead, the state was not involved in education policy-making at all. In Athens, education was aimed at intellectual and aesthetic improvement. The Roman idea of education focused on virtues and on craftsmanship. When Christianity gained cultural hegemony and political dominance over education in medieval times, education was basically provided on religious grounds. The institutional organization of education became the privilege of the church and was dominated by religious forces (Weymann *et al.* 2007).

With the advent of the Renaissance, Humanism and the Enlightenment a secular curriculum and science began to shape education policy. A growing interest in the systematic utilization of science and education in favour of the wealth and power of nations and the progress of humankind prevailed over religious beliefs. Education was increasingly used by the emerging modern state to integrate the population by means of literacy, religious lectures, basic arithmetic, a national language and narrative. The rising sovereign nation state thus ultimately made education its own political domain (Weymann *et al.* 2007). With the institutionalization of education through formal education systems and the establishment of national curricula, the nation state managed to incorporate education into its realm of sovereignty. The standard worldwide model today is characterized by a national curriculum and formally established education institutions (Meyer *et al.* 1992, 1997).

Today, at least in the OECD world, education forms part of the normative good of the welfare state. It developed into a useful instrument of the intervention state to provide for economic growth and to decrease or legitimize social inequality. By and large, the emerging modern state took responsibility for the provision of education at each of the three levels – outcome, regulation and operation (Hurrelmann *et al.* 2007): In many states, the process of nation building led to the fully fledged responsibility of the state over outcome (in terms of numbers and skills of graduates), over regulations (in terms of laws, professional status, acknowledgment of organizations and curricula) and over operations (at least in the field of public education).

As a means for national integration and as a key tool to improve economic growth, education denotes a core element of the nation state's sovereignty and autonomy. Furthermore, the nation state shapes and disseminates through education the idea of a common history of the people. Education has also become a valuable instrument to improve competitiveness of the national economy – a tool to produce grand surpluses and wealth by coordinated human capital investment (Weymann *et al.* 2007: 232).

The challenges of globalization for the regulatory powers of the state, the increasing importance of international organizations, and the rise of transnational and private actors all play a part in transforming the role of the nation state as the fundamental organizing principle of modern societies. Many citizens have been accustomed to seeing the state as the main, and sometimes even exclusive, provider of collective goods, services and values. However, today even core domains of national policy-making, among them education policy, are increasingly shared amongst a variety of actors. Internationalization and privatization seem to be challenging the nation state's dominant role in education policy-making. These processes might alter the landscape of this field substantially and also create tensions between the national and the international level of education policy-making, as well as between public and private providers of educational services.

Market rules are increasingly penetrating domestic education systems. This 'marketization' of education is economically promoted as a worldwide competition for students, research and provision of services. The ongoing negotiations about further international liberalization in education, as envisioned by GATS, facilitate such processes and provide the political and legal framework for more deregulation and commodification (see Chapter 8, this volume). These developments have an enormous impact on the field of education as they allow the increasing privatization of education, new kinds of international and private providers and new forms of delivery through offshore campuses and the World Wide Web.

Moreover, in response to the advent of the knowledge society, pressures on the labour markets and challenges triggered by the globalization process, the education sector is increasingly shaped by internationalization today. International organizations have gained increasing importance in the reform processes of national education systems, for example the EU and the OECD. The Bologna Process – today closely associated which the EU – involves the standardization of degree structures in higher education with the goal of creating a single European Higher Education Area, while the OECD's PISA project regularly evaluates the performance of 15-year-old students in different national education systems. Both international pressure and international organizations triggered extensive public debates and compelled policy-makers to restructure their national education systems (see Chapters 3, 5, 9 and 10, this volume; Jakobi and Martens 2007; Martens and Wolf 2006).

This short account of the rise and fall of the 'golden-age of nation state' (Hurrelmann *et al.* 2007) dominance over education may suffice to indicate that the concept of governance is particularly helpful in investigating education policy in today's post-national constellation. The current reforms go far beyond the redefinition – often economization – of educational targets. They have culminated in the introduction of new forms of governance: international and national rankings, for example, are used to outline common goals and benchmarks for education systems. Such instruments tend to elude state control and influence domestic priorities. Moreover, new instruments of quality assurance, such as evaluation and accreditation processes, have been put in place and further weaken state influence. Above all, the involvement of private actors and non-state agencies is giving education policy-making a completely different shape.

Studying education with the analytical toolbox of political science

The following chapters of this volume contribute to the overarching search for common patterns of change in specific fields and at different levels of educational reforms which may affect the future role of the state. Moreover, each of them shows how, why, and with what kind of consequences education policy-making is currently being transformed by new actors, new political agendas and in an increasingly complex multilevel setting. The different contributions illustrate these changes in education politics from the angles of political science's different sub-disciplines; three chapters are compiled in each part to illustrate different approaches to the subject matter.

The contributions to Part I are dedicated to *comparative education politics*. They analyse political settings in different countries and shed light on the conditions and consequences of introducing new forms of governance. All chapters underline the importance of existing institutional settings in establishing new governance instruments. Whether a political system is more or less open to political change also influences the adoption of specific instruments, and the history and tradition linked to the national education system determine how far trends linked to privatization and internationalization are actually realized.

Michael B. Klitgaard's study deals with the introduction of school vouchers in the United States and Sweden (Chapter 2). School vouchers have faced severe resistance in the United States where the programme has not been adopted as a national educational reform, while the social democratic welfare state of Sweden adopted a universal and national public voucher scheme in the early 1990s. Klitgaard explains this phenomenon by referring to the concept of veto points. He argues that the varying output from political processes on school vouchers in the United States and Sweden can be explained by the different ways political institutions affect decision-making in these two countries. The introduction of new governance instruments – in this case the privatization of school choice – is thus not determined by how far the overall ideology of a welfare system corresponds with it, but it is a matter of political institutions and their flexibility.

Michael Dobbins compares the development of higher education systems in Central and Eastern Europe (Chapter 3). He assesses the impact of international and national factors on changing higher education policies in Bulgaria, the Czech Republic and Romania. These countries share the common experience of communist rule with a highly centralized and ideology based higher education policy, but have now come under the influence of western models. Focusing on issues of university autonomy, the chapter draws on three ideal types of governance for addressing the direction of policy drift: the 'Humboldt' model of academic self-regulation, the market-oriented model, and the state-authority model. His analytical framework enables him to show why, how and to what degree convergence has taken place by means of mechanisms such as transnational communication and institutional isomorphism – that means without binding rules and legislation. The actual realization of governance instruments that are the subject of international transfer thus comes in different shapes and sizes, depending on historical legacies and the nature of transnational interlinkages. Dobbins' chapter delivers a further argument for a strong role of established institutions in the introduction of new governance modes.

Christine Hudson's study directly addresses the core controversy of the governance debate about the future of the state (Chapter 4). In order to give a differentiated account of the change from government to governance she develops a general conceptual map of possible directions and dimensions of changes in governing. An important feature of this approach to capture change in a differentiated way are Kooiman's (2000) three orders of governing which distinguish between the generation and implementation of new and 'better' educational policies (first-order governing), the re-distribution of institutional competencies (second-order governing) in order to create favourable structural conditions for the introduction of such new educational policies, and the re-framing of the standards of appropriateness by which these policies can be measured (meta governing). Using a comparative approach she explores the reform of state instruments towards more private regulation in education in a group of Nordic welfare states. She provides strong empirical evidence against those who claim that governance is eclipsing government, and concludes that rather than relinquishing its control, the state is finding new ways of regulating education by adapting to changing circumstances and, whilst bringing in new actors, still keeping the government in governance. Despite trends towards privatization in governance, northern countries thus continue to dedicate a prominent role to the state as an actor in public policy.

In Part II, education policy-making is analysed as a topic of *public policy analysis and public administration*. In accordance with the special focus of this sub-discipline, the different chapters deal with the way policy-makers, administration and the public shape the programmatic content of education policy and its implementation. As the contributions show, policy actors, their interests and logics are crucial in realizing changes in governance. The chapters provide a close analysis of how education policy is developed from rather abstract ideas and goals to the concrete visible political change.

Katrin Toens analyses the development of curricular governance in German higher education (Chapter 5). In the context of the Bologna Process, the inherited state-authorized system of study reform in Germany has been replaced by a decentralized system of quality assurance with private accreditation agencies. The chapter provides a policy analysis of the power struggles and 'modes of governance' underlying this shift, starting from the assumption that a deeper understanding of these reforms depends on the examination of domestic conditions during the pre-Bologna stage. In order to examine theses changes, she combines two theoretical approaches to one analytic framework, consisting of sequential policy analysis and the concept of multiple streams. Toens illustrates how the stalemate between the federal state and the Länder was dissolved when new actors, such as the universities' representatives, became involved in higher education governance. Even though the resulting new mode of governance does not indicate a total withdrawal of state power from matters of study reform, it signals a gain of political power for university representatives who have become more important players in German higher education politics.

Emiliano Grimaldi and Roberto Serpieri present a case study about the implementation of a new governance instrument dedicated to the integration and coordination in education policy – the so-called 'Conference of District' in a southern Italian province (Chapter 6). The introduction of this new instrument, promoted by the state in education as well as in other policy areas, is embedded in a general strategy to deal with the crisis of the bureaucratic mode of regulation by constituting 'devolved environments' which increase the relevance of local authorities but also the complexity and diversity of the local educational arenas. The resulting multiplication of networks and the emergence of 'new hybrid modes' of regulation create several challenges, in particular the growing need for integration and coordination, for which the conferences are supposed to provide answers. The authors use Giddens' structuration theory as a theoretical framework in order to focus on the unintended consequences of the implementation process, the re-structuring of the local system and the role of policy entrepreneurs in terms of strategic conduct. The study shows how difficult the implementation of new governance instruments is, being highly dependent on policy entrepreneurship and the creation of common goals.

Unintended consequences also play an important role in Pertti Ahonen's case study of a reform process of primary schools and secondary schools in Finland's capital city of Helsinki (Chapter 7). Since Finland's successes in the OECD PISA studies have accumulated, the Finnish school system has attracted the particular interest of scholars and practitioners in search of the secret roots of success. In what may be considered a kind of 'de-mystification' of Finnish school policy, Ahonen does not highlight the good outcomes of Finnish education. These outcomes are often the sole focus of international studies and rankings and thereby hide the fact that Finland's education system also operates under conditions that may constitute obstacles to educational reforms. Using the theoretical framework of bounded rationality, Ahonen focuses on the politicization of political processes by influential stakeholders. As the chapter shows, the introduction of new forms of governance is difficult and by no means guaranteed, even when the goals are clear and transparent, and the need for reform is seen.

Part III presents contributions from the perspective of *international relations*. It highlights the multilevel character of education policy-making and its interplay of domestic and intergovernmental processes. While the state and sub-national levels have traditionally been concerned with education policy-making, the section shows how international organizations and processes are become increasingly relevant for the governance of education.

Antoni Verger explores the influence of a diverse set of factors on the outcome of the GATS negotiations in the field of education (Chapter 8). The GATS negotiations transfer education into a field of international governance, involving new actors and introducing extra-educative elements into education regulation, in particular the idea of free trade in education. In the course of a contested process, numerous education stakeholders have opposed and campaigned against GATS in different countries and at the international level. Verger starts from a critical constructivist understanding of the role of ideas in politics and applies it in a comparative perspective to two country case studies; Argentina and Chile. He shows that ideas matter most when they can be linked to specific material and institutional background factors. The GATS negotiations introduce new needs related to the coordination of state activities as well as new power relations within the state. For stakeholders in education policy, the scene becomes increasingly complex, encompassing different levels, backgrounds and approaches to education governance.

Rik de Ruiter approaches the field of education by studying new forms of governance in Europe based on multilateral surveillance of national policies (Chapter 9). Since tools such as international benchmarking, stocktaking and rankings have become more prominent in recent years, he inquires why states use the Open Method of Coordination (OMC) as a new mode for decision-making in education policy. De Ruiter argues that states are particularly likely to use the OMC for issues that are highly salient in the eyes of the policy-makers. If member states face a conflict between an incentive and the reluctance to act on the EU level, they are likely to opt for the OMC. This conflict is also identified as a driving force behind the development of the OMC's infrastructure. The chapter demonstrates how the OMC in education served the conflicting goals of being reluctant towards and pushing for EU involvement. It shows the multifaceted governance of education in European countries, and the strategic use that states make of the different levels.

Alexander-Kenneth Nagel's analysis gives an instructive account of the development of international actors' networks in the course of the Bologna Process (Chapter 10). The Bologna Process aiming at establishing a European Higher Education Area has been exerting significant impact on European higher education systems. Launched as an intergovernmental initiative at the level of national ministries, the process has transcended national interests and has resulted in a hybrid structure of education policy-making between the nation states and the European Union. Moreover, the internationalization of education politics embodied by the Bologna Process has been accompanied by a reconfiguration of the set of political actors. Nagel provides a systematic analysis of the corporate actors and the exchanges of cultural, economic and symbolical capital between them by means of network analysis. He concludes that the Bologna Process has changed governance structures in European higher education and empowered a new set of actors. In sum, the process created a structure of multi-level governance that is fragmented on the vertical axis – ranging from the national to the international level – as well as on the horizontal axis – among public and private stakeholders.

Finally, the contributions of Part 4 – designed as *meta-reflections* – take on the task of critically 'observing the observers'. Political science and its relationship with educational policy-making are the subject of critical meta-reflections from within and outside the discipline. The contributions show that internationalization processes, governance issues or the exploration of a new field in political science are not merely an intellectual exercise, but can have an important impact on democratic decision-making. In the meantime, internationalization can also change the discipline itself, altering specific national educational traditions.

Klaus Dieter Wolf looks at the Bologna reform process from the perspective of normative political theory (Chapter 11). By introducing different normative perspectives with which political science can take on the concept of reform, his contribution shows what the changing evaluation criteria applied by political scientists can tell us about the development of the discipline itself. The reform of higher education in Europe can thus be portrayed as part of a more comprehensive reform project which is characterized by a fundamental shift from traditional appropriateness criteria, such as those derived from democratic theory, to normative standards imported from the neo-liberal discourse of new public management in the political as well as the academic discourse. Employing Kooiman's distinction between first-order, second-order and meta governing again, this shift is empirically illustrated by the re-definition of the basic goals of higher education as well as the creation of new, informal institutional environments to facilitate the implementation of concrete policy measures in accordance with the new ideational frame.

Erkki Berndtson follows the same path and treats his own discipline as the 'dependent variable' (Chapter 12). He shows how the Bologna Process is already changing and may further change the nature of European political science and, in the long run, even reduce the variety of available knowledge to students and researchers alike. The line of argument developed in this chapter is based on the assumption that changes in the structures of education have an impact on the nature of academic disciplines. From the perspective of historical institutionalism, Berndtson starts with the establishment of political science as an independent academic discipline in the United States during the late nineteenth century. He shows that the transformation of the American higher education system that took place at that time was an important factor which gave the new discipline its character. Although strongly influenced by the American model after the Second World War, the European study of politics remained quite heterogeneous until recently. In Berndtson's study, the Bologna Process is not only considered to be a technical project restructuring the European higher education area, but also identified as another example of the introduction of new modes of governance in higher education which will have a profound effect on the nature of existing academic disciplines as well.

Contributors

Pertti Ahonen is a Professor of Public Administration with a special focus on Government Financial Management at the University of Tampere, Finland. He has authored numerous studies on public policy evaluation and reform, politics and management in various welfare sectors including education, the EU and philosophical and methodological issues.

Erkki Berndtson is a Senior Lecturer in Political Science at the University of Helsinki, Finland. He has been long involved with the work of the International Political Science Association's Research Committee on 'The Study of the Discipline of Political Science', currently as the Committee's Vice-Chair. His research interests include the history of political science, politics of higher education, power and democratic theory, architecture and public space as well as US government and politics.

Michael Dobbins is a research assistant at the University of Konstanz, Germany. His research interests include higher education policy, Central and Eastern European affairs, European integration, and EU decision-making. His most recent work has been focused on changing patterns of governance in higher education in transition countries.

Jürgen Enders is a Professor at the School of Management and Governance, and the Director of the Centre for Higher Education Policy Studies (CHEPS), University of Twente, the Netherlands. His background is in political sociology and his major research interests include the governance and management of higher education and research, organizational change in higher education, higher education and work, and the academic profession. He is the co-editor of the books *Higher Education in a Globalising World. International Trends and Mutual Observations* and *Public-Private Dynamics in Higher Education and Research*, and he has published in journals such as *Comparative Education*; *Higher Education*; *Higher Education Policy*; *Leviathan*; *Public Administration*; *Rassegna Italiana di Sociologia* and *Scientometrics*.

Emiliano Grimaldi is a post-doctoral researcher at the Institute of Education, University of London, UK and holds a PhD in Sociology and Social Research from the University Federico II, Naples, Italy. He is working in different research projects on educational governance and leadership in a comparative perspective as well as on the phenomena of school networks, focusing in particular on democratic developments and equity in education.

Christine Hudson is an Associate Professor at the Department of Political Science, Umeå University, Sweden. Her interests in the field of education relate to comparative studies of local education systems in England and Sweden, the role of education in local and regional development, universities and regions, and theories of governance in relation to education in the UK and the Nordic countries. Recent publications include 'Governing the governance of education – the state strikes back?' in *European Educational Research Journal*, 2007, Vol. 6, No. 3; and, together with Anders Lidström, *Local Education Policies – Comparing Britain and Sweden* (Palgrave, 2002).

Anja P. Jakobi is a Senior Researcher at the TranState Research Center 'Transformations of the State' at the University of Bremen, Germany. Her research interests focus on the internationalization of public policy, in particular in the fields of education policy, social policy and crime policies, with an emphasis on international actors. She is author of *International Organizations and Lifelong Learning From Agenda-Setting to Policy Diffusion* (Palgrave, forthcoming). Her latest articles appeared in *European Educational Research Journal, Compare* and in a special issue of the *Politische Vierteljahresschrift*.

Michael Baggesen Klitgaard is an Associate Professor in the Department of Political Science and Centre for Welfare State Research at the University of Southern Denmark. Research interests include the politics of welfare state reforms, comparative public policy and comparative political economy. His recent publications include a book analysing the decision-making process leading to the 2007 local government reform in Denmark. His latest articles have appeared in *West European Politics*, *Scandinavian Political Studies* and *Governance.*

Kerstin Martens is an Assistant Professor of International Relations at the University of Bremen, Germany. Her research focuses on actors and processes of international governance. She heads the research project on 'Internationalization of Education Policy', a 12-year project financed by the German Research Foundation as part of the TranState Research Center 'Transformations of the State' located at the University of Bremen. She is the author of *NGOs and the United Nations – Institutionalization, Professionalization and Adaptation* (Palgrave Macmillan, 2005). She is also co-editor of *New Arenas of Education Governance* and *Transforming the Golden-Age Nation State* (both Palgrave Macmillan, 2007).

Alexander-Kenneth Nagel is a researcher in the project 'Internationalization of Education Policy' within the TranState Research Center at the University of Bremen. His current research interests are policy network analysis and political sociology. Previous research focused on the institutionalization of transnational higher education policy making in the Bologna Process and religious social policy in the United States.

Rik de Ruiter is a post-doctoral researcher at the University of Twente, Department of Political Science and Research Methods. His main research interests are: European integration and new modes of governance, comparative politics, public policy, and international organizations. He holds a doctorate in Social and Political Sciences from the European University Institute, Florence, Italy. His latest article focuses on the development of the OMC e-Europe and is published in *West European Politics*.

Roberto Serpieri is an Associate Professor of Sociology of Education at the University Federico II, Naples, Italy. He has recently published books and articles on educational leadership and governance, focusing on the discursive shifts occurring in the education field in Italy and UK as well as on the spaces for democratic developments in education. He is the author of *Senza leadership: un discorso democratico per la scuola* [Without Leadership: a Democratic Discourse for the School] (FrancoAngeli, 2008) and *Governance delle politiche scolastiche* [School Policy Governance] (FrancoAngeli, 2008).

Katrin Toens is an Assistant Professor of Political Science at the University of Hamburg, Germany where she teaches political theory and German politics. Her recent work focuses on the analysis of the Bologna Process in German higher education politics. Previous research includes a study on the application of the distributive principles of social justice to social policy reforms in Germany and the United States.

Antoni Verger is a postdoctoral researcher of the AMIDSt (Amsterdam Institute for Metropolitan and International Development Studies) of the Universiteit van Amsterdam, Netherlands. He has been awarded a PhD in sociology from the Universitat Autònoma de Barcelona (UAB) for his work on WTO/GATS and Higher Education. His principal research topics are globalization and education politics, in particular in the context of GATS, as well as education and international development..

Klaus Dieter Wolf is a Professor of Political Science, Darmstadt University of Technology, Germany. He was President of the German Political Science Association (DVPW) from 2003–2006 and Non-North American Member of the Governing Council of the International Studies Association (ISA). He is also the Deputy Director of the Peace Research Institute Frankfurt (PRIF) and Principal Investigator in the Cluster of Excellence 'Formation of Normative Orders'. He is author of numerous studies on issues of transnational governance. He is also co-editor of *Die neuen Internationalen Beziehungen* (Nomos, 2003), *Macht und Ohnmacht internationaler Institutionen* (Campus, 2007) and co-author of *Die Vergesellschaftung des Regierens* (Leske+Budrich, 2003).

Preface and acknowledgements

The Eurovision Song Contest is not the best environment for creating a scholarly book – as one of us editors would say. Strange musicians play even stranger songs, and the world is divided into enthusiasts and those who are more than reluctant to share these emotions. Thinking back to the initial workshop of which this book is the outcome and which was scheduled by the ECPR parallel to the contest, we remember the friendly spirit of Helsinki in the spring, where all the foreigners seemed to be either political scientists or music fans – in rare cases even both, as was the case for two of the editors.

In this context, we arrived in Helsinki for the Joint Session 'Reforming Education Policy – Internationalization, Privatization – Governance', and we were looking forward to meeting political scientists who were also involved in researching education. As we had discovered in the years before, this is still a rather small community, but our workshop proposal was well received by the ECPR organizing committee and workshop applicants, and we had a fantastic session. A recurrent theme was why education has remained such an under-researched and 'homeless' topic on the agenda of political science. When we started thinking about it with many scholars interested in this question, we were quickly convinced that a book on this issue could be an important step in moving education more towards the heart of political science research. Time will show whether we were right.

If this goal is ever ultimately reached, it is also due to the broad support that we received during our project. First, we would like to thank all authors in this volume for their enthusiasm, their continuous support, their timeliness and willingness to revise manuscripts even after they had already been revised twice. Also, we would like to thank those workshop participants whose contribution could not become part of this volume. They provided very valuable insights and helped us formulate our thoughts.

An editors' meeting was held in Seeheim-Jugenheim, and Anja P. Jakobi and Kerstin Martens would like to thank Klaus Dieter Wolf for the friendly welcome and the pleasant working atmosphere we enjoyed at his home. Other support came from the collaborative research centre 'Transformations of the State' at the University of Bremen which financed a follow-up workshop, and from Maren Sennhenn and Julia Engelbrecht who supported us in its organization. Moreover, in summer 2008, the colloquium at the centre provided constructive comments on a first version of our introduction. We are also grateful for having profited from Michael Dobbins' language skills. The series' editor Thomas Poguntke and our publisher Routledge organized a very efficient review process, and the comments of two anonymous reviewers proved extremely helpful for refining our arguments.

Moreover, our thanks go to Toni Verger and Erkki Berndtson for their extensive feedback on the introduction and the conclusions, as well as to other authors who commented on the piece and the volume as a whole. We are also grateful for the support of Johannes Münnighoff, Maren Sennhenn and Ina Shakhrai, who assisted us in the editing process. Finally, we thank the Social Science Research Center (WZB) in Berlin, in particular Jutta Allmendinger and Rita Nikolai, which enabled Kerstin Martens to work on this book during a visiting scholarship in November 2007.

Anja P. Jakobi, Kerstin Martens and Klaus Dieter Wolf
Berlin, Bremen and Darmstadt, 2009

Series editor's preface

Discovering education as a neglected field of political analysis should be a bit like looking for snow in the arctic (well, at least before the age of global warming). After all, conflicts over who controls education were at the very heart of nation building and cleavage formation. The German *Kulturkampf* is but one of many examples of how modern states were taking control over the institutions of education, and many of these conflicts have left their traces in modern party systems. To be sure, more contemporary conflicts about the wearing of head-scarves in schools and universities in Turkey and France are reflections of exactly the same line of conflict. Furthermore, virtually all those who have a right to vote in modern democracies have been to school. And many of them have children who go either to school or to university.

As a result, there is probably no other field of public policy where the over-whelming majority of voters have a direct first-hand experience with or even a current interest in its performance. Hence, we should expect education policy to figure prominently on the political agendas of modern democracies. Even a brief recapitulation of the themes that have figured prominently on the front pages of an admittedly selective sample of countries confirms that this is indeed the case. While the disappointing results of the PISA study sent shockwaves through the German public at the beginning of the new millennium, the plan of the UK Labour government to substantially raise tuition fees for English universities had a similar effect a few years later. Likewise, Italy was shaken by substantial unrest in schools and universities when plans by the Berlusconi government became known in 2008 to impose substantial spending cuts on the education system.

Surely, a theme that has figured so prominently in public debate should have attracted the interest of political scientists. So why is there a need for re-discovery? The editors do not focus primarily on this question, and it is indeed difficult to come up with convincing causal reasons for the surprising disregard. However, they provide persuasive empirical evidence in their introduction for the fact that political scientists have indeed paid little attention to the analysis of education policies for many years while other policy fields like social or envir-onmental policies were given far more attention. This is not to say, of course, that education policy has not attracted attention by academic analysts but they tended to be located in other disciplines, mainly in education studies and sociology. Consequently, the political processes leading to specific education policies were not at the centre of their research. Instead, they focused on the content of such policies, their success or failure and their effects on the social fabric of society.

The current volume sets out to correct this omission by choosing the governance paradigm as the dominant perspective of most of its analyses. To be sure, this choice is convincing and almost self-evident. After all, the dominant trends in education policy over the past decade or so can be summarized by a few catchwords like internationalization, privatization and benchmarking. While empirical reality is always more complex (and often contradictory) than such denominators of seminal trends seem to indicate, there can be little doubt that especially as regards the university sector many modern democracies have moved into a similar direction. While tuition fees were the exception rather than the rule a decade ago, they have become fairly widespread by now. Obviously, they are no indication of a wholesale privatization of higher education but they reflect a shift in the dominant spirit towards a significantly increased regard for the logic of economic efficiency. Similarly, private funding and the logic of new public management have gained substantial weight in the higher education systems of many countries. Overall, this amounts to partial withdrawal of the state and the growing involvement of other stakeholders (like representatives of the business community) in the steering of universities – which is a classic case of moving from government to governance.

However, governance is frequently not confined to the nation state, and the Bologna Process has had profound effects on the structure and the management of higher education in many countries. At the same time, international organizations entered the stage, and the results of the OECD PISA study measuring the achievement of pupils around the globe sparked off heated debates in some countries. International rankings of universities or university departments are another example where private actors have entered the policy process introducing elements of market competition.

This timely volume takes several complementary approaches to the analysis of education policy, including the perspectives of comparative politics, policy analysis and International Relations. It concludes with a section that takes a step back from this and reflects on the wider implications of the findings of the book from a theoretical perspective. As Klaus Dieter Wolf emphasizes in Chapter 11, 'it is overdue to re-establish political science as the leading discipline for generating the normative foundations of the educational reform discourse, rather than leaving it to the economists and their followers among policy analysts'. May the current volume indeed turn out to be something like the starting gun for a movement towards a more intense and reflected debate about the directions of educational reform.

Thomas Poguntke, Series Editor
Florence, January 2009

Jürgen Enders takes the outsider's perspective of an expert in higher education. As a sociologist, he reflects on what political science has achieved in researching the field of education, and he formulates what it should and could contribute in the future (Chapter 13). He argues that current political reforms of education systems as well as conceptual developments in the study of the governance of public sectors provide new windows of opportunity for a more fruitful relationship between political science and educational research. Starting from the points of departure from this introductory chapter, Enders reflects on why education traditionally has not been a main focus of political science, nor was the political process at the heart of education research. These are puzzling observations given the important role of education in modern nation-states, and also with regard to the recent major educational reforms that offer important insights to shifts of governance. The challenge ahead for Enders is thus how both political science and educational research can overcome their mutual neglect and evaluate together the processes and outcomes of reforms in education in terms of effectiveness and democratic legitimacy. He provides an attempt of how such barriers between the disciplines could be overcome.

In their conclusion, the editors take stock of what has been achieved by the contributions to this volume. They bring together the results about education reform processes in order to link them to the general debate on governance (Chapter 14). They also take these findings as a starting point for further conclusions along the lines of the two central themes of this volume: First, the authors focus on what political science can contribute to the analysis of education policy – more specifically: 'What do we know more about education policy when we analyse it from a governance perspective?' Second, they focus on how the subject can enrich the discipline by reversing the first question to 'What do we know more about politics after having analysed education policy?' Finally, based on these findings, as well as from a general perspective on research on education policy, future areas of research are outlined that promise to be particularly fruitful for further inquiry. In sum, by providing answers to these questions, this volume introduces education into the field of political science – a long overdue exercise.

Note

1 Details of data generation: SSCI, query from February 2008; search criteria: years 1970–2007, TI = 'education policy' (respectively: TI = 'social policy' or TI = 'environmental policy'), articles only; refined: political science only. We thank Maren Sennhenn for research assistance.

References

Alexander, K.L., Entwistle, D.R. and Olson, L.S. (2007) 'Lasting consequences of the summer learning gap', *American Sociological Review*, 72, 3: 167–180.

Allmendinger, J. and Leibfried, S. (2003) 'Education and the welfare state', *Journal of European Social Policy*, 13, 1: 63–81.

Andersen, V.N. (2007) 'Transparency and openness: a reform or education policy?', *Scandinavian Political Studies*, 30, 1: 38–60.

APSA (2007) 'Task force on political violence and terrorism'. Online, available at: www.apsanet.org/section_571.cfm.

Bache, I. and Flinders, M. (eds) (2005) *Multilevel Governance*, Oxford: Oxford University Press.

Becker, G.S. (1964) *Human Capital: A Theoretical and Empirical Analysis, with Special Reference to Education*, Chicago: University of Chicago Press.

Benz, A. and Papadopoulos, Y. (eds) (2006) *Governance and Democracy*, London: Routledge.

Benz, A., Lütz, S., Schimank, U. and Simonis, G. (eds) (2007) *Handbuch Governance. Theoretische Grundlagen und empirische Anwendungsfelder*, Wiesbaden: VS Verlag.

Busemeyer, Marius R. (2007) 'Determinants of public education spending in 21 OECD democracies, 1980–2001', *Journal of European Public Policy*, 14: 582–610.

Callan, E. (2005) *Creating Citizens. Political Education and Liberal Democracy*, Oxford: Oxford University Press.

Collins, R. (1979) *Credential Society: A Historical Sociology of Education and Stratification*, New York: Academic Press.

Dahl, R.A. (2005) *Who Governs? Democracy and Power in an American City*, 2nd edn, New Heaven and London: Yale University Press.

Dale, R. (1989) *The State and Education Policy*, Milton Keynes: Open University Press.

Dale, R. (1999) 'Specifying globalization effects on national policy. A focus on the mechanisms', *Journal of Education Policy*, 14, 1: 1–17.

Dale, R. (2005) 'Globalisation, knowledge economy and comparative education', *Comparative Education*, 41: 117–149.

Dale, Roger and Robertson, Susan (2002) 'The varying effects of regional organizations as subjects of globalisation of education', *Comparative Education Review*, 46: 10–36.

DVPW (2007) 'Politik & Wirtschaft in der Lehrerausbildung', position paper of the German Political Science Association (DVPW) and the German Society of Political Science (DGfP), Osnabrück.

Genschel, P. and Zangl, B. (2007) *Die Zerfaserung von Staatlichkeit und die Zentralität des Staates*, TransState Working Paper 62/2007.

Goodin, R.E. and Klingemann, H.-D. (eds) (1998) *A New Handbook of Political Science*, Oxford: Oxford University Press.

Graz, J.-C. and Nölke, A. (eds) (2008) *Transnational Private Governance and its Limits*, London: Routledge.

Heidenheimer, A.J. (1981) 'Education and social security entitlements in Europe and America', in P. Flora and A.J. Heidenheimer (eds) *The Development of Welfare States in Europe and America*, New Brunswick and London: Transaction Press, 269–306.

Henry, M., Lingard, B., Rizvi, F. and Taylor, S. (2001) *The OECD, Globalisation and Education Policy*, Paris: Pergamon.

Hill, M. (2006) *Social Policy in the Modern World. A Comparative Text*, Malden: Blackwell.

Hurrelmann, A., Leibfried, S., Martens, K. and Mayer, P. (2007) 'The golden-age nation state and its transformation – a framework for analysis', in A. Hurrelmann, S. Leibfried, K. Martens and P. Mayer (eds) *Transforming the Golden Age Nation State*, Houndmills: Palgrave Macmillan, 1–23.

Jakobi, A.P. (2007a) 'Converging agendas in education policy – lifelong learning in World Bank and International Labour Organization', in K. Martens, A. Rusconi and K. Leuze (eds) *New Arenas of Education Politics – The Impact of International Organisations and Markets on Educational Policy Making*, Houndmills: Palgrave Macmillan, 95–114.

Jakobi, A.P. (2007b) 'The knowledge society and global dynamics in education policy', *European Educational Research Journal*, 6: 39–51.

Jakobi, A.P. (2009) *International Organizations and Lifelong Learning from Agenda-Setting to Policy Diffusion*, Houndmills: Palgrave Macmillan (forthcoming).

Jakobi, A.P and Martens, K. (2007) 'Diffusion durch Internationale Organisationen: Die Bildungspolitik der OECD', in K. Holzinger, C. Knill and H. Joergens (eds) *Transfer, Diffusion und Konvergenz von Politik. Politische Vierteljahresschrift*, Special Issue, Wiesbaden: VS Verlag, 247–270.

Jary, D. (2005) 'UK higher education policy and the global "Third Way"', *Policy and Politics*, 33, 4: 637–655.

Kallo, Johanna and Rinne, Risto (2006) *Supranational Regimes and National Education Policies – Encountering Challenge*, Helsinki: FERA.

Katznelson, I. and Milner, H.V. (eds) (2002) *Political Science. State of the Discipline*, New York: Norton.

Kooiman, J. (ed.) (2000) 'Societal governance: levels, modes, and orders of social-political interaction', in J. Pierre (ed.) *Debating Governance*, Oxford: Oxford University Press, 138–164.

Kooiman, J. (2003) *Governing as Governance*, London: Sage.

Leibfried, S. and Zürn, M. (2005) *Transformations of the State?*, Cambridge: Cambridge University Press.

McGuinn, P. (2006) *No Child Left Behind and the Transformation of Federal Education Policy 1965–2005*, Lawrence: University Press of Kansas.

McMahon, W.W. (2003) *Lifelong Learning in Developing Countries. An Analysis with Estimates of Private Returns and Externalities*, Washington, DC: World Bank.

Mäding, H. (1989) 'Federalism and education planning in the Federal Republic of Germany', *Publius: The Journal of Federalism*, 19: 115–131.

Manna, P. (2006) *School's in: Federalism and the National Education Agenda*, Washington, DC: Georgetown University Press.

Martens, K. and Weymann, A. (2007) 'The internationalization of education policy – towards convergence of national paths?', in A. Hurrelmann, S. Leibfried, K. Martens and P. Mayer (eds) *Transforming the Golden Age Nation State*, Houndmills: Palgrave Macmillan, 152–172.

Martens, K. and Wolf, K.D. (2006) 'Paradoxien der neuen Staatsräson. Die Internationalisierung der Bildungspolitik in der EU und OECD', *Zeitschrift für Internationale Beziehungen*, 13, 2: 145–176.

Martens, K., Rusconi, A. and Leuze, K. (eds) (2007) *New Arenas of Education Governance. The Impact of Markets and International Organizations on Education Policy Making*, Houndmills: Palgrave Macmillan.

Meyer, J.W. and Ramirez, F.O. (2003) 'The world institutionalization of education', in J. Schriewer (ed.) *Discourse Formation in Comparative Education*, Frankfurt am Main: Peter Lang, 111–132.

Meyer, J.W., Boli, J., Thomas, G.M. and Ramirez, F.O. (1997) 'World society and the nation-state', *American Journal of Sociology*, 103, 1: 144–181.

Meyer, J.W., Kamens, D. and Benavot, A. (1992) *School Knowledge for the Masses*, Bristol: Falmer Press.

Mintrom, M. (2000) *Policy Entrepreneurs and School Choice*, Washington, DC: Georgetown University Press.

Mok, K. (2001) 'Education policy reform', in L. Wong and N. Flynn (eds) *The Market in Chinese Social Policy*, Houndmills: Palgrave Macmillan, 88–111.

Ohmae, K. (1995) *The End of the Nation-state: The Rise of Regional Economics*, New York: Free Press.

Opielka, M. (2006) 'Einleitung', in M. Opielka (ed.) *Bildungsreform als Sozialreform. Zum Zusammenhang von Bildungs- und Sozialpolitik*, Wiesbaden: VS Verlag, 7–10.

Patterson, J.T. (2001) *Brown vs. Board of Education. A Civil Rights Milestone and its Troubled Legacy*, Oxford: Oxford University Press.

Rigby, E. (2007) 'Same policy area, different politics: how characteristics of policy tools alter the determinants of early childhood education policy', *Policy Studies Journal*, 35, 4: 653–669.

Robertson, S.L., Bonal, X. and Dale, R. (2002) 'GATS and the education service industry: the politics of scale and re-territorialization', *Comparative Education Review*, 46: 472–496.

Rosenau, J.N. (2004) 'Strong demand, huge supply: governance in an emerging epoch', in I. Bache and M. Flinders (eds) *Multi-Level Governance*, Oxford: Oxford University Press, 31–48.

Scharpf, F.W. (1991) 'Die Handlungsfähigkeit des Staates am Ende des zwanzigsten Jahrhunderts', *Politische Vierteljahresschrift*, 32, 4: 621–634.

Schmidt, M.G. (2003) 'Ausgaben für Bildung im internationalen Vergleich', *Aus Politik und Zeitgeschichte*, 6–11.

Schuetze, H.G. (2006) 'International concepts and agendas of lifelong learning', *Compare*, 36, 3: 289–306.

Schuppert, G.F. (ed.) (2006) *Governance-Forschung. Vergewisserung über Stand und Entwicklungslinien*, Baden-Baden: Nomos.

Strange, S. (1996) *The Retreat of the State. The Diffusion of Power in the World Economy*, Cambridge: Cambridge University Press.

Walkenhorst, H. (2008) 'Explaining change in EU education policy', *Journal of European Public Policy*, 15: 567–587.

Weymann, A., Martens, K., Rusconi, A. and Leuze, K. (2007) 'International organizations, markets and the nation state in education governance', in K. Martens, A. Rusconi and K. Leuze (eds) *New Arenas of Education Governance – The Impact of International Organisations and Markets on Education Policy Making*, Houndmills: Palgrave Macmillan, 229–241.

Witte, J. (2006) *Change of Degrees – Degrees of Change. Comparing Adaptions of European Higher Education Systems in the Context of the Bologna Process*, Enschede: University of Twente.

Wolf, K.D. (2006) 'Private actors and the legitimacy of governance beyond the state. Conceptional outlines and empirical explorations', in A. Benz and Y. Papadopoulos (eds) *Governance and Democracy*, London: Routledge, 200–227.

Zürn, M. (1998) *Regieren jenseits des Nationalstaates*, Frankfurt/Main: Suhrkamp.

Part I

Comparative education politics

Exploring legacies and institutional settings

2 Veto-points and the politics of introducing school vouchers in the United States and Sweden

Michael Baggesen Klitgaard

Introduction

Within comparative political analysis it is often presumed that liberal ideology strongly embeds the American nation and biases the political culture of the country against large government, towards personal freedom and individual choice. Scandinavians, on the other hand, are supposed to be more egalitarian and to hold collectivist values that translate into a positive vision of a dominating state that regulates significant parts of peoples' lives (Steinmo and Watts 1995: 331; Rothstein 1998; Moe 2001: 15). From this perspective, two decades of institutional reforms in primary school education in the United States and Sweden pose an intriguing puzzle. For generations, both countries have operated universal public school systems according to which all citizens have the right to attain free and compulsory education. In the beginning of the 1980s, educational reform movements began, however, to suggest changes in this traditional form of primary education, and the issue of school choice in general and school vouchers in particular caused harsh conflicts in the following two decades (Klitgaard 2007b). Moving from a centralized way of governance to a market-like model, school vouchers represent a financial arrangement in which students are provided with a tuition certificate that can be used to attend public or private schools participating in the program (NCSPE 2003). Vouchers concentrate, so to speak, the idea of a new mix between public and private, or state and market, embraced by dominant public sector reform prescriptions produced by, for example, the OECD since the 1980s (Premfors 1998; Pollit and Bouckeart 2004). Vouchers guarantee education, but they do not determine where to go to school. This decision remains at the individual level, so that school choice is privatized, while the educational service can be provided by either public agencies or private entrepreneurs.

School vouchers were debated regularly in the American Congress and during all presidential election campaigns since the early 1980s, but have developed only in a sporadic fashion, meaning that some limited voucher programs are established in a few states and cities while a nation-wide program on several occasions has been rejected (Moe 2001). In contrast to the United States, Sweden however adopted national and universal public school vouchers in the beginning of the 1990s. Today the Swedish school system therefore allows for extended competition and school choice between public and private providers of basic education (Blomqvist and Rothstein 2000; Blomqvist 2004). A central Swedish welfare policy, historically aimed at increasing social and economic equality in the Swedish society (Rothstein 1996), is in other words transformed into a policy in which the market forces play a significant role in matters of governance and regulation. In the United States, on the other hand, it has been very difficult to advance a policy that appears as tailor-made to the dominant political culture of the country. The intention of this chapter is to explain why the output from the politics of school vouchers in the United States and Sweden varies to this extent. Why was a universal voucher-program established nation-wide in Sweden, while successful implementation of vouchers in the United States is limited to a few states and cities?

Answering these questions is of general interest for political science, as the puzzle pushes a couple of well-established theories about policy determinants to their limits. There is, for example, a lack of systematic correlation between (non-)adoption of school vouchers and variables as partisan politics and path-dependency in the policy field. The argument of this chapter is that these different developments are a result of the different institutional settings in which the politics of vouchers unfolded. A multitude of institutional veto-opportunities in American policy-making constrained the federal government from realizing its preferences, while very few veto-points provided Swedish governments with a formidable degree of independent policy capacity (Weaver and Rockman 1993). Federal US governments are constrained by presidentialism, bicameralism and federalism, while federalism at the same time facilitates policy innovations at a lower level of government (Martin 2008).

The present contribution is arranged as a matched comparison between a positive and a negative case, which is a strategy of comparative analysis allowing for generalization from even small-*n* structured comparisons (Mahoney and Goertz 2004: 653). The first section discusses shortly some alternative explanations to understand the output from school policy-making. The second part elaborates further on the veto-point argument, while the third section consists of a comparative study of school policy-making in the United States and Sweden since the 1980s. The fourth and final section highlights the conclusions and discusses the potential of generalizing broadly to the process of restructuring principles of governance in welfare service provision.

How to explain the politics of vouchers?

Contemporary discussions on policy developments in economically advanced democracies contain a scholarly dispute about the causal effects of, on the one hand, partisan competition and ideological preferences of government, and on the other the impact of institutionalized policy legacies (Pierson 1994; Allan and Scruggs 2004). Regarding traditional politics matters arguments, conservative and right-winged governments are normally associated with positive views on market-type solutions in provision of public services, whereas social democratic and left-winged governments are seen as more skeptical toward such arrangements. Several scholars have for example identified causal relations between the strengths and ideologies of parties and the share of national incomes spent on social welfare as well as the institutional characteristics of welfare systems (Korpi 1988; Hicks and Swank 1992; Huber *et al.* 1993). If this conclusion is brought into contemporary analysis of the politics of welfare state and public sector reforms, it is reasonable to suggest conservative governments are more likely to adopt school vouchers and related school choice policies than more left-leaning governments.

Republican administrations in the United States between 1981 and 1993 endorsed the idea of school vouchers and presented on several occasions legislative initiatives to the Congress. However, Republican governments never succeeded in implementing public voucher models and school choice nation-wide (Chubb and Moe 1990). In Sweden, on the other hand, a fully developed voucher scheme was implemented by the conservative government in 1992. The decisive move toward vouchers, however, was made when the social democratic government in 1990 introduced a new principle of school funding, allowing private schools to attract public funding on equal terms with public schools (Klitgaard 2007a). In other words, what conservatives failed to accomplish in the United States during 12 years in power was initiated by a social democratic government in Sweden, which makes it difficult to see the strict lines between traditional arguments about the role of politics and real-world developments during the period investigated here.

The politics matters thesis, attributed strong explanatory power in studies of welfare state expansion, was strongly challenged by the concept of *path-dependency* when scholars in the early 1990s began to analyze the reversal process of welfare-state contraction (Pierson 2000). The basic idea of this concept is that policy choice at t_2 depends on the situation at t_1 as policies mobilize political constituencies and interests, and become part of the political foundation upon which subsequent choices are made. Hence, if two democracies diverge in their approach to reform public schools and other types of welfare programs, this may depend upon varying initial starting points for such reform activities (Rothstein and Steinmo 2002: 2).

A universal public school system, attached with strong user groups and well-organized professionals with strong interests in preserving the system has however been the dominating educational institution in both countries for generations. Elaborated theories of path-dependency do include reflections about the dynamics of radical outbreaks of change (Mahoney 2000). If we however accept the idea that the situation at t_1 determines future developments in a policy field, we should expect similarity rather than variation between the United States and Sweden, as their policy legacies in this particular field are quite similar. The problem that moreover arises with these type of arguments, at least when they come in stylized versions, is a problem of crypto-determinism. Once a certain policy path is established, it is presumed to be locked in and to stay in equilibrium as actors are inclined to adjust their strategies to accommodate the prevailing pattern (Thelen 1999: 385).

Thus, in contrast to expecting particular policy outputs to precisely reflect the preferences of a whatever-colored government, or as more or less predetermined by previously established policy legacies, this contribution emphasizes the importance of formal institutions in public policy-making. Certainly, American and Swedish governments of different colors shared a preference for introducing school choice into largely similar structures of existing school policy. However, extremely different institutional platforms left them with varying resources for translating such a preference into policy.

Institutions and veto-points in school policy decision-making

The welfare state crisis in the 1970s and early 1980s put decision-makers in economically advanced countries under increased pressure to develop new modes of regulating the public sector (Pierre 1993; Premfors 1998: 142). Quasi-market arrangements, including a stronger reliance on private entrepreneurs as service-providers and freedom of choice for citizens, were seen as one among other appropriate policy tools to increase public-sector efficiency and to make public agencies more responsive toward citizen preferences (Pollit and Bouckeart 2004).

As mentioned before, school vouchers concentrate this idea, and are believed by voucher proponents to improve the quality, cost-efficiency and responsiveness of schools as they allow for parental choice and competition between public and private institutions (Chubb and Moe 1990). The voucher policy has thus been a central but disputed issue on the reform agenda in many OECD countries (OECD 1994, 2002), which to varying degrees have succeeded in implementing it to national systems of education. But why is this so? Why is it that some governments in some countries stand out as more efficient in transforming reform preferences into legislation, while others are more constrained?

During the 1990s, scholars located the answer to this question by analyzing how institutional rules structure policy-making processes. Institutional rules are given with the constitutional organization of a polity. Does the constitution, for example, divide power between mutually independent branches of government, or is power concentrated within the hands of the executives? This question is, basically, about the length of the decision-making chain. As noticed by Immergut, political decisions are not single decisions made at one point in time, but typically require successive affirmative votes along a chain of decisions. The fate of legislative proposals thus depends upon the number and location of veto-opportunities along this chain (Immergut 1992: 63; Tsebelis 1995). Veto-opportunities, or veto-points, are areas of institutional vulnerability in the political process where the mobilization of power and interests has an opportunity to influence the process and the outcomes (Thelen and Steinmo 1992: 7). This chapter advances a theoretical argument particularly based on Immergut's perspective on institutions as the rules of the game. The assumption is that pref-

erences, goals and interests of actors are formed independently of the institutions; yet institutions affect their strategic opportunities to achieve the desired
policies (Immergut 1992: 231).

Division versus concentration of political power has first to do with the organization of the central authorities. Do they take the form of a presidential
separation-of-powers system or parliamentarism? Presidentialism separates
political power between the executive and the legislative branch of government,
which furthermore can be controlled by different parties (Bonoli 2001: 241).
This may create political obstacles to governmental ambitions of realizing preferred policy choices since governmental initiatives always face the risk of being
met with a veto from the legislative branch of government. Also, when the electorate installs a parliament controlled by the president's party. American presidents, for example, are directly elected and their government cannot be brought
down by a no-confidence vote in the Congress. Congress members are thus freer
to vote in the interests of their constituency and against their own government
without running the risks of voting it out of office (Weaver and Rockman 1993:
13; Bonoli 2001).

Political power in parliamentary systems is more concentrated since executive authority emerges from and is responsible to legislative authority. This constitutes a political system characterized by mutual dependence between the
executive and legislative branch of government (Strøm 2000: 264). Governments
need to control a parliamentary majority not only to move into office but also to
stay there. This structure enhances partisan discipline, and will often allow the
government to form a parliamentary majority in support of government-
sponsored policy proposals, even when the government's parliamentary base of
support disagrees with the content of a proposed policy. Compared to presidential systems, political power is thus more concentrated within the hands of the
government in parliamentary democracies, which is an important reason why
such polities are lesser biased toward deadlocks (Goodin 1996; Crepaz and
Birchfield 2000: 210; Strøm 2000).

Different relationships between the executive and legislative branch of government account for a significant part of the varying reform capacity between
advanced democracies (Weaver and Rockman 1993). Yet the organization of
parliaments is also important. Is the parliament unicameral as in Sweden (after
1969), Denmark (after 1953) and Finland, or bicameral as in the United States,
Germany and France? Under unicameralism proposals only have to be approved
in one chamber, and are thus associated with stronger governmental control in
the decision-making process – control which of course is even stronger when
unicameralism is associated with a strong degree of parliamentarism as in, for
example, Sweden and Denmark (Lijphart 1999). If, as in bicameral settings,
members of a first and second chamber possess veto-opportunities and are in a
position to block policy initiatives, governmental efficiency is more inhibited
(Steinmo and Watts 1995).

A third macro-institutional variable with consequences for the reform capacity of central governments relates to the governmental structures. In unitary

states, as for example Sweden, policy-makers are often able to concentrate on the question of 'what is to be done?' and enjoy considerable freedom to implement their preferred policies. This is in sharp contrast to federal systems as in the United States and Germany, in which authorities at the central level coexist with authorities in the units constituting the federation. Since governmental authorities at all levels have a preference for policy control, questions over policy innovations under federalism are likely to be obstructed in political conflicts among competing centers of political authority. Federal political systems tend, so to say, to superimpose the question of 'who should do it?' (Pierson 1995: 451; Castles 1999).

As argued by Martin, however, the view on federalism as constituting an additional veto-point is only partial (Martin 2008). If the central government depends on, for instance, 50 different states in order to achieve a desired policy, these indeed look like 50 different veto-points – but only from the central point of view. The more federalism namely disperses political authority, the more opportunities policy-makers at the lower level of government may have to change the policy. Federalism has, in other words, two faces; it appears as a structure of veto-points that might block centrally planned policy innovations, but it also appears as a structure of access points that encourage policy proposals from policy-makers at lower levels of the government (Martin 2008). As a result, policy innovations under strong federalism are unlikely to evolve regularly nation-wide, rather according to the institutional and political settings in the decentralized political units, which may be highly different.

The subsequent part of this chapter explores whether such institutional arguments account for different outputs from the politics of school vouchers in the United States and Sweden. Insights gained from institutional political analysis lead us to expect the central Swedish government to have much stronger institutional reform capacity than the federal government of the United States. We also expect American federalism to facilitate sporadic policy innovations in the units constituting the federation.

The politics of vouchers in the United States

The Reagan administration entered the White House in 1981 with declared skepticism toward the federal government and launched political strategies of tax cuts, cuts in public spending, welfare state retrenchment and institutional re-arrangements to favor the principles of the market. Another political strategy of the new administration was so-called 'new federalism'. To reduce the central government Reagan intended to shift a good deal of policy activities back to the states (Pierson and Smith 1993).

The Reagan administration's approach to educational reforms is on the one hand in good keeping with the new federalism initiatives. American schools are governed by the educational policies of their respective states, which are responsible for public education according to the Constitution (Chubb 2001: 27). The new conservative government sought to dismantle the Federal Department of

Education and turn further political responsibilities and funding for education over to state governments. On the other hand, the federal government became rather active in stimulating school choice and competition between public and private institutions. When a national commission in 1983 declared the United States a 'nation at risk' because of the poor quality of the educational system (Pappagiannis *et al.* 1992: 12), political controversies over educational policy in general, and vouchers and school choice in particular, were catapulted to the top of the political agenda. During the following years, the issue attracted the attention of the President, presidential candidates, members of the Congress, media, organized interests and think tanks (Cibulka 2000: 151).

As mentioned, the newly elected conservative administration had a strong preference for encouraging a more market-driven American society and school vouchers were a notable instrument in realizing this preference within the sphere of public education. In the years ahead, the American school debate of course came to involve several elements, but most of them became subordinated to the debate about vouchers and school choice. Those in favor of school choice saw universal public vouchers as a strategy for racial de-segregation, the way to improve academic standards, and to increase institutional efficiency (Moe 2001: 27–28). Opponents of vouchers argued instead that exactly such problems are aggravated with opt-out options to the private sector (Ravitch 2001; Boyd and Lugg 1998).

As mentioned before, the conservative administration of the early 1980s was not completely dedicated to the idea of a new federalism in relation to the school choice issue (Moe 2001: 25, 36–37). While the first Reagan administration reduced federal support for public education, it proposed too, in 1983, a program that would increase federal support for private education – either through tuition tax credits or through public vouchers (Henig 1994: 72). This program was however refuted by a Democratic Congress – as was another program proposed in 1985. A third attempt was made in 1986 and this time with a much more modest program that would have given local school districts the option to use vouchers, without requiring them to do so. It would also have left the decision to the local districts whether to allow such vouchers to be used for private schools. But the result was the same – it never made it through the Congress, controlled by a Democratic Party through which extremely skeptical teachers' unions exerted enormous resistance (Moe 2001: 27). The unsuccessful initiatives made by the White House in this period demonstrate exactly the problem central governments in fragmented institutional settings often face. Because the Democratic Congress serves as a veto-point, which voucher proposals have to pass, the Republican President could not form a sufficient majority in favor of this policy. Moreover, the Republican President could not even count on strong support from Republican Congress members (Henig 1994: 72). Conservative elected officials often have constituents who are in the suburbs, fairly satisfied with their schools, and not pressuring for reforms (Moe 2001: 34).

In the beginning of the 1990s, the first President Bush, who had stated his intention to become the 'Education President' (Henig 1994: 90), made another push for public vouchers. He began his term by pushing for public school choice instead of supporting vouchers, but during the election year of 1992 he launched his 'G.I. Bill for Children', which would have provided $1,000 vouchers to children from low-income families – an idea that went nowhere in a still Democratic Congress. The voucher issue continued to be a central issue in all presidential election campaigns throughout the 1990s, and in 1998, the now Republican controlled Congress successfully enacted a bill authorizing vouchers for children from low-income families in Washington, DC. This bill was, however, vetoed by President Clinton (Moe 2001: 36–37).

In the shadow of national deadlocks, notable developments occurred only regionally and locally. The first public voucher programs were introduced in Milwaukee in 1990, and designed for use by children from low-income families (Mintrom 2000: 24). A similar program was subsequently established in Cleveland in 1996, and the first statewide voucher program introduced in Florida in 1999, restricted to students from failing public schools. After Florida came the state of Colorado in 2003, passing a voucher plan to provide vouchers for students from low-income families with low academic performance (Levin and Belfield 2003).

Although policy innovations in some states often diffuse to others (Berry and Berry 1999), state autonomy and strong federalism in school policy makes it uncertain to which degree that will happen with school vouchers. Federalism may indeed serve as a veto-point from a national point of view, but it may also facilitate policy innovations at local levels of government. This second face of federalism is an important reason for the irregular development of school vouchers in the United States. It has been argued that when the United States Supreme Court in 2002 ruled that the Cleveland voucher program (*Zelman* v. *Simmons-Harris*) does not violate the Establishment Clause of the First Amendment, a green light was given for the development of vouchers elsewhere. Yet the Supreme Court ruling does not abrogate the application of restrictive provisions in state constitutions, which vary widely. Some can be interpreted as permissive to this policy innovation whereas most others are either very restrictive or at best uncertain (Kemerer 2002: 2). In 2003 the Colorado voucher plan was for example struck down, as it was judged to violate the Colorado Constitution by depriving local school boards of control (Levin and Belfield 2003: 9). Consistently, public attitudes have not been overwhelmingly positive toward school vouchers. Local referenda on vouchers have in fact been defeated by sizeable margins, with political opposition easily mobilized (Belfield and Levin 2002; Kenny 2005).

The success of the voucher movement in American school policy has altogether been relatively limited – at least so far. Not only compared to what Swedish governments achieved in the same period but also compared to the achievements of the American charter school movement. Charter schools are public schools of choice, supported by public funds and enjoying a greater freedom from regulations than traditional public schools (NCSPE 2003). The first state to adopt charter school legislation was Minnesota in 1991, and charter schools have grown rapidly since. According to the Center for Educational Reform, 40 states and Washington, DC have adopted charter school legislation by 2007, and about 4,000 charter schools are serving more than a million children (The Center for Educational Reform 2007). Charter schools have won support from various proponents and faced much less resistance than the voucher movement, as they to a lesser degree threaten to undermine the public institutions (Moe 2001: 40). As much as a choice reform, charter schools should also be seen as a decentralization of management to the schools though, going hand-in-hand with other forms of school-based management principles introduced during the 1990s.

The politics of vouchers in Sweden   *Brief overview.*

In the late 1970s, the Swedish public sector was increasingly exposed to criticism for bureaucratic red tape. Against this background, the Social Democratic Party returned in 1982 to office after six years in opposition and launched a comprehensive reform program to facilitate a series of governance reforms. The Social Democratic Party in particular had strong political incentives to do so. For the first time in 44 years, the party lost office in 1976 – partly caused by the electorate's increasingly critical attitude toward the public sector that especially developed under Social Democratic rule between 1973 and 1976 (Petterson 1977: 199–205). The dominant explanation for the historical political change in 1976 was accordingly that perception of the public sector and the welfare state as a rigid bureaucracy first and foremost invalidated the Social Democratic Party in terms of voter mobilization. Incumbency 44 years in a row made it difficult to identify the borders of the party and the beginning of the state (Mellbourn 1986: 12–13; Antman 1993: 52; Pierre 1993). Hence, since public sector and welfare state activities did not accord precisely enough with citizen preferences (Gustafsson 1987: 179–180), the Social Democrats had a strong incentive to modernize this traditionally unsurpassable political asset of the party (Klitgaard 2007a).

The state-dominated and centrally regulated public school system soon became a salient issue on the reform agenda. The dominating principle laid down in this system during the post-war era was to provide all children with a standardized and high-quality form of basic education. Only 0.2 percent of the pupils were enrolled to private schools in the early 1980s. In the second half of the 1980s, the Swedish study of power and democracy conducted a major survey of the Swedish population's attitudes toward possibilities of influencing the public services they use. This survey demonstrated above all a feeling of lack of influence in relation to public schools. The attitudes toward schools were, for example, that it was difficult to influence the teaching offered to one's children and to choose a school according to one's own preferences (Petterson *et al.* 1989: 262). Various policy proposals for school policy reforms launched in different party and government programs since 1982 were then passed on to the arena of decision-making. The proposals did not become subjects of decision-making beforehand, as strong disagreements existed between the leaders of the

Social Democratic Party, which is the government, and several social democratic backbenchers. Internal party disagreements were settled in the late 1980s though, which allowed the government to initiate a decision-making process that fundamentally altered the structures of the Swedish school system.

In 1988, responsibilities for public primary schools were delegated to municipalities, while the role of central state authorities was reduced to formulating general political goals, financial funding, and overseeing the quality of public schools through evaluations (Proposition 1988/89:4: 9). Decentralization was guided by the principle that schools should have an opportunity to develop special academic or pedagogical profiles, and to conduct education according to the needs and demands of the local environment (Proposition 1988/89:4: 53–56). In the autumn of 1989, municipalities came in charge of school personnel (Proposition 1989/90:41: 12), and a new funding system was introduced in 1990/1991 (Proposition 1990/91:18: 25). The new funding system gave municipalities an unspecified block grant, though earmarked for schools and educational purposes. With this, municipalities were given more freedom to dispose of resources and organize public schooling.

New forms of school choice also evolved. Since schools were given an opportunity to develop special profiles, they were also obliged to meet individual preferences of school choice as far as practically and economically possible (Proposition 1988/89:4: 53–7). Nevertheless, school choice was not restricted to a choice between only public schools. Due to the new funding system, private schools were given the possibility of attaining public funding on equal conditions with public schools. As mentioned, the Social Democrats had a harsh internal discussion about public funding of private schools during the 1980s, as the 'traditionalists' of the party feared this would undermine the principles of the universal welfare state. When the government bill proposing a new funding system was debated in a parliamentary committee, the Center Party, which was the primary political alliance of the government, proposed that municipalities should allocate resources in accordance with a principle of needs to all schools, public or private (Betænkning 1990/1991: 23). The government did not oppose this, and enacted in practice a voucher model allowing parents and pupils to choose between public and private, but publicly financed, schools.

During this process, shifting Social Democratic governments broke with the traditional corporatist and consensus-oriented policy-making style. Teachers' unions and other organized interests on several occasions were left in the cold without efficient opportunities to influence the legislative process (Lindbom 1995: 71; Klitgaard 2004). Thus, a characteristic feature of the Swedish process is that the Swedish government, different than American governments sharing a preference for vouchers, had the institutional and political strength to pass its policy proposals through the parliament. As internal disagreements were settled and sufficient alliances created with other parties in the parliament, the government was able to follow its policy preferences and implement desired changes to the public school system on the basis of a stable majority.

In 1991, a Conservative government coalition came to power and abandoned the principle of needs testing in order to grant private schools public funding. This government decided that private schools should have the right to receive an amount per pupil of 85 percent of the average costs of a pupil in public schools, and to charge parents an additional school fee. When the Social Democrats returned to office in 1994, they reduced this to 75 percent due to the economic crisis, but decided in 1996 that private schools should be granted public funding per pupil corresponding to the costs per pupil in public schools. In connection to this, it was also decided that private schools no longer could charge parents for an additional school fee (Klitgaard 2007b). This institutional overhaul of the Swedish public schools caused an increase in the number of private schools from 166 in 1993 to 596 in 2006.[1]

Conclusion

The introduction of new governance instruments is not necessarily bound to how far they correspond to the overall ideology of an education or welfare system. The varying success of shifting governments in the United States and Sweden in introducing a voucher scheme to the systems of primary school education, and thus allowing for choice and competition between public and private schools is highly correlated with these countries' different institutional rules for political decision-making. In the 1980s and beginning of the 1990s Republican American presidents experienced that even modest voucher programs were rejected by a Democratic Congress – a veto-point such programs had to pass to become legislature. These programs were rejected by the legislators because the president's party did not control the Congress, but also because an independently elected president could not even rely on legislators from his own party. This is altogether in good agreement with the theory of separation-of-powers systems and fragmented decision-making structures. Later in the 1990s, a congressional majority in favor of school vouchers was actually formed by a now Republican-controlled Congress. In the meantime, however, a Democratic president had moved into the White House, from where voucher plans now met a veto. Divided American government structures have indeed been a major obstacle to the voucher movement, and prevented a national program from being implemented (Moe 2001: 27). However, to the extent that federalism serves as another veto-point, it has an additional facet. Some state constitutions have been permissive to school vouchers, and voucher programs of a different scale and character have flourished in some parts of the country. However, exactly because of the different rules at the lower levels of government, a further flourishing of school vouchers in the United States must be expected to be as sporadic as it has been to this point.

Swedish governments were in comparison more efficient in transforming policy proposals into real programs when they had settled with internal disagreements. They controlled a majority of the parliament, which was the only requirement to enforce a new financial structure in school policy. Even the traditionally close ties between the Social Democratic Party and the unions did not serve as a veto-point in connection to this policy-making process. If the unions and other opposing interests for example had exploited an opportunity to influence decision-makers in, for instance, a second chamber, an independently elected president, or autonomous political authorities at a lower level, they would have had more opportunities to gain access to the process and modify or even obstruct the government. However, the crux of the matter is exactly that they did not have such possibilities. When the government decided to use its parliamentary majority, teachers' unions could do no more than organize a demonstration outside the parliament as the legislative process went on inside (Lindbom 1995).

The Swedish decision-making process on school vouchers and related educational reforms is, on the one hand, a special case measured against Swedish standards with a traditionally high degree of inclusion of societal interests through a variety of commissions. Only one school policy commission was formed in the period of 1988–1991, and the Minister of Educational Affairs explained this break with Swedish traditions of policy-making as a means of increasing governmental control over the process and preventing obstructions from the organized interests (Lindbom 1995: 74; Klitgaard 2004). On the other hand, governance reforms in the Swedish school system fit into a general pattern of such reforms conducted during the period. In healthcare, for example, purchasers and providers have been split, which has resulted in a construction where politically controlled boards buy healthcare services from providers competing with each other. Today, Swedish citizens can therefore choose not only between different schools but also between different providers of primary healthcare and hospitals (Blomqvist and Rothstein 2000). Such reform developments are also prominent in childcare and eldercare (Green-Pedersen 2002).

Correspondingly, the United States displays relatively low reform activity in other areas too. Conservative governments during the 1980s generally did not achieve radical retrenchment or a major shift toward private sector provision of social welfare, although they did succeed with moderate retrenchments at the edges of the Medicare program (Pierson and Smith 1993: 501). Likewise, the Clintons' ambitions of establishing a national health insurance scheme also failed to be implemented (Steinmo and Watts 1995). Thus, different outputs from policy-making on school and educational policy in the two countries broadly emphasize a well-known conclusion from comparative public policy research. Divided structures of decision-making inhibit policy-makers from realizing their preferences, as they have to pass a variety of veto-points during the process (Castles 1999; Immergut 1992; Pierson 1994; Bonoli 2001). Governments in unified systems are, in comparison, provided with more institutional and political degrees of freedom to transform formulated policy goals into legislation. Hence, the politics of vouchers in the United States and Sweden illustrates the tremendous impact political institutions have for public policy developments.

Note

1 Statistics on private schools in Sweden are available online at www.skolverket.se/content/1/c4/95/93/Frist-skolor070125.pdf.

References

Allan, J.P. and Scruggs, L. (2004) 'Political partisanship and welfare state reform in advanced industrial societies', *American Journal of Political Science*, 48, 3: 496–512.

Antman, P. (1993) 'Vägen till systemskiftet – den offentliga sektorn i politiken 1970–1992', in R.Å. Gustavsson (ed.) *Köp och sälj, var god svälj?*, Stockholm: Arbetsmiljø-fonden, 19–65.

Belfield, R. and Levin, H.M. (2002) *Does the Supreme Court Ruling on Vouchers in Cleveland Really Matter for Education Reform?*, Columbia University: National Center for the Study of Privatization in Education. Online, available at: www.ncspe.org.

Berry, F.S. and Berry, W.S. (1999) 'Innovation and diffusion models in policy research', in P. Sabatier (ed.) *Theories of the Policy Process*, Boulder: Westview Press, 169–200.

Betænkning (1990/91) UbU17. *Vissa frågor avseende skolväsendet*. Online, available at: www.riksdagen.se/Webbnav/index.aspx?nid=34.

Blomqvist, P. (2004) 'The choice revolution: privatization of Swedish welfare services in the 1990s', *Social Policy & Administration*, 38, 2: 139–155.

Blomqvist, P. and Rothstein, B. (2000) *Velfärdsstatens nya ansikte*, Stockholm: Agora.

Bonoli, G. (2001) 'Political institutions, veto points, and the process of welfare state adaptation', in P. Pierson (ed.) *The New Politics of the Welfare State*, Oxford: Oxford University Press, 238–264.

Boyd, W.L. and Lugg, C.A. (1998) *Markets, Choice, and Educational Change*. Online, available at: www.personal.psu.edu/faculty/i/6/i6b/marketschoice.htm.

Castles, F.G. (1999) 'Decentralization and the post-war political economy', *European Journal of Political Research*, 36, 1: 27–53.

Chubb, J.E. (2001) 'The system', in T.M. Moe (ed.) *A Primer on Americas Schools*, Stanford: Hoover Press, 15–42.

Chubb, J.E. and Moe, T.M. (1990) *Politics, Markets & Americas Schools*, Washington, DC: The Brookings Institution.

Cibulka, J.G. (2000) 'The NEA and school choice', in T. Loveless (ed.) *Conflicting Missions*, Washington, DC: The Brookings Institution, 150–173.

Crepaz, M.M.L. and Birchfield, V. (2000) 'Global economics, local politics. Lijphart's theory of consensus democracy and the politics of inclusion', in M.M.L. Crepaz (ed.) *Democracy and Institutions. The Life Work of Arend Lijphart*, Ann Arbor: University of Michigan Press, 197–221.

Goodin, R. (1996) 'Institutionalizing the public interest. The defense of deadlock and beyond', *American Political Science Review*, 90, 2: 331–343.

Green-Pedersen, C. (2002) 'New public management reforms of the Danish and Swedish welfare states: the role of different social democratic responses', *Governance*, 15, 2: 271–294.

Gustafsson, L. (1987) 'Renewal of the public sector in Sweden', *Public Administration*, 65, 2: 179–192.

Henig, J.R. (1994) *Rethinking School Choice*, New Jersey: Princeton University Press.

Hicks, A.M. and Swank, D. (1992) 'Politics, institutions, and welfare spending in industrialized democracies, 1960–82', *American Political Science Review*, 86, 3: 658–674.

Huber, E., Ragin, C. and Stephens, J.D. (1993) 'Social democracy, Christian democracy, constitutional structure, and the welfare state', *American Journal of Sociology*, 99, 3: 711–749.

Immergut, E. (1992) 'The rules of the game: the logic of health policy-making in France, Switzerland and Sweden', in D. Steinmo, K. Thelen and F. Longstreth (eds) *Structuring Politics. Historical Institutionalism in Comparative Analysis*, Cambridge: Cambridge Studies in Comparative Politics, 57–89.

Kemerer, F.R. (2002) *The U.S. Supreme Court's Decision in the Cleveland Voucher Case: Where to From Here?*, Columbia University: National Center for the Study of Privatization in Education. Online, available at: www.ncspe.org.

Kenny, L.W. (2005) *The Public Choice of Educational Choice*, Columbia University: National Center for the Study of Privatization in Education. Online, available at: www.ncspe.org.

Klitgaard, M.B. (2004) 'At beskytte et politisk våben. Når Socialdemokratiet dekollektiviserer den universelle velfærdsstat', unpublished PhD dissertation, University of Aalborg.

—— (2007a) 'Why are they doing it? Social democracy and market oriented welfare state reforms', *West European Politics*, 30, 1: 172–194.

—— (2007b) 'Do welfare state regimes determine public sector reforms? Choice reforms in American, Swedish and German schools', *Scandinavian Political Studies*, 30, 4: 444–468.

Korpi, W. (1988) *The Democratic Class Struggle*, London: Routledge & Kegan Paul.

Levin, H.M. and Belfield, C.R. (2003) *The Marketplace in Education*, Columbia University: National Center for the Study of Privatization in Education. Online, available at: www.ncspe.org.

Lijphart, A. (1999) *Patterns of Democracy. Government Forms and Performance in Thirty-Six Countries*, New Haven and London: Yale University Press.

Lindbom, A. (1995) *Medborgerskapet i Velfärdsstaten*, Stockholm: Almqvist & Wicksell International.

Mahoney, J. (2000) 'Path dependence in historical sociology', *Theory & Society*, 29, 4: 507–548.

Mahoney, J. and Goertz, G. (2004) 'The possibility principle: choosing negative cases in qualitative research', *American Political Science Review*, 98, 4: 653–670.

Martin, I. (2008) *The Permanent Tax Revolt: How the Property Tax Transformed American Politics*, Stanford: Stanford University Press.

Mellbourn, A. (1986) *Bortom det starka samhället*, Stockholm: Carlssons.

Mintrom, M. (2000) *Policy Entrepreneurs and School Choice*, Washington, DC: Georgetown University Press.

Moe, T.M. (2001) *Schools, Vouchers and the American Public*, Washington, DC: The Brookings Institution.

NCSPE (2003) *Frequently Asked Questions*, Columbia University: National Center for the Study of Privatization in Education. Online, available at: www.ncspe.org.

OECD (1994) *School: A Matter of Choice*, Paris: OECD.

—— (2002) *What Works in Innovation in Education. School: A Choice of Direction*, Paris: OECD/CERI.

Pappagiannis, G.J., Easton, P.A and Owens, J.T. (1992) *The School Restructuring Movement in the USA: An Analysis of Major Issues and Policy Implications*, Paris: International Institute for Educational Planning.

Petterson, O. (1977) *Väljarne och Valet*, Stockholm: Statistiska Centralbyrån.

Petterson, O., Westholm, A. and Blomberg, G. (1989) *Medborgernas Makt*, Stockholm: Carlssons.

Pierre, J. (1993) 'Legitimacy, institutional change, and the politics of public administration in Sweden', *International Political Science Review*, 14, 4: 387–402.

Pierson, P. (1994) *Dismantling the Welfare State. Reagan, Thatcher and the Politics of Retrenchment*, Cambridge: Cambridge University Press.

—— (1995) 'Fragmented welfare states: federal institutions and the development of social policy', *Governance*, 8, 4: 449–478.

—— (2000) 'Increasing returns, path-dependence, and the study of politics', *American Political Science Review*, 94, 2: 251–267.

Pierson, P. and Smith, M. (1993) 'Bourgeois revolutions? The policy consequences of resurgent conservatism', *Comparative Political Studies*, 25, 4: 487–520.

Pollit, C. and Bouckeart, G. (2004) *Public Management Reform: A Comparative Analysis*, Oxford: Oxford University Press.

Premfors, R. (1998) 'Reshaping the democratic state: Swedish experience in comparative perspective', *Public Administration*, 76, 1: 142–159.

Proposition 1988/89:4, *Skolans utveckling och styrning*. Online, available at: www.riksdagen.se/Webbnav/index.aspx?nid=34.

Proposition 1989/90:41, *Ansvaret för skolan*. Online, available at: www.riksdagen.se/Webbnav/index.aspx?nid=34.

Proposition 1990/91:18, *Om vissa skollagsfrågor m.m.* Online, available at: www.riksdagen.se/Webbnav/index.aspx?nid=34.

Ravitch, D. (2001) 'American traditions of education', in T.M. Moe (ed.) *A Primer on Americas Schools*, Stanford: Hoover Press, 1–14.

Rothstein, B. (1996) *The Social Democratic State*, Pittsburgh: Pittsburgh University Press.

—— (1998) *Just Institutions Matter*, Cambridge: Cambridge University Press.

Rothstein, B. and Steinmo, S. (eds) (2002) *Restructuring the Welfare State. Political Institutions and Policy Change*, New York: Palgrave Macmillan.

Steinmo, S. and Watts, J. (1995) 'It's the institutions – stupid. Why comprehensive national health insurance always fails in America', *Journal of Health Politics, Policy and Law*, 20, 2: 329–372.

Strøm, K. (2000) 'Delegation and accountability in parliamentary democracies', *European Journal of Political Research*, 37, 3: 261–289.

The Center for Educational Reform (2007) Online, available at: www.edreform.com/index.cfm?fuseAction=section&pSectionID=5&CFID=9557161&CFTOKEN=53724891.

Thelen, K. (1999) 'Historical institutionalism in comparative politics', *Annual Review of Political Science*, 2: 369–404.

Thelen, K. and Steinmo, S. (1992) 'Historical institutionalism in comparative politics', in S. Steinmo, K. Thelen and F. Longstreth (eds) *Structuring Politics. Historical Institutionalism in Comparative Analysis*, Cambridge: Cambridge University Press, 1–32.

Tsebelis, G. (1995) 'Decision making in political systems: veto players in presidentialism, parliamentarism, multicameralism and multipartism', *British Journal of Political Science*, 25, 3: 289–325.

Weaver, K.R. and Rockman, B.A. (eds) (1993) *Do Institutions Matter? Government Capabilities in the United States and Abroad*, Washington, DC: The Brookings Institution.

3 Comparing higher education policies in Central and Eastern Europe

Michael Dobbins

Introduction

The institutions of higher education across Europe are currently subject to tremendous pressures for reform, triggered primarily by increased international competition and the so-called Bologna Process. Against the background of increasing student numbers, dwindling state funds and external competition, European universities have been in a state of transition at latest since the 1990s. To increase efficiency and competitiveness, the methods and instruments of higher education management are being redesigned, while governments are delegating regulatory activities to the universities and other institutions (Goedegebuure *et al.* 1993: 9). Governance of higher education has thus been subject to many changes, and international models have played a large role in the restructuring process.

This comparative study[1] addresses how pre-existing models, the socio-economic transition, and the Bologna Process have impacted on the evolution and governance of higher education (HE) in Central and Eastern Europe (CEE), and in particular three new EU members – the Czech Republic, Romania and Bulgaria.[2] Governance, as conceived here, comprises patterns of control, coordination and the allocation of autonomy between the state, professoriate, university management, and other societal actors. The radical makeover of the economy, political system and production patterns after 1989 entails gargantuan institutional tasks for nascent democracies within an extremely compact timeframe. Unlike their western counterparts, CEE universities are faced with a constellation of 'simultaneous transition' (Offe 1993; Radó 2001): Not only are the institutions challenged by the burdens with which Western Europe is also struggling, for example massification, funding or output (Neave 2003a: 20), but also dilemmas particular to their special circumstances, such as dismantling a system of manpower planning and the restoration of autonomy.

My analysis falls back on three historical and contemporary visions of university governance – the originally French state-control model, the German-based model of academic self-rule and the Anglo-American market-oriented model (Clark 1983). Although these models no longer exist in pure form, they remain anchored in modern-day university practice and collective memory, functioning as poles towards which the systems may converge (Olsen 2005). By examining the potential diffusion of western models into CEE, I address the phenomenon of transnational convergence in a policy area traditionally regulated exclusively at the national level (Field 2003; Neave 2003b). This enables us to assess whether the external dimension has facilitated policy convergence by means of mechanisms such as transnational communication and institutional isomorphism – that is without binding rules and legislation.

The chapter proceeds as follows: I first briefly outline the theoretical framework to explain policy change and/or inertia, before drawing up indicators for the three models of HE governance. I then present three brief country reports, before assessing the direction and degree of convergence.

Theoretical framework

My analysis proposes a policy convergence approach, which integrates both the historical starting points of the examined countries and the channels and mechanisms of policy change. Convergence is understood as 'the tendency of societies to grow more alike, to develop similarities in structures, processes, and performances' (Kerr 1983: 3). A number of explanatory factors for convergence have been discussed in the literature (Tews 2002: 8; Holzinger and Knill 2005), among them transnational communication, which is likely to be the most crucial mechanism in higher education. Despite the absence of binding legislation and direct coercion, transnational communication may facilitate the exchange of information and experiences, as well as mutual lesson-drawing and learning among national policy-makers.

To address the degree of convergence, I draw on *institutional isomorphism.* Isomorphism stresses how units in a population are compelled to become more alike when faced with the same environmental challenges (DiMaggio and Powell 1991: 66). Normative isomorphism views convergence as a consequence of professionalization, as the collective struggle of actors to define the conditions and methods of their work (Larson 1977 cited in DiMaggio and Powell 1983: 70). The logic is that groups of policy-makers from different backgrounds share a common perception of pressures and strategies for adaptation (DiMaggio and Powell 1983). Mimetic isomorphism is driven by uncertainty, in particular when organizational technologies and processes are poorly understood, goals ambiguous and future developments uncertain (DiMaggio and Powell 1983: 151).[3]

Following the assumption of the convergent effects of isomorphism, the nature and depth of HE networks existing in the pre-Bologna and Bologna phase are examined. Before Bologna, a high degree of diversity is expected in terms of the nature of the policy networks. This is substantiated by their loosely coupled and highly fragmented nature and because there was no supranational level of HE in Europe to provide guidance and mutual coordination to CEE countries. Thus, although isomorphic processes are expected in the early transformation phase, they were mediated through scattered and porous networks, and may shift policies in different directions. I argue that the Bologna Process has particularly enhanced the conditions for isomorphism, with convergence being a likely effect. It has created a tightly knit transnational regime that facilitates communication and the elaboration of norms and common solutions. To avoid looking like laggards, national HE systems are likely to embrace practices regarded as legitimate and successful in the broader environment (DiMaggio and Powell 1991: 70). Hence, isomorphism is a common strategy for laggards, such as new EU countries, to 'catch up' during the integration process.

However, isomorphic processes are by no means automatic and only one of various options. Imitation may be carried out selectively, in line with national opportunity structures. Once underway, the initial intent of transfer or emulation may be watered down by institutional constraints, diminishing the prospects of fully-fledged isomorphism. The obstacles to reform are compounded by the 'bottom-heavy' character of HE, its resistance to change and often 'set-in-stone' administrative culture (Neave 2005: 17). I attempt to accommodate these long-standing traditions by drawing on insights from *historical institutionalism.* By examining procedures, routines and norms embedded in organizational structures, historical institutionalism offers explanations for the distinctiveness of national outcomes (Hall and Taylor 1996: 937) and demonstrates how past decision-making patterns are reiterated in a path-dependent manner. Hence, national politics metabolize, translate and reshape global trends in the face of their cultures, needs and institutional framework (Vaira 2004).

As outlined above, the exogenous forces of change are derived from isomorphism, which is driven by institutional interlinkages. Two types of institutional interlinkages are distinguished. First, I examine academic networks existing in the pre-Bologna phrase, in which the selected countries were networked with different actors at different institutional levels. Second, I address how institutional interlinkages which have burgeoned in the Bologna Process (see Chapter 10, this volume) have impacted national policy-making.

By selecting the Czech Republic, Bulgaria and Romania, I tap into Lijphart's (1971) logic for comparative studies by focusing on 'comparable' cases (see Table 3.1). These include those which are similar in many important characteristics viewed as constants (transformation countries, new EU members), but differ with regard to key variables: legacies from the pre-communist and communist phase and institutional interlinkages.

Table 3.1 Selection of countries

	Czech Republic	*Bulgaria*	*Romania*
Pre-communist pathway	Self-governance	Mixed type	State authority
Communist pathway	Relatively moderate state control	Far-reaching state control	Extreme state control
Pre-1989 networking with (non-communist) countries	No	Limited	Yes (after approximately 1965)

The Czech system was based on Humboldtian principles in the pre-communist phase, while Romania initially adhered to the state-authority model before moving towards the Humboldtian paradigm. Despite traces of German traditions and periodically heavy state control (Kiossev 2001), Bulgaria attempted to put into practice Anglo-Saxon notions of university self-management in the early twentieth century (Gocheva 2002). While all traces of self-management were eradicated in Romania and Bulgaria in the communist phase, Czech academia sustained limited autonomy over academic programmes. Third, countries differed with regard to their integration into international, non-socialist academic networks in the communist phase. The Bulgarian and Czech systems were essentially closed, while Romanian academics were partially permitted to engage in technology transfer and international cooperation (Sadlak 1990).

The empirical study draws on 35 interviews with high-ranking CEE policy-makers, HE experts and various legislative and policy documents.

Convergence towards a common model?

The dependent variable is defined as convergence in governance systems during the transformation and Bologna phase. Although Bologna prompts universities to adapt to changing external and internal demands, it remains ambiguous as to the means for achieving these objectives. The declaration does not bypass issues of university autonomy and governance, but essentially allows the member states to define their course of action. The present HE arena is marked by an array of plausible visions of modern universities. Thus, if European integration triggers convergence to a common model, it remains uncertain on what it may be based and what specific aspects of academic life it may affect. Drawing on models of university governance by Clark (1983) and Olsen (2005), I distinguish between three ideal-types, towards which post-communist systems may converge: the state-authority model, the Humboldt model and the market-oriented model.

In the state-authority model, universities are state-operated institutions marked by strong process control and relatively little autonomy (Clark 1983). The state, acting as a 'guardian' (Neave 1996), coordinates many aspects of HE, such as admission, curricula, nomination of personnel, and actively influences quality assurance and university–business relations (Neave and Van Vught 1991: xi–xxii). This explains the close oversight by the ministry and a high degree of hierarchy.

Founded upon Humboldt's principles, the model of self-governing communities of scholars (Scott 2002: 140–141) implies weak university management and strong collegial control and professorial dominance (de Boer and Goedegebuure 2003: 215). The model ideally is based on a state–university partnership, governed by principles of corporatism and collective agreement. The state remains a potent actor thanks to diverse planning and financial laws. This limits self-governance but enables universities to establish normative and constitutive principles of their own without external design (Olsen 2005: 10).

Market-oriented models contend that universities are more efficient when operating as economic enterprises (Marginson and Considine 2000). The main

State authority

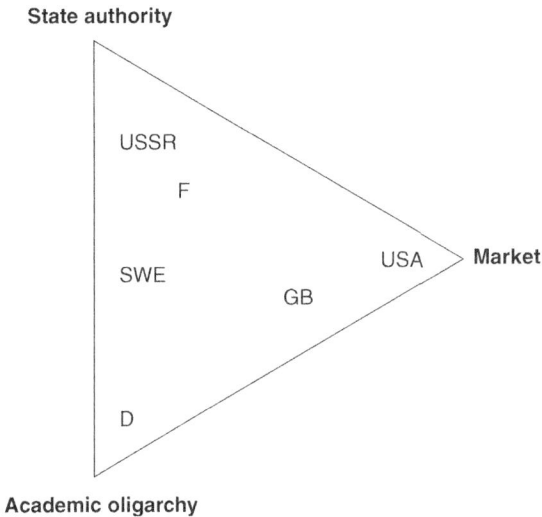

USSR

F

SWE   USA   **Market**

GB

D

Academic oligarchy

Figure 3.1 Clark's coordination triangle (source: adapted and modified from Clark 1983).

thrust of power lies with university management, which strategically positions the institution, while offering academic services to fee-paying students and external stakeholders. Government involvement usually entails incentives and competition-promoting measures, not directives or manpower planning (Olsen 2005: 10).

To distinguish these three ideal-types, I draw up indicators for various aspects of governance. As for *financial governance*, I distinguish between input and output-based systems and between centralized and decentralized systems (Jongbloed 2003: 123). In market models discretion over funds is vested within management level, which strategically allocates them on the basis of productive output. In academic self-rule models, the professoriate enjoys greater control over state and third-party resources, while market-based systems integrate entrepreneurial and investment culture into funding procurement (Clark 1998).

Personnel autonomy grasps the delegation of authority with regard to appointing rectors, university leadership and academic staff and their degree of participation in strategic decision-making process. In the state-authority model, academic and administrative positions are based on state appointment (Burnham 1999: 75). Self-governance models take a more collegial approach, which strongly involves academic staff in the recruitment of personnel (Herrschel 1999: 108), for whom tenure privileges are frequent. Market-oriented approaches see for a greater managerial selection of academic and high-level personnel.

Substantial autonomy (Behrdahl 1990) comprises teaching and research content. The central question is whether teaching and research should be focused on what the academic faculty or state deems most important or what students and the market demand. In self-governance and state-based models, the state functions as a 'gatekeeper' (Herrschel 1999: 999) that sets the institutional framework conditions, while decisions over academic matters are entirely left up to the professoriate with little intervention from university management. Market-based institutions are characterized by strong leverage of university management over admission requirements, institutional parameters and study content.

The Czech Republic: the long shadow of Humboldt

The post-1989 course of events was swift and dramatic. Practically overnight, 'democratic' governance with far-reaching autonomy was introduced, as the academic community mobilized and consolidated to protect and distance itself from the state. Instead of seeking a pragmatic relationship with the state, policymakers, who are academics themselves, placed faith in the self-healing capacity of HE institutions (Interview #2 Czech Ministry 2006). Against this background, policy-makers sought to reinstate the idea of the Humboldtian university, bolstered by internal democratic structures and external buffer organizations. The re-establishment of 'free' universities, like free parliaments (Scott 2002: 144), also allowed for the broad participation of students in representative bodies (Pabian 2007).

The restoration of the chair-based system (Interview #1 Czech Center for Higher Education Studies 2006) quickly transformed the once hierarchical system into a highly fragmented one, in which autonomy over substantial and procedural affairs was fragmented down to the lowest level. The Higher Education Act of 1990 granted universities control over all aspects of substantial autonomy, including teaching and research programmes, admission criteria and all internal structural decisions (Interview Czech University Vice-Rector 2006; Interview #2 Czech Center for Higher Education Studies 2006). With regard to personnel autonomy, the newly established system represented an extreme form of academic self-governance. High and low-level academic staff were elected solely by other high-ranking faculty staff, without state review. This equally pertains to rectors, who were chosen by fellow academics and shared governance authority with them.[4]

The HE Act contained several additional features significant for understanding the governance system. Essentially, anything indicative of central control was banished (Cerych 2002). De Boer and Goedegebuure (2003: 219) even speak of the 'abolition of government'. Yet the diminishment of executive control also applied to the powers of rectors, who were constricted by various buffer organizations, which protected institutions' intellectual independence and capacity for self-governance. The most prominent of these are the Academic Senates, 'democratically elected' bodies consisting of academics and 30–50 per cent students. For policy change, the ministry also required the consensus of the Czech Rectors' Conference and Council of Higher Education Institutions which only included academics, thus no external stakeholders.

Using the terminology of Neave and Van Vught (1991: 251–252), the state relinquished both *product* and *process* control in Czech HE. In fact, the only means for the state to shape the regulatory framework was through funding instruments. The Czech system remained heavily subsidized by the state, which in turn allocated earmarked funds to institutions. Instead of opting for a market-oriented solution with, for example, tuition and contract-based university–business cooperation, the ministry continued to entirely fund HE. Initially, the level of funding remained incremental and negotiation-based (Interview #1 Czech Center for Higher Education Studies 2006). Since 1992 however, university autonomy was enhanced with the switch to lump-sum funding (Pabian 2007; Jongbloed 2003: 128), although performance-based criteria were not yet considered. Thus, with respect to funding, the Czech system remained in line with the Humboldt ideal-type.

The transnational dimension also profoundly affected Czech HE. However, these effects were primarily restricted to quantitative-structural aspects (Pabian 2007). In other words, governance has only been slightly affected by the policy models conveyed through transnational networks. Instead, the Humboldt-oriented path after 1989 was reinforced by three primary motivations: the drive for democracy; pre-communist traditions; and linkages with western countries, Germany and Austria in particular. Although they did not provide a blueprint for reform, references to German and Austrian legislation added substantiation to the Czech model of self-governance (Interview #3 Czech Center for Higher Education Studies 2006). Instead of aligning themselves with the trend towards 'entrepreneurial universities' (Clark 1998; Sporn 2006), policy-makers concocted a novel system of quasi-parliamentary governance and checks-and-balances, clearly motivated by the oversensitivity of the academic community to external intervention (Hendrichová 1995: 65; Interview #2 Czech Ministry 2006).

However, the Czech academic community did become involved in various international undertakings to stimulate reform (Šťastná 2001: 478). Highly instructive for understanding the dynamics of Czech HE is its cooperation with the OECD, which drew up recommendations concerning problematic aspects of the post-1989 system (OECD 1992: 139). Besides the expansion and the modernization of HE, the OECD proposed the establishment of an independent high-level group, that is an advisory *think tank* to address competitiveness and technological progress (OECD 1992; Cerych 2002: 117). Moreover, the OECD called for more efficient management-based internal HE structures and diversified funding.

The expansion of Czech HE was indeed based on the transfer of foreign models. Following the OECD recommendation, a Dutch university association (HBO-Raad) allocated funding for the creation of non-university professional institutions. However, the OECD's appeal for increased strategic management was shrugged off by the academic lobby, fearing the imposition of a masterplan by the state. A similar scenario applies to the recommendation for more efficient internal structures, greater accountability from university managers and the procurement of non-state funding. Instead of devolving greater power to university management, Czech academics came to master the 'art of freedom' and use autonomy to block reforms (Matějů 2004). In fact, changes were only implemented in those areas which did not alter the governance structures established post-1989. Hence, the impact of institutional interlinkages primarily remained restricted to system expansion and 'capacity-building', such as the establishment of international relations departments and continuing education centers (Šťastná 2001: 476; Pabian 2007).

Is the Czech system of governance marked by the same degree of inertia in the Bologna phase? First, the Higher Education Act of 1998 was modified with the objective of stabilizing relations between the state and universities, by giving the state more leverage over 'product control'. This entailed a broader system of programme-based state accreditation (Interview #2 Czech Ministry 2006), while the Act also authorized the creation of private universities. More significant, however, is the array of aspects unchanged post-1999 – despite the more integrative and homogenous supranational framework. These include the power of the professoriate, strong collegial control, nearly exclusive academic representation in governing bodies, and lacking entrepreneurialism in management structures.

Nevertheless, the Bologna Process has dragged the Czech system away from extreme academic self-rule, a development manifested by a current centralization tendency in HE governance (Pabian 2007). Scattered policy-makers have also used Bologna as a discourse argument to bolster a stronger, but still comparatively moderate, neo-liberal agenda. For example, amendments to the HE act triggered by right-wing parliamentarians led to the implementation of the two-tier degree structure, but also stronger ties to knowledge-related enterprises, free and fee-based funding and greater transparency in admissions (Matějů 2001; Pabian 2007). A stronger market orientation is evident with regard to the diversification of funding through strategic investments and contracts with private firms. At the same time, the country is clearly moving from input to output-based funding, inspired – to a large extent – by the British model (Interview #1 Czech Ministry).

Altogether, by adding multilevel reference points, the Bologna Process has changed Czech HE politics, but only incrementally underlying policy and governance patterns (Pabian 2007). The fragmented and relatively isolated system of governance that emerged post-1989 demonstrates a lack of executive leadership and trans-faculty coordination and is slow in meeting needs for flexibility and accountability. This can be explained by the relatively inward-looking nature of the academic community (Interview #2 Czech Center for Higher Education Studies 2006) – likely a consequence of the closed nature of the Czech system in the communist phase. Nevertheless, the Bologna platform has provoked academic policy-makers to partake in 'unconscious inspiration' by foreign trends (Interview #4 Czech Center for Higher Education Studies 2006), leading to a greater sense of problem pressure and the sluggish introduction of market-oriented and managerial instruments. However, the many veto-points and lack of executive steering have clearly upheld the Humboldt-oriented chair system, in which individual faculties and academics are devising their own strategies to adapt to globalization.

Bulgaria: the rocky path towards marketization

The post-1989 path in Bulgaria illustrates that the transition towards university autonomy can be a rocky one. Bulgaria initially followed the same storyline as the Czech Republic with a swift move towards 'academic oligarchy' (Interview Bulgarian University Vice-Rector 2007). However, no higher education act was issued in the initial phase. Instead, policy-makers only legally codified academic autonomy, without a legal framework for system governance. Hence, instead of clear principles and legislation regulating the relationship between the state and HE providers, academics conceived the reintroduction of autonomy as a political action to accelerate the erosion of totalitarianism (Boyadjieva 2007: 112). Substantial matters were determined at faculty level and via academic senates, without government influence. Personnel autonomy was also vested at faculty level. The powers of rectors remained watered down compared to more market-oriented systems.

This led to a situation of unfettered autonomy in which academics pursued a course of fragmented expansion. Individual faculties sought to achieve the status of HE institutions, enabling them to collect tuition fees. Not only did the number of universities increase from five to 40, but student numbers also increased uncontrollably, despite the lack of adequate facilities and staff (Interview Bulgarian University Rector 2007). Instead of establishing effective university management systems, academics utilized the liberal regulations to shield themselves from external control, often demonstrating rent-seeking behaviour in the procurement and management of tuition funds (Interview Bulgarian University Professor 2007). Thus, instead of channelling academic processes towards greater accountability and productivity (Georgieva 2002: 28), universities pursued a strategy of unfettered expansion with autonomy vested at the lower level.

The devolution of power to faculties can partially be attributed to circumstances existing in the communist phase. The abolishment of state regulation enabled individual units to operate independently and hindered the creation of overarching policy. There are also indications that policy-makers drew inspiration from pre-war constellations. Boyadjieva (2007: 116–118) even claims that isomorphic processes came to bear here, as policy-makers strived to design their institutions in line with the only pre-war Bulgarian university in Sofia. After 1989 Bulgarian academics frequently opted not to build on their own university profiles, but adhered to the model regarded as most successful and desirable – the pre-war 'University of Sofia model'. This was facilitated by the widespread view that Sofia was modelled on western traditions. Hence we find a junction here between the two theoretical strands guiding this analysis – historical institutionalism and isomorphism.

With regard to transnational isomorphism, interlinkages with Western Europe initially were weak, as academic policy-makers remained rather 'inward-looking' (Interview Bulgarian University Professor 2007). However, this changed incrementally as a consequence of the re-centralization of Bulgarian HE in the mid-1990s. Unlike their Czech counterparts, Bulgarian academics did not sufficiently insulate themselves from the state or effectively manage their autonomy. With the HE Law of 1995, the pendulum thus shifted back to state control. This was manifested by Uniform State Requirements, a registry of state-authorized programmes on the basis of which the state regulated accession conditions and funding. Suddenly, the state regained control over *system design* and created a control cycle, in which funds were determined by student numbers, and student numbers determined by the state.

While re-centralization initially was aimed at preventing the system from sliding into disarray, the ministry increasingly strived to draw up a reform package to bring the system in line with European standards. Re-centralization enabled the Ministry to seek tighter links to the international level to accompany a more uniform reform strategy and redefine its role in HE. This was exemplified by the World Bank's involvement in Bulgarian education and the Ministry's efforts to emulate the British accreditation model (Interview Bulgarian Ministry 2007). However, the 'ideational inspiration' via transnational platforms by no means translated into effectively functioning institutions. This is exemplified by the accreditation system, as disagreements persisted over program vs. institutional accreditation (Interview Bulgarian Rectors' Council 2007).[5] This was further complicated by frequently shifting governmental coalitions, competing objectives of the ministry, leading to politics of stop-and-go. Moreover, academics, who widely perceived the state as intervening where it should not, e.g. student numbers, structural issues, remained unreceptive to the state-managed strategies for adopting HE to contemporary demands.

Hence, before Bologna Bulgaria found itself stuck between state control and fragmented academic interests, but also increasingly imbedded in a web of transnational networks. The evidence demonstrates that Bologna has not radically transformed Bulgarian HE. However, by introducing an overarching inspirational platform, it has added coherence and direction to previously initiated policies, which were often interrupted and stalled by coalition breakdowns and weak administrative capacity.

The current status quo is best described as a mixed-model of state authority and academic oligarchy, with market-based governance the clear trend. There are manifestations of this shift at the state and university level. The Accreditation Agency, the main vehicle of EU networking, has moved away from a state-serving to output-oriented approach. Previously, focus was placed on the proper implementation of legal regulations, whereas accreditation now aims to stimulate universities to establish their own output-oriented accreditation systems to be evaluated by the agency (Interviews Bulgarian Ministry 2007; Bulgarian University Rector 2007; Bulgarian University Professor 2007). The burgeoning network activity on the Bologna platform has also flanked reforms in the funding system. This includes not only the diversification of funding sources (in 2007 approximately 60 per cent from the state budget and 40 per cent from other sources), but also the fact that since 2001–2002 universities receive money per capita, no longer per professor. However, funding is still subject to a parliamentary decision, then itemized and controlled by the ministry, which now partially pegs allocation to accreditation outcomes (Interviews Bulgarian Ministry #1; #2 2007).

Drawing on the English system, the state has also presented a non-binding blueprint for effective university management and employer relations. As a likely side effect of Bologna, there is a marked trend towards more managerialism, not least with regard to internal allocation of funding. And resulting from the imitation of western practice, the Accreditation Agency and Rectors' Conference have also – with increasing success – organized meetings with business representatives to stimulate synergies between market and academic demands (Interview Bulgarian Ministry #1 2007; Interview Bulgarian University Professor 2007). Obstacles to a more entrepreneurial approach are however the multitude of state regulations and the limited four-year term for rectors, who have little incentive to perform well.

Altogether though, the broader trend towards marketization can be regarded as a spin-off of the Bologna Process and the late, yet swift development of the market itself. This shift towards product control and marketization has prompted the state to partially give back to universities the autonomy taken away in 1995 in exchange for accountability (Interview Bulgarian Ministry #2 2007). Although Bologna has not triggered profound reform at the system's core, the web of networks has enabled policy-makers to more clearly define their aims and expectations in line with readily available examples of best practice (Interviews Bulgarian University Professor; Bulgarian Ministry #2 2007). However, Bulgaria is still marked by its rather underdeveloped and unsystematic policy formulation process, which has lacked critical elements for a successful reform course, for example systematic preponderance of evidence, assessment of potentials and constraints, broad coalition-building and the synergetic leadership of policy entrepreneurs. Bulgarian higher education has instead suffered from lacking transparency in policy formulation and implementation (Interview Bulgarian University Professor 2007). The result has been a patchwork of occasional legislative changes, which despite all incoherencies exhibit a gradual shift towards the market paradigm.

Romania: a textbook case of isomorphism

To a greater extent than its counterparts, the Romanian case demonstrates how learning and flexible adaptation inspired by transnational networking can provide an impetus for paradigmatic change and a successful reform course. In the pre-communist phase Romania was marked by the disproportionate role of the state in HE (Scott 2002: 140–141; Sadlak 1990: 7), although the Humboldt model became more predominant between 1920 and 1950 (Interview UNESCO-CEPES 2006). During the communist phase, remaining traces of academic autonomy were abolished, while universities were transformed into labour-force breeding units in line with ideological norms (Mihailescu and Vlasceanu 1994: 76). However, as a consequence of Ceauşescu's 'divorce' from Moscow, a slight liberalization of the academic sphere took place and academic cooperation with the west developed rapidly, enabling academics to participate in technology transfer (see Sadlak 1990).

Unlike the Czech and Bulgarian cases, no extensive reforms to uproot the logic of the system were pursued immediately after 1989 (Nicolescu 2002: 92–93). Universities were granted de facto autonomy, yet only in a limited and inconsistent manner. For example, matters of substance remained the prerogative of the state. Hence, the Ministry continued to establish goals, strategies and an overarching framework for universities (Interviews Former Romanian Minister/ University Rector 2006; UNESCO-CEPES 2006). In view of weak self-management traditions in Romania, the state demonstrated great reluctance in granting universities greater procedural and substantial autonomy. Accustomed to acting with restraint vis-à-vis an omnipotent state, academia also was unable to mobilize and push for more self-management powers.

By the mid-1990s, public HE was still state-controlled and state-funded, while individual institutions functioned under the pressure of corruption, instead of societal accountability, competition and transparency (Marga 1998). At this point, drastic changes were triggered as a result of domestic problem pressure, lesson-drawing and ministerial activism. Subsequent to reforms initiated by Education Minister Andrei Marga, the state relinquished its role as a system designer and sought inspiration from market-based systems to impose more competitiveness and entrepreneurialism. The ministry was restructured according to management methods and reforms introduced to promote new teaching methods and performance-based criteria (Marga 2002: 130). Moreover, the reform package entailed a switch away from formula funding to global lump-sum funding. The ministry encouraged HE institutions to attract additional non-state funds and introduce tuition (Interview Romanian Ministry 2006). The evidence suggests that isomorphic effects already came to bear before Bologna, as international trends were continually referred to during reform negotiations and Romanian policy-makers overtly feared looking like a HE laggard – in particular with imminent prospects for intensified EU cooperation (Interviews Romanian University Vice-Rector 2007; Romanian University Rector). While the introduction of moderate study tuition was inspired by American practice, the British model was most attractive to Romania with regard to lump-sum funding and external procurement.

Yet historical legacies also continued to shape Romanian HE, some of which actually facilitated market-based governance. This is the case with the tight collaboration between industries and HE, which is not only the consequence of the ministry's support measures (as taxation incentives), but also the forced collaboration between universities and industry under Ceauşescu (Interviews Romanian University Vice-Rector 2007; Romanian University Vice-Rector 2007). Moreover, academics have turned to the Humboldt-orientation of the interwar phase (Sadlak 1990: 1) as inspiration to strengthen their collective interests vis-à-vis the state. As a result, an 'academic oligarchy' had indeed snowballed in the 1990s (Interview UNESCO-CEPES 2006), which resists the influence of external stakeholders and the abolition of tenure privileges. Although the chair model has returned to some institutions, many universities have relatively successfully established management structures to counterbalance the professorial lobby and provide strategic leadership over fragmented faculties. Interestingly, the strengthening of the management level is also the result of isomorphic processes, as Romanian universities have been keen to emulate two institutions broadly regarded as successful in procuring external funding, benefiting from international networking, and with regard to research output – Babeş-Bolyai University of Cluj-Napoca and Alexandru Ioan Cuza University of Iaşi (Interview Former Romanian Minister/University Rector 2006).

Bologna has accelerated and reinforced the market-oriented trend in Romanian HE, having side effects on numerous issues. Policy-makers tend to view the Bologna Process as a means of changing the functioning of universities and bringing them in line with the demands of globalization and the knowledge economy (Interview Romanian Ministry 2006). The reform course consolidated under the Bologna banner has been defined as a springboard to move Romania closer to Europe, and lend legitimacy to its HE system.

The pressure to join the EU – combined with the normative environment of Bologna – has prompted the ministry and HE community to increasingly focus on institutional performance (Interview Romanian Ministry 2006). A new system of accreditation inspired by guidelines conveyed through the Bologna Process was hence established in 2006, although the level of external stakeholder participation remains uncertain (Interview Romanian Ministry 2006). The Bologna Process has also strengthened the autonomy of the country's universities. The state has relinquished control over accession conditions, size, personnel affairs and research profiles, which are now determined exclusively by university management in cooperation with individual faculties. The rector's position has also been strengthened, allowing for performance-based fund allocation.

Altogether, the Bologna Process combined with the willingness to emulate western practice has accelerated marketization trends in Romanian HE. If passed, current legislation would represent the most far-reaching expression of entrepreneurialism in the three examined countries, as the law prescribes close cooperation between universities and businesses. This is envisioned not only at the university level, but also by means of a National Strategic Council for HE, which would enable the ministry to nominate business representatives to exert leverage over policy development (Interview Romanian Ministry 2006).

Comparative conclusions

Altogether, the study has revealed moderate convergence towards the market-oriented model during the Bologna Process. The early transformation phase was marked by convergence towards the Humboldtian self-rule model, which only emerged to a lesser extent in Romania. Hence Romania was the only country in which the communist legacy of vertical control still shaped policy-making, while Bulgaria also took a swift 'detour' back towards state control (see Figure 3.2). In terms of governance, the European dimension had the strongest isomorphic

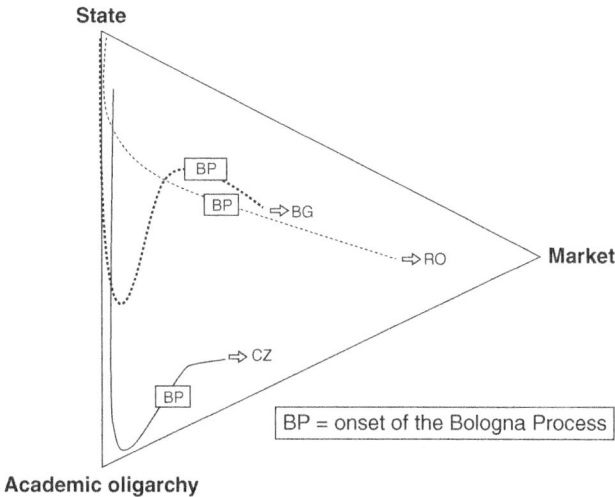

Figure 3.2 Post-communist policy developments applied to Clark's Triangle.

impact in Romania, triggering a rapid, consistent shift towards market-oriented governance after 1997. Bulgaria, and to a lesser extent the Czech Republic, have demonstrated an incremental adoption of market-oriented features (e.g. lump-sum, output-based funding in the latter, external stakeholders in the former) during the Bologna Process, but are far from being market-based systems.

The Bologna platform has not stimulated all-embracing convergence, rather a *convergent trend towards market-oriented governance* and the use of an array of market-based instruments, for example private-sector synergies, comprehensive quality assurance. This trend is bolstered by the increasing conviction that the systems no longer can withstand the exigencies of globalization. Above all though, convergence towards western practice has taken place with regard to the role of the state, as the thrust of power has switched from control over substantial matters to evaluation and accreditation. In line with the trend towards the 'evaluative state' (Neave 1998), a shift from *process* to *product* control has taken place. Hence, decreasing centralism and increasing university autonomy have been pegged with greater responsibilities with regard to productive output, with Romania the clear forerunner, followed by the Czech Republic and Bulgaria.

How do the results enhance our understanding of the theoretical framework? The evidence shows that both historical legacies and transnational isomorphic processes have impacted HE. To conclude, I address the conditions under which isomorphic forces have uprooted historical path dependencies.

The Bologna Process has visibly enhanced the emulation of western practice broadly regarded as successful. However, the results reveal that isomorphism is not an automatic reflex and requires other essential 'ingredients' to stimulate policy change. Based on the evidence, these ingredients appear to be:

1   'agents of transfer' at the central level;
2   policy entrepreneurship and executive leadership; and
3   incentives for negatively affected actors.

First, the 'agents of transfer' should be located within the ministry or university management in order to draw up overarching strategies. With its stronger tradition of centralism and weaker professoriate, Romania proved most effective in elaborating a broader strategy for approximation with exogenous institutions. This enabled the ministry to enforce various less convenient policies for academics, for example business ties, external stakeholder participation. While the Czech Republic has certainly not isolated itself from foreign advice, policy change has been decelerated by the insufficient leverage of the ministry over the well-consolidated academic community, omnipotent academic senates and fragmented faculties.

Second, change is contingent on policy entrepreneurs and executive leadership. This entails the capacity to create synergies between international dynamics and national reform. Entrepreneurial foresightedness also requires the ability to assess the constraints and potential for the altered policy course. Precisely this was the case in Romania, but not in Bulgaria. While the Romanian ministry created a broad coalition of academics, governmental policy-makers and university managers for its exogenously inspired reform course, the Bulgarian strategy lacked an effective balance of policy activism and entrepreneurialism. The Czech ministry, by contrast, has opted for 'self-imposed restraint' due to historical sensitivities of academia towards state intervention (Vlk 2006: 152).

Third, isomorphism-driven change not only must be justified and acceptable to the academic community, but is also dependent on incentives granted to affected actors. While the Romanian ministry offered institution-level actors incentives for procuring non-state funding and better performance, the Bulgarian ministry gave universities few incentives to increase efficiency and was even perceived as taking away autonomy from universities. Despite genuine efforts to move closer to the market paradigm, the Bulgarian ministry was unable to build up its steering capacity by granting universities incentives (such as autonomy and financial motivations) in return for support of the reform course and improved performance. Subsequently, university administration and faculties watered down the implementation of the reform proposals. Hence, the Bulgarian case, in particular, offers generalizable insights for our understanding of isomorphism – in the absence of policy entrepreneurship, executive guidance and financial incentives, there are only weak to moderate prospects for large-scale isomorphism in a policy area still shaped by the historically anchored balance of power and historically legitimated perceptions of the role and function of modern universities.

In sum, the governance of higher education has been affected by several developments outlined in the Introduction of this volume: the state-centred model has become increasingly unacceptable, both due to the oppressive nature of former communist models as well as the expansion and costs of higher education. Internationalization processes such as the Bologna Process have provided guidance towards specific models of governing higher education, which are now increasingly reflected in national higher education systems.

Seen from an even broader angle, the analysis has shown that the application of political science tools provides an added value to the study of higher education. The analytical framework has enabled us to go beyond the description of the status quo and focus on why, how, and to what degree convergence has taken place. The selected internal and external factors influencing higher education policy have led us to the realization that policy convergence comes in 'different shapes and sizes' depending on historical legacies and the nature of transnational interlinkages. Moreover, the presented social science framework has generated explanations for the country-specific differences with regard to the speed, depth (that is change or non-change in policy paradigms) and future direction of policy change and convergence. Finally, it has demonstrated that higher education is an ideal empirical field for addressing broader societal trends such as changing patterns of governance, deregulation or re-regulation, and the increasing synergies between the public and private sectors.

Notes

1 This chapter presents the partial results of the research project 'Comparing Higher Education Policies in Central and Eastern Europe'. Special thanks are given to the Fritz-Thyssen-Stiftung for generous funding. I also thank the Chair for Comparative Public Policy (University of Konstanz) and the participants of the ECPR Helsinki Joint Sessions for helpful comments.
2 The analysis is restricted to public universities, since these are the main addressees of governmental policies.
3 DiMaggio and Powell (1983) also stress that certain imposed legal regulations can lead to isomorphism and define such processes as 'coercive isomorphism'. This mechanism is not addressed here because of the non-binding, non-legal nature of the Bologna Process.
4 The shift of authority towards the professoriate was further bolstered by tenure privileges.
5 After the foundation in 1995, operations did not begin until 1998 (Interview Ministry #2 2007).

References

Berdahl, R. (1990) 'Academic freedom, autonomy, and accountability in British universities', *Studies in Higher Education*, 19, 2: 151–164.
Boyadjieva, P. (2007) 'Diversity matters: a lesson from a post-communist country', in G. Krücken, A. Kosmützky and M. Torka (eds) *Towards a Multiversity?*, Bielefeld: Transcript.
Burnham, J. (1999) 'France: a centrally-driven profession', in D. Farnham (ed.) *Managing Academic Staff in Changing University System*, Buckingham: SRHE & Open University Press.
Cerych, L. (2002) 'Higher education reform in the Czech Republic', *Higher Education in Europe*, XXVII, 1–2: 112–121.
Clark, B. (1983) *The Higher Education System*, Berkeley: University of California Press.

—— (1998) *Creating Entrepreneurial Universities: Organizational Pathways of Transformation*, Oxford: Pergamon-Elsevier Science.

de Boer, H. and Goedegebuure, L. (2003) 'New rules of the game? Reflections on governance, management, and systems change', in J. File and L. Goedegebuure (eds) *Real-Time Systems*, Enschede: CHEPS, University of Twente.

DiMaggio, P. and Powell, W. (1983) 'The iron cage revisited', *American Sociological Review*, 48: 147–160.

—— (1991) 'The iron cage revisited', in W. Powell and P. DiMaggio (eds) *The New Institutionalism in Organizational Analysis*, Chicago: Chicago University Press, 63–82.

Field, H. (2003) 'Integrating tertiary education in Europe', *The ANNALS of the American Academy of Political and Social Science*, 2003: 182–195.

Georgieva, P. (2002) *Higher Education in Bulgaria*, Bucharest: CEPES.

Gocheva, Dimka (2002) 'Apologia Declarationis Boloniensis contra murmurantes', International Policy Fellowship Program, Budapest. Online, available at: www.policy.hu/gocheva/text/bologna.html.

Goedegebuure, L., Kaiser, F., Maasen, P., Meek, L., van Vught, F. and de Weert, E. (1993) *Hochschulpolitik im internationalen Vergleich: eine länderübergreifende Untersuchung*, Gütersloh: Bertelsmann Stiftung.

Hall, P. and Taylor, R. (1996) 'Political science and the three new institutionalisms', in *Political Studies*, 44, 1: 936–957.

Hendrichová, J. (1995) 'Recent developments in higher education in Central and Eastern Europe', in K. Hüfner (ed.) *Higher Education Reform Processes in Central and Eastern Europe*, Frankfurt: Peter Lang.

Herrschel, T. (1999) 'Germany: a dual academy', in D. Farnham (ed.) *Managing Academic Staff in Changing University Systems*, Buckingham: SRHE/Open University Press.

Holzinger, K. and Knill, C. (2005) 'Explaining cross-national policy convergence: concepts, causes, and coalitions', *Journal of European Public Policy*, 12, 5: 775–796.

Jongbloed, B. (2003) 'Institutional funding and institutional change', in J. File and L. Goedegebuure (eds) *Real-Time Systems*, Enschede: CHEPS, University of Twente.

Kerr, C. (1983) *The Future of Industrial Societies: Convergence or Continuing Diversity?*, Cambridge: Harvard University Press.

Kiossev, A. (2001) 'The university between facts and norms', *Eurozine*. Online, available at: www.eurozine.com/articles/2001–11–02-kiossev-en.html.

Larson, M.S. (1977) *The Rise of Professionalism: A Sociological Analysis*, Berkeley: University of California Press.

Lijphart, A. (1971) 'Comparative politics and the comparative method', *American Political Science Review*, 9: 682–693.

Marga, A. (1998) *The Reform of Education in 1999*, Bucharest: Agentia Nationala Socrates.

—— (2002) 'Reform of education in Romania in the 1990s: a retrospective', *Higher Education in Europe*, XXVII, 1–2: 123–135.

Marginson, S. and Considine, M. (2000) *The Enterprise University: Governance and Reinvention in Australian Higher Education*, Cambridge: Cambridge University Press.

Matějů, P. (2001) 'Diversified tertiary education and its multi-source financing', in J. Fukač, J. Kazelle and A. Mizerova (eds) *Universities and the Bologna Declaration: A Strategy of Changes*, Brno: VUTIUM.

—— (2004) 'Czech higher education still at a crossroads', *The Prague Post*. Online, available at: www.praguepost.com/P03/2004/Art/1118/opin4.php.

Mihailescu, I. and Vlasceanu, L. (1994) 'Higher education structures in Romania', *Higher Education in Europe*, XIX, 4: 79–93.

Neave, G. (1996) 'Homogenization, integration, and convergence', in L. Meek, L. Goedegebuure, O. Kivinen and R. Rinne (eds) *The Mockers and the Mocked: Comparative Perspectives on Differentiation, Convergence and Diversity in Higher Education*, Oxford: Pergamon.

—— (1998) 'The evaluative state reconsidered', *European Journal of Education*, 33, 3: 265–284.

—— (2003a) 'On the return from Babylon', in J. File and L. Goedegebuure (eds) *Real-Time Systems*, Enschede: CHEPS, University of Twente.

—— (2003b) 'The Bologna Declaration: some of the historic dilemmas posed by the reconstruction of the community in Europe's system of higher education', *Educational Policy*, 17, 1: 141–164.

—— (2005) 'On snowballs, slopes and the process of Bologna', *ARENA Background Paper*, 31 May 2005. Online, available at: www.arena.uio.no/events/seminarpapers/NeaveMAY05.pdf.

Neave, G. and Van Vught, F. (1991) *Prometheus Bound: The Changing Relationship between Government and Higher Education in Western Europe*, Oxford: Pergamon.

Nicolescu, L. (2002) 'Reforming higher education in Romania', *European Journal of Education*, 37, 1: 91–100.

OECD (1992) *Review of Higher Education in the Czech and Slovak Federal Republics. Examiner's Report and Questions*, Paris: OECD.

Offe, C. (1993) *Designing Institutions for East European Transitions*, Public Lecture Series Publications. Collegium Budapest. Online, available at: www.colbud.hu/main_old/PubArchive/PL/PL09-Offe.pdf.

Olsen, J. (2005) *The Institutional Dynamics of the (European) University*, ARENA Working Paper series, 15/2005. Online, available at: www.arena.uio.no/publications/working-papers2005/papers/wp05_15.pdf.

Pabian, P. (2007) 'Europeanisation of higher education governance in the post-communist context: the case of the Czech Republic', unpublished manuscript, Prague: Center for Higher Education Studies.

Radó, P. (2001) *Transition in Education – Policy Making and the Key Educational Policy Areas in the Central-European and Baltic Countries*, Budapest: Open Society Institute. Online, available at: www.osi.hu/iep/papers/transit.pdf.

Sadlak, J. (1990) 'Higher education in Romania, 1860–1990', *Special Studies in Comparative Education*, 27, Buffalo: Graduate School of Education Publications SUNY.

Scott, P. (2002) 'Reflections on the reform of higher education in Central and Eastern Europe', *Higher Education in Europe*, 27, 1–2: 137–152.

Sporn, B. (2006) 'Governance and administration', in P. Altbach and J. Forest (eds) *International Handbook of Higher Education*, Dordrecht: Springer, 147–151.

Šťastná, V. (2001) 'Internationalisation of higher education in the Czech Republic', *European Journal of Education*, 36, 4: 473–491.

Tews, K. (2002) 'Der Diffusionsansatz für die vergleichende Policy-Analyse. Wurzeln und Potenziale eines Konzepts', Forschungsstelle für Umweltpolitik. Manuscript. Report 02–2002. Freie Universität Berlin. Online, available at: www.fu-berlin.de/ffu/download/rep2002_08.pdf.

Vaira, M. (2004) 'Globalization and higher education organizational change', *Higher Education*, 48, 4: 483–510.

Vlk, A. (2006) 'Higher education and GATS: regulatory consequences and stakeholders' responses', Dissertation, CHEPS Universiteit Twente.

4 Transforming the educative state in the Nordic countries?

Christine Hudson

Introduction

Dramatic changes have occurred in education systems in most European countries in recent decades. Education has been challenged by developments taking place in society, politics and the economy. Globalization, the forward march of neo-liberalism, the growth of the knowledge economy and the new middle classes have encouraged the growth of powerful rhetoric around the need for education to be more pluralistic and individualized; and uniform, blanket solutions have been seen as increasingly inappropriate to meet the needs of more diverse and heterogeneous societies. In many countries, this has led to a decentralization of the responsibility for education from the state to local government, schools or the market and a move from detailed regulation to framework legislation as a means of steering education. These developments have been seen as part of the process of governance whereby the state is no longer able to 'go it alone' and is forced to step back and allow other interests to play a role. However, in recent years the 'hollowing out' of the state model has been challenged and more subtle theories of governance have been developed. These suggest that what we are witnessing is not the disappearance of the state but rather its ability to adapt to changing circumstances and find new ways of governing that, whilst bringing in new actors, enable the state to remain an active part of governance. The importance accorded to education, not only in terms of creating and maintaining national identity, but also for economic development suggests that this is an area from which the state will not willingly abdicate.

Utilizing a comparative approach, and drawing on a qualitative analysis of official policy documents, statements and the information database on European education systems, *Eurybase*, the chapter explores these ideas in relation to compulsory education in the Nordic countries of Sweden, Finland, Norway, Denmark and Iceland. These countries have been considered to represent a distinctive type of welfare state, the social democratic or Nordic model (Esping-Andersen 1990) in which education has been characterized by social equality and a strong state role (Antikainen 2006). However, in an era of globalization and neo-liberalism, this model has been seen as challenged by developments such as decentralization, competition, deregulation and privatization and the previously highly centrally controlled Nordic education systems have been municipalized and steering by goals and general grants have been introduced (Telhaug *et al.* 2006; Tjeldvoll 1998). The state's past powerful position in relation to education in these countries makes them an interesting case in which to examine whether it is possible to find support for arguments concerning a shifting rather than shrinking role for the state, in other words, is there still government within governance? Further, although belonging to the same model, there are differences between the countries. Denmark has always had a more pluralistic and less centralized education system (Tjeldvoll 1998) and Sweden has moved most rapidly from a highly centralized to a highly decentralized education system (OECD 2002) which might lead us to expect less government in governance in these countries.

The chapter is structured as follows: it begins by discussing the rise of governance and the development of new, more subtle theories in this field. It then considers whether support for these theories can be found in the field of compulsory education in the Nordic countries. Utilizing Kooiman's (2000) three orders of governing, a general conceptual framework is developed which is then used to analyse changes at the meta-institutional and policy programme levels of education in the five countries. It concludes with a discussion of whether the state, rather than relinquishing its role, is finding other ways of regulating education in the Nordic countries.

Replacing government?

A common theme during the 1990s was the weakening of the nation state's ability to govern (Hudson 2007). It was argued that, whilst remaining the basic unit of economic and political organization, nation states were challenged by changes taking place in both the economy and society. On the one hand, greater economic, political and cultural integration and convergence were moving power upwards away from the state and, on the other, processes of regionalization, fragmentation and decentralization of authority were channelling power downwards (Jessop 2004). The forward march of neo-liberalism with its rhetoric of greater choice, accountability, efficiency, consumer empowerment and privatization of the public sector (Harvey 2007) and reinforced by the rise of the new middle class (Crompton 1998) which enamours individualism and choice were also seen as putting the position of the state into question, challenging its policy-making and steering ability. National government standardized policy solutions were seen as increasingly inappropriate to meet diverging problems and more varied needs. The state's ability to 'fly solo' was questioned in many policy areas, including education (Green 1997), and demands were voiced for greater decentralization of responsibility both to local government and the market to facilitate greater flexibility and responsiveness to differentiated needs and problems.

Government, it was argued, was being replaced by governance, where policy is formulated through interactions between actors in different networks and service provision is shared among a range of agencies, both public and private

(Rhodes 1997; Pierre 2000). In this process, non-state actors become involved in doing more societal coordination for themselves with far less (or even no) central government involvement (Jordan *et al.* 2005), leading to the emergence of governing styles that blur the boundaries between and within public and private sectors. Thus, the essence of governance becomes 'its emphasis on governing mechanisms which do not rest on recourse to the authority and sanctions of government' (Stoker 1998: 17).

However, the view that governance marked the 'withering away' of the state has been increasingly questioned. Loughlin (2004), for example, suggests that governance has always been a part of government 'in the sense that there have always been interest groups from outside the official political system involved in the policy-making system' (Loughlin 2004: 13). Similarly, Dale argues that we need to recognize that the state never did it all anyway and what becomes important is 'what forms of governance … are in place where, and why, and what is the place and role of the state within them' (2005: 129). This brings us to the more nuanced versions of governance theory that have emerged in recent years. Here, rather than abdicating control, the state is seen as altering its methods of steering to adjust to a changing environment and the idea of governing without government is questioned (Davies 2002). Kooiman (2003) argues that what is happening should be interpreted as a deliberate strategy on the part of the state to cope with the increasingly complex nature of today's problems. The state is demonstrating its adaptability to a changing environment and its ability to find new ways of maintaining some degree of control (Hudson 2007). Thus, even if the state has been in flux in recent years, it has still retained many of its core features and is very much alive as an institution of governance (Kooiman 2003), that is, government and governance are closely intertwined (Kohler-Koch 1996).

It has been even been suggested that governance is leading to new forms of government and that regulation should not be rigidly coupled with state steering. Privatization and new public management, often seen as some of the most important driving forces behind governance, may, for example, actually require more and not less regulation (Majone 1996). Indeed 'many of the new policy instruments used require some state involvement (that is, "government"), and very few are entirely devoid of state involvement (that is, pure "governance")' (Jordan *et al.* 2005: 477). Thus Jordan *et al.* argue that governance often complements rather than eclipses government and that there may even be cases of fusion where government and governance merge. From this perspective, the state is seen as being subtly transformed by newer hybrid forms of regulation or 'soft governance' such as self-monitoring (through, for example, benchmarking, peer review and the development of best practice) and societal self-organization (Jacobsson 2002). Indeed Bache (2003) goes as far as to suggest that governance can actually enhance the state's power and shows how central government introduced policies, such as public–private partnerships in the delivery of education, can both accelerated the process of governance and allow the state to achieve its policy goals more effectively. The next section considers these ideas in relation to compulsory education in the Nordic countries.

Features of contemporary Nordic education policy

In order to help us understand changes in the processes of governing, an analytical frame is constructed, drawing on Kooiman (2000) and Wolf (Chapter 11, this volume), composed of three orders of governing. The most abstract level, the meta- or third-order level, concerns the visionary or ideological level – what governs the governors? (Kooiman 2000: 154). Changes at this level form the context for reforms at the other levels of governing – the institutional (second-order) and the policy (first-order) levels (Kooiman 2003). Reforms at the institutional level concern translating the ideational frame developed at the meta-level into institutional practices and procedures (Chapter 11, this volume). Thus they also affect the concrete policy level of measures and solutions. Together these processes at the different levels 'constitute the analytical body of governance' (Kooiman 2000: 160).

The main features of the compulsory education context in the Nordic countries are summarized in Table 4.1. The issue in focus is not whether there have been changes in this context, but rather whether these changes necessarily imply the retreat of the state. Starting with the third-order level, that is the vision for education in the Nordic countries: has the move from a social democratic ideal of a 'school for all' to neo-liberalism's focus on a market agenda in education and an emphasis on individualization, choice and competition, marked a retreat of the state? Next, have the institutional reforms (second-order) aimed at improving efficiency, increasing the diversity of responsibility (decentralization to local

Table 4.1 Education policy context in the Nordic countries

Government of education	*Governance of education*
Meta-level (third-order)	
Social democracy	Neo-liberalism
Focus on:	Focus on:
• levelling out differences (egalitarian)	• social advancement (aspirational)
• school for all (democratic)	• individualization (market)
• social equality	• choice/competition
Institutional level (second-order)	
Centralized	Decentralized
Hierarchical	Multi-level
Standardization	Differentiation
Central control (planning state)	Self-regulation, 'soft' steering (evaluative state)
Policy programme level (first-order)	
Emphasis on:	Emphasis on:
• government measures	• partnership (public/private)
• uniform, standardized solutions	• pluralistic, individualized solutions
• inputs	• outputs (measuring performance)
• inspection	• evaluation (quality control)

Source: reworked from Hudson (2007).

government and the market) and new forms of steering introduced as a consequence of the shift at the meta-level marked a shrinking state role in education, or are the institutions of the state still present, but in a less direct way? Finally, at the more concrete, first-order level of governing, education policies and measures have been introduced to deal with the perceived increasing complexity and diversity in society that focus on more pluralistic, individualized solutions and on measuring and evaluating outputs. Have these meant a reduction in the state's regulatory role or have new more indirect control mechanisms appeared?

The demise of the planning and the rise of the evaluative state?

Meta-order governing

Turning first to the meta- or third-order level of governing, the Nordic countries, Sweden, Finland, Norway, Denmark and Iceland, are regarded as forming a particular type of welfare state – the social-democratic model, although there are country-specific versions of this model (Antikainen 2006; Kautto *et al.* 2001). Ideal-typically, it is characterized by a strong role for the state, comprehensive welfare policies with high quality services and generous benefits, active labour-market policies promoting full employment and an emphasis on social justice, equality, an equitable distribution of wealth and universalism (Esping-Andersen 1990; Tjeldvoll 1998). However, a powerful rhetoric emerged during 1980s and 1990s concerning the unmanageability of these highly developed, extensive welfare states, and their inability to meet the new challenges presented by, for example, globalization (Micheletti 2000). At the meta- or third governing level, a clear influence from these changes can be discerned in the vision for education. Developments such as the knowledge economy, the growth of the new middle class, the spread of neo-liberalism and the appearance of a new post-industrial labour market (Ahonen 2002) have been seen as undermining the social-democratic Nordic model. The growth of New Public Management with its focus on accountability, effectiveness, value for money, standards and quality assurance also emphasized the need to cut back state involvement and to increase the variety of actors involved in the provision of welfare services (welfare pluralism). These tendencies often coupled with more individualized demands, emphasize greater freedom of choice and individual rather than collective solutions. Taken together, these changes have been regarded as challenging the basic tenants of the Nordic welfare state, that is the tradition of solidarity (Kautto *et al.* 2001) and the belief in, and institutional support for, social egalitarianism (Blomqvist 2004).

Further, it has been argued that the loss of the social-democratic hegemonic hold on Nordic politics, the expansion of the EU and the growth of transboundary problems (making the countries more porous) have weakened the position of the state and meant that the Nordic countries are no longer able to plan their futures in the way they could in the early post-war years. Thus Michelletti (2000: 275) contends that 'big government is being transformed into big governance' with an increasing involvement of non-governmental actors in securing the well-being of the Nordic societies and economies.

Education, as a significant part of the social democratic model, has been no exception to this ideological shift (Tjeldvoll 1998). However, whilst there have clearly been changes in the vision for education, have the demands for more pluralistic, individualized, market-oriented education meant the demise of the educative state? Does the greater involvement of other actors in education mean the retreat of government within the governance of education?

Second-order governing

Turning to the institution building or second-order level of governing, at first glance the answer would appear to be yes. The responsibility for education has been transferred to local government, to schools and individuals (headteachers, teachers, pupils and parents) and to the market in all five countries. The previously closely defined, state-run, regulatory systems with strict regulation of, for example, curriculum content, student/pupil numbers and resources have become more loosely described in the regulations, framework legislation has been introduced and there has been a move towards a more decentralized, goal-oriented, result-driven education system (Johannesson *et al.* 2002; Hudson and Lidström 2002). The actors involved in education have also been broadened with the opening up of opportunities to establish independent schools and the provision of greater scope for parental involvement in schooling. Sweden can perhaps be seen as the foremost illustration of this trend as, according to the OECD (2002), it has in the last three decades shifted from having a highly centralized and detailed national government control of school matters to having one of the most decentralized educational systems among the OECD countries.

However, if we look more closely, there is evidence to suggest that despite far-reaching decentralization, all central control has not been relinquished in the Nordic countries. There are, indeed, some indications that the introduction of goal steering was also accompanied by some centralizing tendencies. Koritzinsky (2001) in the case of Norway and Ahonen (2001) in the case of Finland point out that a number of the reforms associated with the introduction of Management by Objectives had the effect of concentrating power. Indeed Koritzinsky (2001) suggests that the Norwegian Ministry of Education actually obtained more centralized political and administrative control over the education system as a result of the reforms. Similarly Ahonen (2001: 182) argues that the reforms in Finland in the early 1990s meant that power was not only transferred down to local self-government, it was also transferred up to the state departments. These were given 'planning and evaluation tasks that traditionally had been done by ad hoc nominated, politically representative committees'. In other words, the state bureaucracy could still exercise a steering function over education and possibly even strengthen this role through its responsibility for evaluation.

Indeed, all five countries have reformed their central administrative organization to strengthen their supervisory function through evaluation. Beginning with

Sweden and Denmark, the two countries we speculated might have witnessed the sharpest retreat of the state, we find evidence to suggest the contrary. The 2003 reform of the Swedish National Agency for Education (NAE), for example, gave it a supervisory role with responsibility for educational inspection and for ensuring compliance with the provisions of the Education Act (Eurybase 2006/2007b; 2007/2008a; 2007/2008b; 2007/2008c). This rebuilding of a strong and effective inspectorate can be seen as reassertion, at least to some extent, of the state's direct regulatory role. The NAE is playing an increasingly important part in the monitoring and evaluation of schools and, from 2004 onwards, schools have been obliged to use the evaluation criteria drawn up by the NAE (Eurydice 2004: 80). Further, the NAE is charged with collecting educational statistics that can be used as comparative indicators for schools. The NAE was reformed yet again in 2008 and, as well as reaffirming its responsibility for following up and evaluating compulsory education, it was given a role in ensuring quality assurance in school development. The direct regulation of schools was further strengthened through the establishment of a new separate government authority, *Skolinspektionen* (The National Agency of School Inspection), charged with the supervision and quality control of schools. This new agency is to contribute to the better achievement of educational goals and quality in schools through regular inspection and publication of its findings.[1]

In Denmark, evaluations are explicitly considered to have a control function informing stakeholders about the quality of education (Eurybase 2007/2008a). To this end, an independent institution under the Ministry of Education, the Danish Evaluation Institute (EVA), was set up in 1999 with responsibility for the systematic and mandatory evaluation of teaching and learning at all levels of the educational system. 'Quality assurance of Danish education is the main focal point of EVA, and the primary task is to initiate and conduct evaluations in the educational sector' (CIRIUS 2006). The evaluative function has been further strengthened with regard to compulsory education in that, in 2006, the Agency for the Evaluation and Quality Development of Primary and Lower Secondary Education was set up under the Ministry of Education with responsibility for improving the evaluation culture in Danish schools; contributing to the documentation and analysis of school results; disseminating best practice; and for overseeing the municipalities' quality assurance of public schools.[2] Within this agency, an advisory board has taken over, from EVA, the function of initiating evaluations in the compulsory school sector.

The other Nordic countries have also established organizations responsible for evaluation and, even if their direct control is less blatant, these institutions nevertheless exercise a central regulating function. In Finland, a separate Council for Educational Evaluation was established under the Ministry of Education in 2003 (Eurybase 2007/2008b). Its function is to organize external evaluations of 'the operations and activities of education providers and educational policy, and arrange the publication of such evaluations' (Lyytinen and Hämäläinen 2005: 2). Even Iceland has established an evaluation and supervision division in the Ministry of Education and increased decentralization and schools' greater responsibility for evaluating their own activities are seen as requiring the ministry to monitor activities more closely than before (Ministry of Education Science and Culture 2005). In Norway, the Norwegian Directorate for Education and Training, set up in 2004, has the overall responsibility for supervising education, implementing legislation and regulations and developing, organizing and implementing the national system for quality assessment (Eurybase 2006/2007a). The Directorate's control function is also discernable in that it is responsible for monitoring the County Governors (the extended arm of the state) who are charged with supervising the schools and safeguarding the rights of pupils in order to ensure equity in education in all parts of the country. Further, it is responsible for all national statistics concerning primary and secondary education, making these public and for using them to continuously assess the status of Norwegian education.

Thus it could be argued that the changes that have taken place in the central organizations in all the Nordic countries to improve their capacity for evaluation from the end of 1990s onwards have been working to reinforce the state's regulatory function in education both directly and indirectly. They have provided both subtle and less subtle means for the state to obtain information on the extent to which educational goals are being met and to ensure compliance with them.

First-order governing

At the policy programme or first-order level of governing, it might also seem at first as if the state has retreated. All the Nordic countries have introduced national curricula that are largely framework documents specifying the broad aims and guidelines for education and leaving room for interpretation and adaptation to local circumstances by local authorities, schools and teachers (see Eurybase 2006/2007a and b for the respective countries). However, the introduction of such documents cannot unambiguously be interpreted as the retreat of the state as central government still retains overall curricular control. Indeed Koritzinsky (2001) points out that the Norwegian national curricula introduced in 1994 (upper secondary education) and 1997 (compulsory education) had for the first time the formal status of legal directives. Further, there are signs that the other Nordic curricula are once more becoming more regulatory, for example, the 2004 Finnish national core curriculum contains more specific guidelines and a more detailed contextual framework compared with the 1994 curriculum (Eurybase 2007/2008b).

Further, whilst the direct control of the input side of education appears to have been relaxed, a new emphasis has been put on regulating outputs. All the Nordic counties continue to have instruments to check that the teaching of basic skills in primary and secondary schools is up to standard, but now the focus has moved to measuring the quality of the results. Indeed Simola *et al.* (2002) argue that, in the new educational governance discourse, evaluation is seen as an essential tool assuring quality. Turning to Sweden, the focus on evaluating results is can be seen clearly in the annual School Quality Reports[3] (Eurybase

2006/2007b), where schools have to describe how well they are doing in relation to the national objectives, that means there is an internal audit and assessment of the school's performance (Skolverket 2005). A central regulating function can be discerned in this quality assurance process as the NAE aims at systematically strengthening quality assurance in education and is developing standardized measures for assessing results (Eurybase 2006/2007b).

Sweden is also in the vanguard with regard to standardized testing among the Nordic countries. National tests are used to clarify educational goals, make examination criteria more tangible, and form a basis for analysing the extent to which these goals have been achieved nationally, locally and at the school level (The Swedish National Agency for Education 2006).[4] Although national tests are not new in Sweden,[5] what is new is the increased availability of information concerning the results of these tests and the greater opportunities for making comparisons between schools and municipalities. The NAE has developed an online information system, *SIRIS*, containing information on results and quality which has been in operation since 2001. The focus on the need for improved accountability in education figures clearly in SIRIS's aims. These include making it easier for schools and municipalities to identify where they can make improvements by examining their own performance and comparing themselves with others; as well as providing the public with a better understanding of how schools perform. Whilst 'league tables' of schools are not produced in Sweden, the use of tests for monitoring and accountability (and hence control) has been seen, in Sweden, as introducing a different and conflicting purpose into the system, one that compounds questions about validity, reliability and equity in assessment (Björklund *et al.* 2004). In the past, testing tended to play a comparatively minor role in the education system, mainly serving to support fairness and consistency in teachers' marking. However, given greater parental choice, the growth of competition between schools, and a possible increase of public distrust in teachers, Söderberg *et al.* (2004) suggest that assessments designed for summing up student achievement may become a means for checking up on schools and teachers.

Iceland has had national tests at the end of compulsory education since 1977, however, national tests were also introduced in 2001 in Years Four and Seven (for Icelandic and mathematics). Since 1993, an independent institute, the Educational Testing Institute, has been responsible for the development, implementation and grading of national tests and for making results public (Eurybase 2007/2008c). Although they are not used as 'aggressively' as in Sweden, national tests represent nevertheless a means of centralized control that can be used to assess and compare how well schools are meeting national goals. National tests are of more recent origin in the other Nordic counties. In Norway, they were introduced in 2004 as part of the new National Quality Assessment system intended to clarify the school's responsibilities (Eurybase 2006/2007a). The tests in reading, writing, English and mathematics are carried out in the beginning of Years Five and Eight and, as in Sweden, there is an emphasis on making the results public. These are published on a special website which contains various data concerning primary and secondary schools. According to the Norwegian Directorate for Education and Training, the website is intended to be a resource for schools and municipalities in relation to the systematic evaluation and development of education and contribute to quality assessment and development within schools. However, although it is targeted mainly at headteachers, school administrators and politicians, is also open to parents, pupils and the public in general (Skoleporten 2006)[6] and thus offers potential as a means of soft, indirect regulation of school performance.

Denmark is in the process of moving closer to Sweden in its use of quality controls. Compulsory national tests were introduced in 2007 in primary and lower secondary education[7] in order to enhance the evaluation culture in the *folkeskole*, the compulsory level of education (Eurybase 2007/2008a). Again, as in Norway, Sweden and Iceland, there is a strong emphasis on making information readily available to parents and pupils and, by providing improved access to comparable information on education and schools, enabling individuals to make informed choices and a special website (evaluering.uvm.dk) has been set up. The provision of systematic information to schools is intended to enable them to compare themselves with other schools, learn from the experience of others, and in this way promote the spread of good practice (Eurybase 2007/2008a). All schools are required to have a website containing detailed information about their educational provision, publish grade averages for individual subjects and levels as well as all other information deemed relevant for assessing the quality of the teaching provided. Further, annual school quality reports with similar aims to the Swedish were also introduced in 2007.

Although Finland has a well-developed evaluation system and evaluation has been statutory in all sectors of education since 1999 (Eurybase 2007/2008b), it has dragged its feet when it comes to introducing standardized testing and evaluation. Tests are used for diagnosis and improvement (and never for 'naming and shaming') and there has been considerable discussion about whether results should be made public. Finland has, however, created a national test bank so it is possible to check levels of skill and knowledge in school subjects. 'Obligatory national testing has, however, never been applied in the Finnish comprehensive' (Rinne *et al.* 2002: 650). Indeed, according to Aho *et al.* (2006), Finland has not followed the Anglo-Saxon accountability trend, but has instead developed the idea of *flexible accountability* in which the focus is on deep learning and not on testing. They argue that a culture of trust has developed in the Finish education system which means that 'the Ministry of Education and the National Board of Education, believes that teachers together with principals, parents, and their communities know how to provide the best possible education for their children and youth' (Aho *et al.* 2006: 138). As Rinne *et al.* (2002) point out, the new means of control and assessment are not as burdensome or as strict as in many other countries.

However, despite the lack of league tables in the Nordic countries it is, nevertheless, possible to compare schools' performances. This possibility enables not only the state to regulate the 'output' of schools; it also allows parents and the public in general to exercise a controlling function on its behalf. Further, all the countries have introduced internal or self-evaluation for municipalities and schools, often including both pupils and parents. Whilst this implies a decentralization of responsibility, it also opens up potential for central steering either directly through the provision of specific guidelines or an evaluation 'model' or, more subtly, through training courses, consultation services and materials and information services disseminating 'best practice' and 'tool-kits'. Swedish schools, for example, have been given responsibility for following up and evaluating their activities. They have to produce a work plan covering their activities, a yearly report on how these plans are implemented as well as an annual quality report (Eurybase 2006/2007b). Teachers, other staff and even pupils and parents, participate in drawing up these quality reports. However, a central regulating function can be discerned as the reports are supposed to assess the extent to which the goals set up by the state are being achieved and make proposals for necessary changes if these are not being met. Schools are 'encouraged' to use the national tests as a guide and the self-evaluations are to contain common and comparable measures of, for example, the national test results (Bjöklund *et al.* 2004). Further, the NAE also publishes general advice and comments on how schools should present quality standards and improvements in their written reports.

In Denmark, the requirement for systematic self-evaluation and follow-up is a central principle in the Danish approach to quality (Eurybase 2007/2008a). A model for schools' self-evaluation has been developed by the Danish Evaluation Institute. The model is set out in its publication *A Key to Change: School Improvement through Self-evaluation* (The Danish Evaluation Institute 2002) which is intended to guide the school through the evaluation process and make clear the types of issues that need to be tackled in the self-evaluation (Leth Nielsen and Munch Thorsen 2003). In common with Sweden, central guidance is also apparent in the newly introduced school quality reports. Icelandic schools are also required, by law, to carry out self-evaluations and the Icelandic Ministry of Education, Science and Culture has responsibility for investigating the self-evaluation methods used by the schools (Ministry of Education, Science and Culture 2005). To this end, it has published a booklet *Sjálfsmat skóla* [Schools' Self-Evaluation]. This lists criteria for self-evaluation,[8] suggestions for implementation, and a checklist and guidelines for writing the final report (Ministry of Education, Science and Culture 2004). Norway too has a mandatory requirement for all schools to evaluate, on a regular basis, how far the organization and implementation of the school's activities are in line with the objectives of the curriculum. Again the guiding hand of the state is felt in that the aim is to evaluate the extent to which the teaching and learning at a school correspond to the aims and principles of the curriculum (Eurybase 2006/2007a). Finland once again deviates somewhat here in that, although schools and other education providers have a statutory duty to evaluate their own activities following national guidelines (Eurybase 2007/2008b), it is up to local government to inform national government of the findings – if it chooses.

Conclusions

At first glance, it might seem that national government in the Nordic countries has been relaxing its strict control on education, blurring the boundaries between public and private and opening up for pluralism and choice and letting 'flowers of many kinds blossom'.[9] However, if we look more closely at what has been happening, it becomes apparent that the state is still active within the governance of education. Although there have been changes at the meta-level of governing with a shift towards a more neo-liberal vision for education, this has not meant the disappearance of the state at the institutional and policy programme levels of governing. It is the expression of the state's presence that has changed and, rather than reneging on its responsibility for education, it appears to have been finding new, often more indirect steering methods. Thus we seem to be witnessing the state's metamorphosis and not its vanquishment. This is very much in line with the more nuanced versions of governance theory that have emerged in recent years. The powerful discourse around the importance of education for a country's well-being and competitiveness in the global market has presented the state with a quandary – education is too important for the state to relax its hold completely yet, at the same time, its means of regulation must not constrain the potential for finding new ways of meeting or adapting to increasingly diverse and changeable societies and problems. One way of doing this appears to be to shift the focus of control to the output side of education and, at the same time, introducing more subtle 'soft' forms of steering. Linked to this is the increased use of evaluation and quality control. In particular, the development of internal or self-evaluation methods whereby the schools regulate themselves in line with centrally devised guidelines seems to be a particularly effective method on the part of the state.

Further, although there were some variations discernable in the extent to which the state was maintaining its presence in the different countries, it was not in the way expected. Sweden and Denmark, rather than providing the greatest support for the retreat of the state argument, were, in the Swedish case, witnessing a 'return of the state' and, in the Danish case, soft-regulation even appears to be leading to a stronger centralized presence in education. Thus in the Nordic countries, the state is clearly maintaining government in the governance of education.

The issues discussed here have wider implications for political science in general. Increasing societal diversity and complexity require more nuanced responses in which the state interacts with other actors in the making and implementing of public policy. The greater complexity, interdependency and diversity of policy-making and implementation found in relation to education are also reflected in other policy areas.

Notes

1 www.skolinspektionen.se/sv/Om-oss (accessed 25 October 2008). *Skolinspektionen* was set up 1 October 2008 and there is not yet an English version of the webpage.
2 http://skolestyrelsen.dk/om%20styrelsen/opgaver.aspx (accessed 21 December 2007).
3 Introduced in 1997.
4 www.skolverket.se/sb/d/170 (accessed 26 September 2006).
5 They are obligatory in Year Nine and optional in Year Five and concern English, Maths, Swedish and Swedish as a second language.
6 www.skoleporten.no/templates/default.aspx?id=2011&epslanguage=NO.
7 During the nine years of compulsory schooling, ten compulsory national tests will be conducted in Danish, English, mathematics and the natural sciences.
8 These are also published in the general section of the National Curriculum Guide for primary/lower secondary schools.
9 Speech Delivered by Lu Ting-yi, Director of the Propaganda Department of the Central Committee of the Chinese Communist Party, on the Party's Policy on Art, Literature, and Science, 26 May 1956.

References

Aho, E., Pitkänen, K. and Sahlberg, P. (2006) *Policy Development and Reform Principles of Basic and Secondary Education in Finland since 1968*, Washington, DC: The World Bank, Education Working paper series, No. 2: May 2006.

Ahonen, S. (2001) 'The end of the common school? Change in the ethos and politics of education in Finland towards the end of the 1900s', in S. Ahonen and J. Rantala (eds) *Nordic Lights: Education for Nation and Civic Society in the Nordic Countries 1850–2000*, Helsinki: Finnish Literature Society, 175–203.

—— (2002) 'From an industrial to a post-industrial society: changing conceptions of equality in education', *Educational Review*, 54, 2: 173–181.

Antikainen, A. (2006) 'In search of the Nordic model in education', *Scandinavian Journal of Educational Research*, 50, 3: 229–243.

Bache, I. (2003) 'Governing through governance: education policy control under New Labour', *Political Studies*, 51: 300–314.

Björklund, A., Edin, P.-A., Fredriksson, P. and Krueger, A. (2004) *Education, Equality, and Efficiency – An Analysis of Swedish School Reforms during the 1990s*, IFAU – Education, Equality, and Efficiency Report, 28 January 2004.

Blomqvist, P. (2004) 'The choice revolution: privatization of Swedish welfare services in the in the 1990s', *Social Policy and Administration*, 38, 2: 139–155.

CIRIUS (2006) *The Danish Education System*, Copenhagen: CIRIUS.

Crompton, Rosemary (1998) *Class and Stratification*, 2nd edn, Cambridge: Policy Press.

Dale, R. (2005) 'Globalisation, knowledge economy and comparative education', *Comparative Education*, 41, 2: 117–149.

Danish Evaluation Institute (2002) *A Key to Change: School Improvement through Self-evaluation*, 23, Copenhagen: Danish Evaluation Institute.

Davies, J. (2002) 'The governance of urban regeneration: a critique of the "governing without government" thesis', *Public Administration*, 80, 2: 301–322.

Esping-Andersen, G. (1990) *The Three Worlds of Welfare Capitalism*, Oxford: Polity Press.

Eurybase (2006/2007a) *The Education System in Norway*, The Information Database on Education Systems in Europe. Online, available at: http://eacea.ec.europa.eu/ressources/eurydice/eurybase/pdf/0_integral/NO_EN.pdf.

—— (2006/2007b) *The Education System in Sweden*, The Information Database on Education Systems in Europe. Online, available at: http://eacea.ec.europa.eu/ressources/eurydice/eurybase/pdf/0_integral/SE_EN.pdf.

—— (2007/2008a) *The Education System in Denmark*, The Information Database on Education Systems in Europe. Online, available at: http://eacea.ec.europa.eu/ressources/eurydice/eurybase/pdf/0_integral/DK_EN.pdf.

—— (2007/2008b) *The Education System in Finland*, The Information Database on Education Systems in Europe. Online, available at: http://eacea.ec.europa.eu/ressources/eurydice/eurybase/pdf/0_integral/FI_EN.pdf.

—— (2007/2008c) *The Education System in Iceland*, The Information Database on Education Systems in Europe. Online, available at: http://eacea.ec.europa.eu/ressources/eurydice/eurybase/pdf/0_integral/IC_EN.pdf.

Eurydice (2004) *Evaluation of Schools Providing Compulsory Education in Europe*, Brussels: Directorate-General for Education and Culture, European Commission.

Green, A. (1997) *Education, Globalization and the Nation State*, Basingstoke: Palgrave Macmillan.

Harvey, D. (2007) *A Brief History of Neoliberalism*, Oxford: Oxford University Press.

Hudson, C. (2007) 'Governing the governance of education – the state strikes back?', *European Educational Research Journal*, 6, 3: 266–282.

Hudson, C. and Lidström, A. (2002) *Local Education Policies, Comparing Sweden & Britain*, London: Palgrave.

Jacobsson, K. (2002) *Soft Regulation and the Subtle Transformation of States: The Case of EU Employment Policy*, SCORE 2002–04, Stockholm: Stockholm Centre for Organizational Research.

Johannesson, I., Lindblad, S. and Simola, H. (2002) 'An inevitable progress? Educational restructuring in Finland, Iceland and Sweden at the turn of the millennium', *Scandinavian Journal of Educational Research*, 46, 3: 325–339.

Jessop, B. (2004) 'Hollowing out the "nation-state" and multilevel governance', in P. Kennett (ed.) *A Handbook of Comparative Social Policy*, Cheltenham: Edward Elgar, 11–25.

Jordan, A., Wurzel, R.K.W. and Zito, A. (2005) 'The rise of "new" policy instruments in comparative perspective: has governance eclipsed government?', *Political Studies*, 53, 3: 477–496.

Kautto, M., Fritzell, J., Hvinden, B., Kvist, J. and Uusitalo, H. (2001) 'Conclusion: Nordic welfare states in the European context', in M. Kautto, J. Fritzell, B. Hvinden, J. Kvist and H. Uusitalo (eds) *Nordic Welfare States in the European Context*, London: Routledge, 262–272.

Kohler-Koch, B. (1996) 'The strength of weakness: the transformation of governance in the EU', in G. Sverker and L. Lewin (eds) *The Future of the Nation State*, Stockholm: Nerenius and Santerus, 169–210.

Kooiman, J. (2000) 'Societal governance: levels, modes and orders of social-political interaction', in J. Pierre (ed.) *Debating Governance: Authority, Steering, and Democracy*, Oxford: Oxford University Press, 138–164.

—— (2003) *Governing as Governance*, London: Sage.

Koritzinsky, T. (2001) 'Education reforms in Norway in the 1990s: civic pluralism and national unity in decision-making and curriculum contents', in S. Ahonen and J. Rantala (eds) *Nordic Lights: Education for Nation and Civic Society in the Nordic Countries 1850–2000*, Helsinki: Finnish Literature Society, 204–225.

Leth Nielsen, K. and Munch Thorsen, K. (2003) *Development of Methods of Self-Evaluation in the Danish School Sector*, ICSEI Australia.

Loughlin, J. (2004) 'The "transformation" of governance: new directions in policy and politics', *Australian Journal of Politics and History*, 50, 1: 8–22.

Lyytinen, H.K. and Hämäläinen, K. (2005) *Developing National Evaluation of Education in Finland*, The Finnish Educational Evaluation Council Policy Outlines, 17 March 2005.

Majone, G. (ed.) (1996) *Regulating Europe*, London: Routledge.

Micheletti, M. (2000) 'End of big government: is it happening in the Nordic countries?', *Governance*, 13, 2: 265–278.

Ministry of Education, Science and Culture (2004) *Findings of Evaluation of Self-evaluation Procedures in Primary/Lower Secondary Schools 2001–2003*, Reykjavík: Ministry of Education, Science and Culture.

—— (2005) *The Ministry of Education, Science and Culture in Iceland*, Reykjavík: Ministry of Education, Science and Culture.

OECD (2002) *Education at a Glance*, Paris: Organization for Economic Co-operation and Development.

Pierre, J. (ed.) (2000) *Debating Governance: Authority, Steering, and Democracy*, Oxford: Oxford University Press.

Rhodes, R.A.W. (1997) *Understanding Governance. Policy Networks, Governance, Reflexivity and Accountability*, Milton Keynes: Open University Press.

Rinne, R., Kivirauma, J. and Simola, H. (2002) 'Shoots of revisionist education policy or just slow readjustment? The Finnish case of educational reconstruction', *Journal of Education Policy*, 17, 6: 643–658.

Simola, H., Rinne, R. and Kivirauma, J. (2002) 'Abdication of the education state or just shifting responsibilities?', *Scandinavian Journal of Educational Research*, 46, 3: 247–264.

Skolverket (2005) *Inspecting for Improvement – a Brochure about the National Agency for Education's Educational Inspectorate*, Stockholm: Skolverket.

Söderberg, S., Wirén, E. and Ramstedt, K. (2004) *The Role of Evaluation, Assessment and Inspection in Swedish Educational Policy*, Berlin: Sixth Conference of the European Evaluation Society (EES) 'Governance, Democracy and Evaluation', 30 September–2 October 2004.

Stoker, G. (1998) 'Governance as theory', *International Social Science Journal*, 50, 155: 17–28.

Telhaug, A., Oftedal, M., Odd, A. and Aasen, P. (2006) 'The Nordic model in education: education as part of the political system in the last 50 years', *Scandinavian Journal of Educational Research*, 50, 3: 245–283.

Tjeldvoll, A. (ed.) (1998) *Education and the Scandinavian Welfare State in the Year 2000: Equality, Policy, and Reform*, New York: Garland.

Part II

Education in public policy analysis and public administration

Winding roads to implementation

5 Modes of governance in German curricular reform

Examining transformative change before the Bologna Process

Katrin Toens

Introduction[1]

Since the turn of the century the German higher education system has undergone visible structural change in the politics of curricular reform. Political decisions in this field do not only impact on the capacity of higher education institutions to adapt their study programs to a changing environment. They also affect the ability of single disciplines to survive under the financial constraints of fiscal crisis and state measures of austerity. The roots of the traditional curricular reform instrument date back to the post-1945 period when a foreseeable massive increase of university students began to capture the attention of educational reformers. In 1954, the Standing Conference of the Ministers of Culture and the West German Rectors' Conference created the Joint Commission for the Order of Studies and Examination.[2] From the late 1970s onward the Joint Commission coordinated discipline specific curricular reforms on the national level. Even though the rather time-consuming and inefficient curricular reform procedure was highly criticized, the Joint Commission continued to work until its replacement with the current accreditation system in the year of 2002.

The displacement of the traditional curricular reform instrument provides an interesting case for further research. It does not only exemplify the rare breakdown of a long-established reform bureaucracy, but it also signals the reluctant opening of the traditional German approach to quality assurance for internationally enforced standards and guidelines. The following contribution examines this major change. It addresses the questions of who served as a main driving force, and what motivated action?

Turning to current research debates on higher education reform, the attention paid to the Bologna Process (see for instance Nagel 2006; Witte 2006; Walter 2006) creates the impression that domestic structural change was caused by intergovernmental reform activities on the European level. Some studies make it even explicit by arguing that intergovernmental action in sovereignty-burdened policy fields, such as education, are driven by a new *raison d'état* (Martens and Wolf 2006; see also Wolf 2000). The basic assumption is that actors from the federal government created an outside pressure on the national power balance in order to overcome domestic reform barriers. No doubt, the Europeanization pressure of the Bologna Process did play a role, particularly in a later stage of domestic reforms (see Toens 2008). But this should not lead to the neglect of internal causes as well as bottom-up mechanisms of change, created by non-state actors.

This chapter is based on a counter-thesis to the argument that Europeanization pressure was the decisive driving force of domestic structural change. I will show that there was a time parallel between exogenous change pressure, created by the Bologna Process, and endogenous driving forces. These endogenous driving forces were firmly rooted in domestic politics, they came from within the German Rectors' Conference, and they date back before the beginning of the Bologna Process at the turn of the century. This renders the Bologna Process a context factor instead of an independent determining force of domestic policy change.

The analysis in this chapter provides evidence for the above hypothesis. It is designed as a single case study of the transition phase from the traditional state authorized curricular reform instrument to the German accreditation system. For the extraction of data I used qualitative methods, combining expert interviews with the analysis of secondary literature as well as documents, published by the relevant representative actors and organizational units of German curricular reform. The chapter addresses the overarching themes of this volume in the following two ways. First, by drawing attention to the institutional reorganization of curricular reform it provides insight into the power struggle and mode of governing accompanying change. Furthermore, the analysis sheds light on issues of internationalization and privatization from a bottom-up perspective of Europeanization. From this perspective, the internationalization of higher education politics as well as the partial privatization of public services in quality assurance is perceived as an instrumental policy agenda of former university rectors and presidents who seek to extend their political control over the institutional reorganization of higher education in Germany.

The chapter is divided in two main sections. The next section will set the stage by specifying the research question and theoretical frame of reference. After a brief clarification of the term governance, two approaches are introduced in order to construct an analytical framework for examining transformative change in a pre- and early stage of the Bologna Process. The first approach is historical institutionalism that has recently been modified to serve the analysis of the endogenous change mechanisms (Streeck and Thelen 2005). Second, the policy analytical concept of multiple streams (Zahariadis 1999; Rüb 2007) is introduced as a complementary tool for identifying micro-level aspects of policy change. In the empirical section of part three these approaches are applied to the replacement of the inherited institutional settings in the politics of curricular reform with the current accreditation system. This section provides evidence for the central hypothesis that the most important causal factors of structural change are rooted in domestic politics.

Setting the stage

Nowadays policy change is most frequently analyzed from perspectives of governance. In political science the term governance is used to emphasize a shift from the nation state as the traditional locus of political action to multi-level, multi-actor settings of policy-making. The increased complexity and de-nationalization of political steering renders governance perspectives as analytically important. Yet they have become criticized for a lack of systematic attention to the power aspects of recent state transformations (Greven 2007; Deitelhoff and Geis 2007). Critics draw attention to a naïve understanding of policy-making in governance studies that tend to perceive politics as neutral problem solving. Their main accusation is that these studies remain rather indifferent to questions regarding the actual scope of state withdrawal from decision-making power as well as the consequences of the informal participation by non-state actors for the democratic legitimacy of political decisions. In order to avoid these problems without denying the added value of governance perspectives I will apply a concept of governance that is based on the distinction of first, second and third-order governing (Kooiman 2003; see also the Introduction to this volume; Chapter 11, this volume). My main focus is on forms of action that fall under the category of second-order governing. Second-order governing concerns the institutional organization of issue-specific policy-making, such as curricular reform in our case, whereas first-order governance deals with problem-solving and opportunity creation in the narrower space of certain issue-domains. Thus, 'in second order governing the institutions in which first order governing takes place are the objects of governance: their design, maintenance and care for' (Kooiman 2003: 10).

If second-order governing in the field of curricular reform is the dependent variable or explanandum, I look at power struggles in search for explanatory factors. The desire to gain power in the Weberian sense (the ability to impose one's will upon others) is assumed to be an important driving force of institutional change. Power is nothing static. Particularly in mass democracies it is not ascribed to certain people or institutions once and for all. As a matter of fact, to take power for granted is the best way of losing it. Power is constantly under attack, and it must be permanently politically established and re-established. Those who are close to the powerful can be expected to be the most creative in finding ways of redirecting power to their advantage.

In order to analyze shifting modes of second order governing in German curricular reform I will use a historical institutionalist approach, called sequential policy analysis (Streeck and Thelen 2005; see also Trampusch 2007).[3] The approach fits the concept of power as something fluid and constantly under attack. It is based on a grounded and realistic concept of an institution, resembling Max Weber's definition of a ruling organization (*Herrschaftsverband*). From this perspective institutions are continuously created and recreated by the interaction of a great number of rule makers and rule takers with limited cognition and control of the overall course of policy change. The translation of institutional relations into interactions between identifiable social actors does not only make institutions eminently accessible to empirical research. It also captures important features of incremental endogenous change. This is done by means of distinguishing between rules and their implementation or enactment as well as by identifying 'the gaps between the two that are due to or open up opportunities for strategic action on the part of actors' (Streeck and Thelen 2005: 13).

The particular kinds of endogenous transformative change that are relevant to the analysis in this chapter are grasped by the concepts of institutional drift and displacement. Drift is the 'neglect of institutional maintenance in spite of external change resulting in slippage in institutional practice on the ground' (Streeck and Thelen 2005: 31). Thus change is triggered by the mechanisms of deliberative neglect. Particularly when deliberative neglect is practiced over longer time-periods, it results in a growing lack of 'the design, maintenance and care' for institutions that were referred to earlier by the term 'second order governing' (Kooiman 2003: 10). Depending on issue salience or the amount of political attention, resting on a particular policy field, drift could easily cause social dissatisfaction that crystallizes to a lack of political acceptance over time.

The application of the concept of institutional drift to the history of German curricular reform sheds a different light on institutional change than conventional studies on the stalemate in the federal-*Länder* relations of German educational politics (see Lehmbruch 2000; Scharpf 1988). Instead of emphasizing stalemate as a consequence of mutually blocking parties one can identify the kind of institutional erosion that results from deliberative neglect and the involved political non-decisions. Non-decisions or the lack of adapting institutions to a changing environment become just another kind of policy input that, in the long run, is powerful enough to gradually unleash transformative change. The lack of maintenance and care for institutions contributes to their erosion behind the surface of formal integrity.

If drift directs attention to the erosion of institutions, the concept of displacement points to the 'rising salience of subordinate relative to dominant institutions' (Streeck and Thelen 2005: 31). Mechanisms of displacement or defection are triggered by 'institutional incoherence opening space for deviant behavior, [the a]ctive cultivation of a new "logic" of action inside an existing institutional setting, [and/or the i]nvasion and assimilation of foreign practices' (Streeck and Thelen 2005: 31). The case of German curricular reform provides a good example for the fact that both mechanisms, drift and displacement, can complement each other. In that case, drift provides an opportunity structure for canalizing policy change toward displacement. Thus, the intentional framing of drift as self-reinforcing mechanisms of policy failure could easily discredit reform suggestions that start from national experience or make domestic resistance against invasion and the assimilation of foreign practices collapse more easily.

From an analytical perspective, the model of multiple streams provides a linkage to the concepts of drift and displacement. This model is particularly well equipped to analyze policy change at a micro level by focusing on policy entrepreneurs and how they manipulate and channel institutional change in a favored direction. The underlying idea that there are independent streams of decision-making, consisting of problem perceptions, suggested solutions and opportunities to connect both to decisions (Cohen *et al.* 1988; Kingdon 1984; Zahariadis 1999; Rüb 2007). In my view this concept has recently gained relevance due to the growing importance of different levels of policy-making. From the analytic perspective of the multiple streams approach, multi-level governance adds perceptions of problems and solutions to the policy-making process. It thus increases the opportunities for manipulating political decisions through the connection of streams. Problems and solutions that are created on the European level of politics do not automatically penetrate national politics. It requires people, who pull them into the domestic policy-making process. Actors who decisively pull in international and/or European perceptions of problems and solutions by means of connecting streams are serving as change agents or policy entrepreneurs. In the next section the discussed approaches are applied to the analysis of transformative change in a pre-Bologna stage of German curricular reform.

From traditional curricular reform to accreditation

The replacement of the traditional institutional settings of curricular reform, represented by the Joint Commission, with the current accreditation system provides a good example to show transformative kinds of endogenous change that resemble the concepts of institutional drift and replacement. Change took place below the surface of institutional stability. Contrary to the appearance of a rather sudden displacement, the Joint Commission was gradually dismantled and phased out over a time period of about a decade. A small group of university representatives, situated within the German Rectors' Conference, acted as policy entrepreneurs by using opportunity structures in the mid-1990s to work toward the displacement of the traditional institutional settings with an accreditation system modeled on selected bits and pieces of foreign experience. Almost a decade before the Bologna declaration of 1999, these people were able to profit from internal factors, such as a history of institutional drift as well as a political climate of anxiety emerging from the fear of not being internationally competitive. If these were the conditions of policy change, its driving force was the gain of political influence by former university rectors and presidents who helped to transform the German Rectors' Conference from a rectors' club to an international policy actor.

In what follows I will first give a brief overview of the historical development of the federal arrangement of curricular reform that served as a predecessor of the current accreditation system for about half a century. The aim is to identify the relevant actors and the power relations between them in order to tackle the issue of how this relates to the development of institutional drift.

Institutional drift in the politics of curricular reform

The origins of the current system of educational federalism in Germany date back to the period of decentralized reconstruction after World War II when the *Länder* governments and their respective ministries of education emerged as the most powerful actors in higher education politics. The Constitution of the Federal Republic of Germany allocates the power of supervision of educational institutions to the *Länder* level because education is considered an element of cultural diversity. In order to set guidelines for the required minimum norms in the education system the *Länder* decided to establish the Standing Conference of the Ministers of Culture that should later become the institutional location for the coordination of nationwide curricular reforms.

In 1949, the Rectors' Conference emerged as a key actor in German higher education politics. According to its self-understanding the Rectors' Conference serves as a representative body of all higher education institutions. Since the mid-1970s this has included universities of applied sciences (*Fachhochschulen*). The gain of influence over the years is related to the growing involvement of university representatives, serving as advisors to the federal state and *Länder* governments. The inception of a number of hybrid institutions that combine the engagement of all three parties (the federal government, the *Länder* and the universities) proves the importance of university representatives in German higher education politics. The most prestigious of these hybrid institutions is the German Council of Science and Humanities, the foundation of which signaled 'the beginning of a period in which the academic expertise was put more or less on equal footing in councils, in which government was represented as well' (Teichler 1991: 32).

In the late 1950s, a period of system-wide initiatives began that were geared toward the adaptation of higher education to the non-Humboldtian conditions of mass education. The shared initiative of the Standing Conference and the West German Rectors' Conference to establish the Joint Commission falls into this period (see Commission for the Order of Examination and Studies 1982). However, it took several attempts until the Joint Commission was finally used to coordinate nationwide curricular reforms. What favored this development was a revival of a reformist climate in the mid-1960s that led to the increased engagement of the federal government in higher education politics. The first Higher Education Framework Law in 1976 signaled the federal state competency to set guidelines regarding various issues of higher education to be regulated homogeneously in the respective laws of the *Länder*. The Framework Law gave instructions for the establishment of the Joint Commission to serve the nationwide coordination of curricular reforms. The Joint Commission was set up by *Länder* agreement in 1978. According to this agreement, it served the following goals:

1   the implementation of Art. 9 of the Framework Law that asked the *Länder* governments to guarantee equal standards of higher education at all universities in the Federal Republic in order to allow for student mobility;

2   the coordination of discipline-specific curricular reform commissions, involving representatives of the federal state, the *Länder*, universities and the labor market; and

3   the updating of curricula by means of creating discipline-specific curriculum framework orders and adapting them to the changing developments in science and the labor market (Standing Conference of the Ministers of Culture 1978).

The establishment of the Joint Commission falls into the period of cooperative federalism, signifying the concerted political planning of the federal government and the *Länder*. However, due to the *Länder* who protected education as a core domain of their competence, the Joint Commission was basically under their control.[4]

The production of discipline-specific curriculum framework orders was less problematic compared to the actual procedure of bringing them into effect. Procedures were known as extremely bureaucratic and time-consuming from the beginning onward. A proposal from such a commission had to pass the Joint Commission in order to receive the status of a draft. It was then sent for comment to all universities and education ministries of the *Länder*. After receiving comments, the proposal was modified and sent to the Standing Conference of the Ministers of Culture for approval (Teichler 1991: 38). Due to the veto power of the ministerial *Land* bureaucracy and the lack of prompt response by the externally involved universities the creation of a curriculum framework order took on average nine years and sometimes even longer. Most curriculum framework orders were already outdated before they reached the university level for implementation. Given this, the instrument of federal curricular reform operated although everyone involved recognized its dysfunctional characteristics (see also Witte 2008). This raises the question of why, over all these years, there has remained a lack of structural reform. Instead of a reform in procedural rules, there was a continuous growth of the curricular reform bureaucracy. At its peak, the procedural steps amounted to 42 (Interview Standing Conference of the Ministers of Culture #2, 2007). Adding the need for consensus with the externally involved *Länder* ministries and universities, the number of procedural steps approximately doubled. These mechanisms of bureaucratization were a symptom of institutional drift. If the enactment of institutions changes 'not by reform of rules, but by rules remaining unchanged in the face of evolving external conditions' (Streeck and Thelen 2005: 31), the result is institutional drift.

The curricular reform bureaucracy of the Joint Commission fulfilled the hidden task to reach a maximum transparency and consensus among the representatives of the federal state, the *Länder* and universities (Interview Standing Conference of the Ministers of Culture #2, 2007). Consequently, the institution drifted away from its original goal to adopt curriculum framework orders to the developments of science and the professional world. Instead, the Joint Commission was increasingly geared toward the neutralization and absorption of potential conflict between the involved parties. If conflict emerged at all, it became routinized in repeated quarrels about profane issues, such as whether the average study duration should be nine or ten semesters or what word to use in order to describe the practical orientation of university studies (Interview Standing Conference of the Ministers of Culture #2, 2007; see also Schreiterer 1989: 162, 320).

What all this amounted to was a division of power and authority between state and university representatives, which served both parties. On the one side, the *Länder* were able to demonstrate regulatory power vis-à-vis the federal government in order to defend their political autonomy. On the other side, university academics were able to refer to their expertise in order to defend their subject domains against state intrusion. In the end, institutional dynamics became increasingly dependent on a self-referential curricular reform community that increasingly lost its grip on social reality underneath the cover of formal integrity. As a result the Joint Commission became more and more vulnerable to outside attacks (Schreiterer 1989: 202).

Altogether, the period of institutional drift was characterized by a relatively strong unity of university representatives behind the Humboldtian tradition to defend the freedom of research and teaching by individual academics.[5] Part of the problem of institutional drift was created by the indifference of state actors, who insinuated the incompatibility of this tradition with the requirements of mass education without seriously challenging it. As noted earlier, the unresolved tension between representatives of the *Länder* governments and the universities provided a significant reason for institutional drift. The very emergence of drift can be taken as evidence that public administrators gave primacy to the academic community and its demand for a high degree of academic latitude. The next section will show that the consensus behind this traditional model started to crumble when a group of university representatives within the German Rectors' Conference split off from the traditionalist academic community by means of pushing for the institutional displacement of the Joint Commission. Since the professional organizations of professors, such as the Union of University Academics and the Umbrella Organization of Academic Subject Networks (*Allgemeiner Fakultätentag*), were national organizations, which dealt primarily with routine legal services and university affairs, they were ill-prepared to defend the status interests of their members politically in the increasingly internationalized reform struggle.

Institutional displacement in the context of internationalization

Institutional drift alone did not trigger the dissolution of the Joint Commission. The drifting away of institutions from their original policy goals had been accepted from the beginning onward. If anything, time made a difference because the costs of institutional drift grew over the years. But additional factors were required to prepare for structured change. Among them was a shift in the problem perception of political elites that was triggered in the early 1990s by the following two factors. First, university studies became more important to the private economy due to the parallel trends of the privatization of employment intensive state enterprises (i.e. postal services and railway) and the so-called academization of labor in the growing private service sector. Given this, economic actors and their political representatives in higher education, such as the Confederation of German Employers' Association and the business community's innovation agency for the German science system, called *Stifterverband*, pressured for a more efficient and outcome-oriented organization of studies and learning structures (Witte 2006: 164). After reunification this pressure was more directly targeted toward universities. Numerous previous attempts to expand practice-oriented studies at universities of applied sciences had failed before due to strict resistance by the academic communities in the universities. This contributed to the fact that politicians began to expect regular universities to take a larger share of responsibility for practice-oriented higher education. Second, from 1992 onward, globalization was more strongly perceived within the ministerial bureaucracy. At least on the federal state level this has triggered a shift in perception from a rather inward-looking problem definition to an outward-looking awareness of an increasingly competitive international context that could no longer be ignored (Interview Federal Ministry of Education and Research #2, 2006). In 1993, the publication of several independent action plans for structural reforms signaled a growing readiness for change on the part of political elites (Mentges 2004). In the mid-1990s, the situation came to a head. Foreign policy elites scandalized the relatively low percentage of foreign student enrolment at German universities (Interview Ministry of Education and Research of Lower Saxony #2, 2007).

The issue domain of curricular reform, however, provides a good example for the fact that the change of problem perception did not automatically lead to policy change. What was lacking was a clear vision of alternatives as well as people who were strategically positioned to push such a vision and to rally the potentially conflicting interests of state officials from the central government, the *Länder* and academia behind it. Such a combination of change triggering factors emerged in the German Rectors' Conference at the beginning of the 1990s. A key figure in this context was the professor and previous university rector Hans-Uwe Erichsen. Erichsen was the President of the German Rectors' Conference from 1990 until 1998. During his period of office he contributed to the transformation of this organization from a rectors' club into an international policy player (Interview German Rectors' Conference #6, 2006; see also Landfried 2003: 124). He energetically got involved in international networks of quality assurance. In order to infiltrate international ideas into the domestic policy arena Erichsen initiated a joint working group of the Standing Conference of the Ministers of Culture and the Rectors' Conference, called the Working Group for the Advancement of the Structure of Higher Education.[6] In retrospect, the working group gradually turned into a key platform for triggering change in the politics of curricular reform.

A decisive reason for the key role of the working group is that it fulfilled several functions at once. First, it served the spread of new ideas from its informal inner circle to the larger community of higher education politics. The inner circle of the working group was formed by Klaus Landfried, a previous university president who served as the president of the German Rectors' Conference after Erichsen's period of office had ended, the General Secretary of the Rectors' Conference, Josef Lange, the Minister of Education in Rhineland-Palatinate, Jürgen Zöllner (a former university president), and his State Secretary Doris Ahnen (formerly chair of the grassroots student organization ASTA at the same university as Zöllner). These four members of the inner circle acted as important change agents. Most of what has actually been accomplished during the official meetings of the working group has been an input of the pre-discussions during numerous informal gatherings of its inner circle (Interview German Rectors' Conference #7, 2007).

A second factor that contributed to the fastening of institutional change was the fact that the inner circle of the working group had direct contacts into the ministerial bureaucracy of the *Länder* to its disposal. This enabled the working group to annul the ponderous ministerial bureaucracy that dominated the committees within the Standing Conference of the Ministers of Culture (Interview German Rectors' Conference #7, 2007). What added to the success of this strategy was the existence of a tight network between university rectors, the presidential office of the German Rectors' Conference and the ministerial bureaucracy of the *Länder*. An indicator for the existence of such a policy network is the fact that majority of the members of the working group's inner circle have had a stunning political career in the ministries of education of the *Länder* after serving in German Rectors' Conference.

Third, the working group triggered innovation in the area of quality assurance. Some of its core members have been involved in a pilot-project of the EU Commission on the evaluation of teaching. A year later, the Rectors' Conference served as the German national agency in this project (German Rectors' Conference 1995). Three years later, the Rectors' Conference started its own project on the quality assurance of teaching. The so-called Project Q became responsible for the international cooperation in this policy field. It has authored numerous publications, and it is currently serving as a German platform for the organization of Bologna conferences.

In the second half of the 1990s the working group set the course for the establishment of the accreditation system. It officially recommended the introduction of bachelor and master degrees and the establishment of an accreditation system to assure the quality of the two-tired study programs in November 1997. After the Fourth Amendment of the Federal Framework Act in August 1998 had opened up higher education to the introduction of the two-tiered degree structure on a trial basis, the working group used this as a reason to push for the fast establishment of an accreditation system with private quality assurance agencies. The vision behind this action was an entrepreneurial concept of university autonomy based on the professionalization and political strengthening of institutional leadership. The adoption of foreign practices, such as external quality assurance, private accreditation agencies and peer review, was one cornerstone of this vision. It served to question the German tradition of status equality among all higher education institutions and university professors. Partly the new vision was put forward in combination with the claim that the political application of the Humboldtian tradition of academic freedom to the whole university sector would nurture a culture of irresponsibility and incompetence among German professors and teaching staff (Interview German Rectors' Conference #8, 2007).

The Fourth Amendment of the Framework Act has brought a decisive change. It abolished the system of curriculum framework orders that had once served as a legal basis for the establishment of the Joint Commission by the *Länder* governments. From then onward it was entirely up to the *Länder* to replace the Joint Commission with the accreditation system (see also Witte 2006: 169). They began with a decision of the Standing Conference of the Ministers of Culture in December 1998, which still did not automatically lead to the displacement of the Joint Commission. The accreditation system was set up in 1999 for a trial period of three years, and it was meant to co-exist with the Joint Commission (Standing Conference of the Ministers of Culture 1999). At that time, nobody truly believed that the Joint Commission would become dissolved. When it finally did, it was again a combination of several factors that contributed to its displacement.

The final meeting of the Joint Commission took place at the Bauhaus University Weimar in September 2002. About a year earlier, the last Chair of the Joint Commission, a former rector of the Bauhaus University, frequently invited consulting experts from the economy and the larger higher education community to confront the protectors of the status quo with the critical viewpoints of experts outside of the Joint Commission. Thus, in the summer of 2001, a correspondence between the Confederation of German Employers' Association and the Joint Commission took place. In this correspondence, the education representative of the Confederation of German Employers' Association suggested the fast dissolution of the Joint Commission and the establishment of private accreditation agencies. In the fall of 2001, the respective representative was invited to join a meeting of the Joint Commission. Additionally, professors from specific disciplines were invited, who accused academic members of the curricular reform commissions to act on behalf of the possessive interests of their faculty instead of advancing curricular reform (Interview German Rectors' Conference #6, 2007).

The harsh criticism of external experts served to undermine the authority of the traditionalists within the Joint Commission who defended academic freedom as a matter of status right.[7] An indicator of the loss of authority on the side of the traditionalists in the Joint Commission was the fact that the working group had been urged frequently to intervene when the representatives of the *Länder* and universities got caught up again in one of these endless quarrels about the average duration of university studies. Interventions did two things. First, they relocated political influence from the traditionalists within the Joint Commission to the modernizers within the working group. Second, they shifted the blame to professors who were accused of taking advantage of institutional drift by using curricular reform as an instrument to manipulate state funding in favor of their specific disciplines. When the Sixth Amendment of the Framework Law in August 2002 ended a trial phase by establishing bachelor and master as regular degrees, this was wind in the sails of the change agents who had used the introduction of the new degree structure in order to question the purpose of the Joint Commission and to declare it unnecessary.

Summary

The findings of this chapter can be summarized in the following four observations. Previous studies referred to the Bologna Process as an outside pressuring force that has been deliberately created by federal state actors in order to overcome domestic reform blockage. This contribution tells a slightly different story. The main forces behind the discussed changes were civil-society actors, who initiated significant reform steps from within the German Rectors' Conference about a decade before the Bologna Process had become relevant to national policy formulation in Germany. It is true that these non-state actors were able to profit from external factors, commonly referred to as globalization and internationalization. It should not be forgotten, however, that these factors have to be brought into national policy-making by domestic policy entrepreneurs in order to become relevant to institutional change. Given this, they rather constitute a contextual instead of determining element of domestic policy change. What made a difference for the course of national policy change was the fear of political elites of being excluded from international developments, their influence on the political reform climate as well as their strategic use of policy drift as a window of opportunity for channeling institutional change into a favored direction. The governance change in German higher education was thus primarily caused by non-state actors, which used internationalization processes as door-openers to realize their objectives.

Second, the trigger of policy drift was a specifically German conflict between the key players in higher education politics, the federal government, the *Länder* and university representatives. I described this conflict in terms of an interpretation struggle about the definition and timeliness of the German tradition of academic freedom. Under the conditions of mass higher education and the resulting increase of regulatory demands, the broad political validity of this tradition came under attack. In the context of cooperative federalism the Joint Commission served as a niche for resolving the emerging tension between the political representatives of the federal government, the *Länder* and the universities. It did so by means of creating procedural rules that comforted all three sides. The fact that the Joint Commission was first attacked from leading circles of the German Rectors' Conference pointed to a growing dissent within the academic community. A lack of political power by the professional associations of professors contributed to the fact that the Rectors' Conference succeeded in bringing forward a particular concept of university autonomy. Instead of defending the individual autonomy of senior academic staff, they supported a concept of university autonomy under the organizational guidance of a strong professionalized university leadership. Not surprisingly, this idea of university autonomy works to strengthen the power of the very status group the initiators of the described institutional displacement originally came from, namely the university presidents and rectors. Effective political strategies led to the fact that particularly this status group quite success-fully extended its networks into the current accreditation system, where some of its members fulfill key tasks in the accreditation council and agencies.

Third, the results of this contribution provide an example for the fact that it is not always public officials who are pressuring toward the abundance of tradi-tional modes of second-order governing. The case study presented in this chapter proves that even though civil-society actors often do act in the 'shadow of hier-archy', they can serve as a major pushing force for changing modes of gover-nance. Civil-society actors can also profit from the federal structures of German policy-making. It was the amendments of the Federal Framework Law that came to the help of the change agents within the German Rectors' Conference. By contrast, these actors could not count on the support of the *Länder* in the Stand-ing Conference of the Ministers of Culture when they first decided to push for the replacement of the Joint Commission with the current accreditation system. Ironically, accreditation has now not only become the main driving force behind the national implementation of the Bologna Process, it also provides a powerful instrument for the self-transformation of the *Länder* governments who contribute to a shift in the modes of governance by delegating public tasks to transnational policy actors and private accreditation agencies.

Finally, the contribution has implications for political science as a discipline, because it challenges dominant perspectives on educational federalism. Previ-ously, the study of policy change has often become neglected due to an exces-sive concern with institutional stasis and non-change. This particularly accounts for traditional historical institutionalist research perspectives, which – if they acknowledge structural change at all – emphasize the role of exogenous forces outside ordinary politics and administrative routine. From the perspective of sequential policy analysis, chosen in this chapter, there is no such thing as insti-tutional stasis. Institutions are always influenced by the (non-)decisions of politi-cal actors who cannot avoid triggering incremental transformative change underneath the cover of the alleged institutional stability.

Notes

1 I thank the editors, the members of the authors' workshop and Helga Welsh for helpful comments on earlier versions of this chapter.
2 In the following: Joint Commission.
3 With reference to Streeck and Thelen, I use the words policy and institution as exchangeable to the extent that both 'constitute rules that can and need to be imple-mented and that are legitimate in that they will if necessary be enforced by agents acting on behalf of the society as a whole' (Streeck and Thelen 2005: 12).
4 In the issue domain of curricular reform the conflicts between both parties were settled by means of shared responsibility and task division. The federal state ministries were

in charge of studies with a state examination (i.e. teaching profession, law, medicine and pharmaceutics), and the Joint Commission concentrated on university studies (diploma and master) only.
5 There are three major historical reference models for higher education in Europe, namely the Humboldtian, the Napoleonic and the Anglo-Saxon (see Neave 2001; Witte 2006: 104). Germany represents the Humboldtian model, which places a comparatively high value on academic freedom (see also Chapter 3, this volume).
6 In the following: working group.
7 In Germany, the freedom of research and university teaching is granted by the Constitution (Art. 5).

References

Cohen, M.D., March, J.G. and Olsen, J.P. (1988) 'A garbage can model of organizational choice', in J.G. March (ed.) *Decisions and Organizations*, Oxford: Blackwell, 294–334.

Commission for the Order of Examination and Studies (1982) *Tätigkeitsbericht 1954–1981*, Bonn: Standing Commission of the Ministers of Culture and the West German Rectors' Conference.

Deitelhoff, N. and Geis, A. (2007) 'Sicherheits- und Verteidigungspolitik als Gegenstand der Policy-Forschung', in F. Janning and K. Toens (eds) *Die Zukunft der Policy-Forschung*, Wiesbaden: VS Verlag, 279–296.

German Rectors' Conference (1995) *Europäische Pilotprojekte für Qualitätsbewertung im Bereich der Hochschulen. Bundesrepublik Deutschland. Nationaler Bericht*, Bonn: Rectors' Conference.

Greven, M.T. (2007) 'Politik als Problemlösung – und als vernachlässigte Problemursache. Anmerkungen zur Policy-Forschung', in F. Janning and K. Toens (eds) *Die Zukunft der Policy-Forschung. Theorien, Methoden, Anwendungen*, Wiesbaden: VS Verlag, 23–33.

Kingdon, J. (1984) *Agendas, Alternatives, and Public Policy*, Boston: Little, Brown and Co.

Kooiman, J. (2003) *Governing as Governance*, London: Sage.

Landfried, K. (2003) 'Perspektiven der Hochschulreform in Deutschland', in G. Färber and S. Renn (eds) *Zehn Jahre Hochschulreform seit dem Eckwertepapier*, Berlin: Duncker & Humblot, 123–130.

Lehmbruch, G. (2000) *Parteienwettbewerb im Bundesstaat. Regelsysteme und Spannungslage im politischen System der Bundesrepublik Deutschland*, Wiesbaden: Westdeutscher Verlag.

Martens, K. and Wolf, K.D. (2006) 'Paradoxien der neuen Staatsräson. Die Internationalisierung der Bildungspolitik in der EU und der OECD', *Zeitschrift für Internationale Beziehungen*, 13, 2: 145–176.

Mentges, J. (2004) 'Zehn Jahre Hochschulreform seit dem Eckwertepapier', in G. Färber and S. Renn (eds) *Zehn Jahre Hochschulreform seit dem Eckwertepapier*, Berlin: Duncker & Humblot, 9–21.

Nagel, A. (2006) *Der Bologna-Prozess als Politiknetzwerk. Akteure, Beziehungen, Perspektven*, Wiesbaden: Deutscher Universitätsverlag.

Neave, G. (2001) 'The European dimension in higher education: an excursion into the modern use of historical analogues', in J. Huisman, P. Maassen and G. Neave (eds) *Higher Eduation and the Nation State. The International Dimension of Higher Education*, Amsterdam/London: Pergamon, 13–74.

Rüb, F. (2007) 'Policy-Analyse unter Bedingung von Kontingenz. Konzeptuelle Überlegung zu einer möglichen Neuorientierung', in F. Janning and K. Toens (eds) *Die Zukunft der Policy-Forschung*, Wiesbaden: VS Verlag, 88–111.

Scharpf, F. (1988) 'The joint decision trap. Lessons from German federalism and European integration', *Public Administration*, 66: 239–278.

Schreiterer, U. (1989) *Politische Steuerung des Hochschulsystems. Programm und Wirklichkeit der staatlichen Studienreform 1975–1986*, Frankfurt/M.: Campus.

Standing Conference of the Ministers of Culture (1978) *Agreement of the Länder on the Formation of a Curricular Reform Commission According to § 9 of the Higher Education Framework Law*, 16 February 1978.

—— (1999) *Strukturvorgaben für die Einführung von Bachelor-/Bakkalaureus- und Master-/Magisterstudiengänge*, 5 March 1999.

Streeck, W. and Thelen, K. (2005) 'Introduction: institutional change in advanced political economies', in W. Streeck and K. Thelen (eds) *Beyond Continuity. Institutional Change in Advanced Political Economies*, Oxford: Oxford University Press.

Teichler, U. (1991) 'The Federal Republic of Germany', in G. Neave and F. Van Vught (eds) *Prometheus Bound*, Oxford: Pergamon Press, 29–50.

Toens, K. (2008) 'Hochschulpolitische Interessenvermittlung im Bologna-Prozess. Akteure, Strategien und machtpolitische Auswirkungen auf nationale Verbände', in B. Rehder, T.v. Winter and U. Willems (eds) *Interessenvermittlung in Politikfeldern. Vergleichende Befunde der Policy- und Verbändeforschung*, Wiesbaden: VS Verlag.

Trampusch, C. (2007) 'Sequenzorientierte Policy-Analyse. Warum die Rentenreform von Walter Riester nicht an Reformblockaden scheiterte', in F. Janning and K. Toens (eds) *Die Zukunft der Policy-Forschung*, Wiesbaden: VS Verlag, 259–278.

Walter, T. (2006) *Der Bologna-Prozess. Ein Wendepunkt europäischer Hochschulpolitik?*, Wiesbaden: VS Verlag.

Witte, J. (2006) *Change of Degrees and Degrees of Change. Comparing Adaptations of European Higher Education Systems in the Context of the Bologna Process*, Twente: CHEPS/UT.

—— (2008) 'Parallel universes and joint themes: reforms of curricular governance in the Bologna context', in A. Amaral, P. Maassen, C. Musselin and G. Neave (eds) *Bologna, Universities and Bureaucrats*, Dordrecht: Springer.

Wolf, K.D. (2000) *Die Neue Staatsräson – Zwischenstaatliche Kooperation als Demokratieproblem in der Weltgesellschaft*, Baden-Baden: Nomos.

Zahariadis, N. (1999) 'Ambiguity, time and multiple streams', in P.A. Sabatier (ed.) *Theories of the Policy Process*, Boulder: Westview Press.

6 Decentralizing education policy in Italy

Entrepreneurship and networks implementation

Emiliano Grimaldi and Roberto Serpieri[1]

Introduction

This chapter deals with a case study concerning the introduction of new governance structures in the field of education at the regional level in Italy. In essence, it analyses the implementation process (Pressman and Wildavsky 1973) of a new policy-making institution, established by a local authority in order to cope with the increasing need for integration and coordination among the actors of the reformed education system (Kooiman 2000). The new institution replaced an older, more centralized governance structure in a local educational arena. Our aim is to show to what extent the new policy-making body is an effective tool for the governing of the local educational arena and how it reshaped the arena itself. We use structuration theory (Giddens 1984; Cohen 1989) as a theoretical framework in order to focus both on the unintended consequences of the implementation process, the restructuring of the local system and the role of policy entrepreneurs in terms of strategic conduct.

In the last decade, in education as well as in many other policy areas, some states promoted change in the governing structures by adopting a variety of strategies (Derouet 2000; Newman 2001; Ball 2006). In many cases the reforms constituted 'devolved environments' where an increasing relevance is attributed to local authorities (Rhodes 1997) responding to the crisis brought about by the bureaucratic mode of regulation (Pierre 2000: 2; Peters 1996). Within this mainstream, the reform of the Italian education system initiated in 1997 has significantly increased the complexity and diversity (Kooiman 2000; Kickert *et al.* 1997) of the local educational arenas. The Italian reforms pursued a decentralization of the education system, introducing school autonomy and devolving a relevant part of the 'old' functions of the Ministry of Education to local authorities such as regions (the largest), provinces (intermediate local government) and municipalities.[2] There has been, then, a growing differentiation of the actors involved in the governing processes in terms of their goals, intentions and powers (Kooiman 2000: 140). The architecture of the relationship among them has been characterized by the emergence of interdependencies. Governing in this context often means steering multiple agencies and sharing objectives, resources, activities and even power (Bryson and Crosby 1993; Jessop 1997). The main feature of these changes is the multiplication of networks (Rhodes 2000; Börzel 1998) and the emergence of 'new hybrid modes' of regulation (Kooiman 2000). In many Italian local educational arenas, the hybridization between hierarchies and horizontal networks faced several challenges (Newman 2005). In particular the growing complexity and diversity created the need for integration and coordination (Kooiman 1993: 254–257). The production of shared meanings as well as the fine-tuning of different objectives, interests and actions often became crucial in order to accomplish policy objectives, solve problems or create opportunities.

Our case study is about the implementation of an instrument of integration and coordination, the so-called 'Conferences of District', in a southern Italian province. This governing process was promoted by a local policy entrepreneur and includes all the relevant actors (above all public ones) of the local educational arena. It has the general aim of sharing decisions concerning the governing of the system. Adopting ideas drawn up by structuration theory (Giddens 1976, 1979, 1984; Cohen 1989) we try to highlight to what extent the conferences represent a way of providing answers to the challenges generated by the increasing diversity and complexity of the governance arena. We will show how this kind of implementation process is intended to promote patterns of reflexive regulation (Giddens 1984) in order to manage 'either synergies or conflicts' (Sterling 2005: 147). Furthermore, the analysis will highlight the unintended consequences of the establishment of such governing institutions, focusing also on the 'space for manoeuvre' (Ball 2006) for policy entrepreneurs and the shape they give to the unfolding of the implementation process.

Theoretical framework, case selection and methods

As a consequence of the reform of the education system in Italy, provinces became relevant actors in the governance of education. They are actually in charge of, first, the management of school buildings; second, the annual local educational planning (opening, closing or merging schools, opening or closing curricula in specific schools etc.); and third, the governing of vocational guidance.

The case of the southern Italian province we present is widely considered as an innovative experience of governance in education (Grimaldi *et al.* 2006) at the national level. As established by law, the province divided its territory into nine districts, identified on the basis of socio-economic similarities. They then created a new policy-making institution, that is a so-called 'conference', for each district. Formal members of the conferences are the councillor for education (who leads it) and some of her staff, the headteachers and the mayors of that district, representatives of the regional ministerial bureaucracy, the local confederation of industry, provincial job centres and local workers' unions. The conference represents a formally established 'collective actor' intended to involve all the relevant stakeholders of the local educational field in the decision-making processes regarding educational planning and school buildings. Conferences meet during the year on a provincial convocation in order to discuss about and make decisions on these issues. The province itself has the power to set the meeting agenda. At the end of each year a general 'conference of districts', involving previous elected representatives of each district, takes place and summarizes the decisions and proposals made by each conference, all of which should be the basis for the province's annual educational plan.

We chose to analyse the experience of one of the nine districts. The district we sampled is made up of nine different municipalities and 12 schools. The related conference includes the provincial councillor and her staff, nine mayors, 12 headteachers and three representatives of the other categories (in total 28 people). The district-in-focus[3] was chosen through a *theoretical sampling* (Silverman 2000) based on indicators regarding:

1   the previous experience of collective activities of coordination;
2   the quality of the school buildings;
3   the richness of the educational supply.

The quality of the buildings is quite good: 55 per cent of them require minor interventions. The average number of students for each school is 765 (the maximum established by the law is 900). The choice of available courses is wide and well distributed. However the dominant characteristic is the legacy of an experience of coordination between the mayors and the headteachers of two municipalities on vocational guidance as well as the running of a research project funded by the province on the local schools networks. In other words, this district seems to be recognizable as a case of a 'partnership-rich' area (Sterling 2005), where it is possible to identify the conditions for an effective establishment of an instrument of integration and coordination such as the conferences.

The research was characterized by a *mixed-method design* and included lengthy contacts within the field (three years). It has so far led to the collection of documents; transcribed in-depth interviews with the provincial councillor, her staff and most of the headteachers involved; observations of the conferences as well as of workplace practices in the provincial offices. The materials have been examined through an *in-depth discourse analysis* (Fischer and Forester 1993). The aim was to identify *interactive sequences* that had a recognizable main character or purpose and the prevailing *scripts* (Barley and Tolbert 1997) or types of encounters. The analysis followed a *process tracing* method (George and Bennett 2005), in order to generate data on processes, events and actions that link putative causes to observed effects.

In order to show to what extent the conferences represent a way for implementing new modes of coordination and integration, we chose to adopt structuration theory as a framework of analysis (Giddens 1976, 1979, 1984; Cohen 1989; Stones 2005). As Kooiman (2000), Rhodes (2000) and Hay (2002) argue, in the studies regarding policy implementation there is very often a lack of conceptualization of the mutual relations between structure and agency. Sometimes the structural aspects are privileged by focusing on systemic features of the institutional patterns, as happens in the structuralist accounts, or stressing a new determinism in reconstructing, *ex post*, the role of the structures, as in the perspective that reificates policy networks or in network analysis. In other cases the exclusive focus on the role of the agency (intentionalism) denies the significance of structural or contextual factors (Hay 2002: 165). The structuration theory, in our opinion, makes available a general and rich conceptual framework that allows interpretation of the complex interaction between the creativity inherent in the human agency and the constraining role of the structural aspects of social life, which avoid the risk of reification. Furthermore, it highlights the role of the actors' capacity for reflexive monitoring and intervention on the contexts of their interactions, as well as the relevance of the unintended consequences in social life.

In our case, structuration theory made available a set of conceptual tools that allowed us to look deeper inside the process in focus. It led us to examine the implementation of the new policy-making institution and the related decision-making processes as sets of recursive social practices that imply the production and communication of meanings, the use of power (through the enactment of resources-facilities) and the actualization of norms (that are related sets of rights and obligations) (Giddens 1976: 145). As the only analytically separable aspects of social practices, all of them have been considered as constituent moments of the interaction within the conferences.

Coherently, our attention was focused at the beginning on the 'strategic conduct' (Giddens 1984) of the main actors involved in the meetings in the district, that is the way they reflexively monitor their interactions and make efforts of reflexive regulation of the contexts within which they act. This allowed us to identify the role of the policy entrepreneurs (Roberts 1992) in the implementation process. Furthermore, each interactive sequence identified was analysed also in terms of outcomes of the interwoven strategic conducts of the actors involved. Focusing on some unintended consequences of social interaction we pointed out some relevant changes the establishment of the conferences caused in the governing networks of the local educational system.

As suggested by Cohen (1989: 208), the local governing system was interpreted as a network of *position-practices and relations*, that is to say as a set of:

1 positional identities defined in terms of identifying criteria and associated with a series of prerogatives and obligations;
2 clusters of practices through which these positional identities are made clear in recognizable ways;
3 ranges of other position-practices with which a given position-practice is necessarily or contingently interrelated as the holder enacts prerogatives or obligations;
4 institutionalized aspects of reciprocities through which position-practice relations occur (Cohen 1989: 210).

Consistently, the changes enacted by the establishment of the conferences were interpreted as transformations of the set of position-practices and their relations that made up the local educational arena, highlighting the coordination and integration effects of the new practices implemented.

Structuration theory thus gave us the possibility of overcoming the dualism between structure and agency, highlighting the process of mutual intertwining of agential and structural factors that fostered political change and reproduction.

Phases of implementing the new governing institution

In Figure 6.1 we show the interactive sequences identified within the unfolding of the practices in the conferences. Each sequence will be described below in detail.

The decision to establish the conferences

In 1996, the provinces became responsible for all high school buildings and their requirements, while since 1998 they have also been in charge of local educational planning. As briefly described above, they were faced with a complex *horizon of action* (Stones 2005). Starting from the two main provincial functions in education, the school building ownership and educational planning, we will try to define this horizon in terms of *position-practices and relations* (Cohen 1989).

Concerning the first function, the provinces' decisional practices depend strongly on national government which controls and distributes financial resources. However, they are also interdependent on the municipalities, owners of most of the schools buildings before 1996 and still responsible for urban building planning. The network of interdependent position-practices in which the province is enmeshed also includes the headteachers who manage the auton-

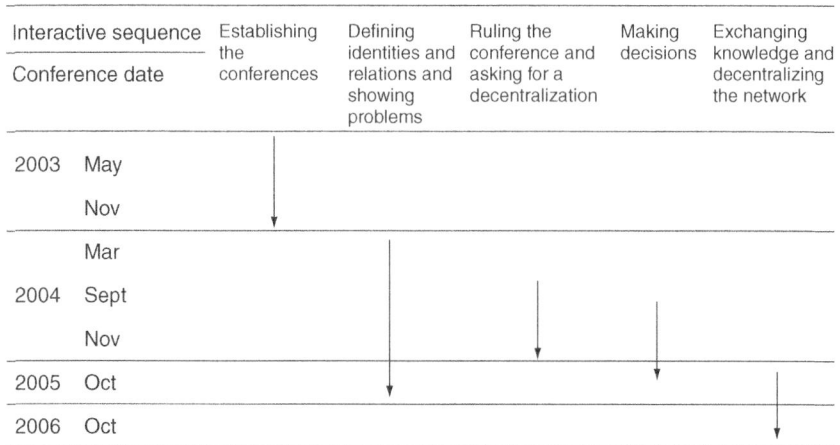

Interactive sequence / Conference date	Establishing the conferences	Defining identities and relations and showing problems	Ruling the conference and asking for a decentralization	Making decisions	Exchanging knowledge and decentralizing the network
2003 May					
Nov					
Mar					
2004 Sept					
Nov					
2005 Oct					
2006 Oct					

Figure 6.1 The interactive sequences within the conferences.

omous schools and who refer to the province for their needs. The horizon of action regarding educational planning is even more complex since provincial decision-making is strictly interdependent on that of the region. The provincial annual planning must in fact be approved by the region, which also has the possibility of changing decisions. The whole educational planning is strongly linked to national government through the position-practice of the ministerial regional director, who controls the human resources and the budget of the schools. Headteachers and municipalities here depend on this chain of actors to meet their needs, but can also mobilize the public to support their requests and exert pressure. In the case of our province, data show how, at the beginning of the implementation process, the main coordinating mechanism still remains the hierarchy. The relations are top-down oriented and the horizontal networks established by the reforms encounter difficulties and resistances in being stabilized.

Within this context of interdependencies, in the year 2000, the councillor and her staff responsible for education in the province started to reflect on the national reform and to apply it. They looked at the reform as an incentive for the provinces to obtain a relevant role in the governing of education. In order to achieve this result, they created the districts and the conferences as a new 'locus of dialogue', new devices of coordination. The experience of the conference started in late 2003 and since then they have met several times each year (with decreasing frequency as will be shown later). Since the beginning, a strong ambiguity characterized both the purposes of the conferences and the issues they were called on and expected to discuss or decide about. The conferences were defined, in fact, at the same time as consultative bodies, places of discussion and proposal making as well as decision-making locus. The issue was not exactly defined and seemed to coincide with the whole set of functions the province was in charge of.

Defining identities and relations and highlighting problems

The first conference of the district took place in March 2004. Since then, the actors of the district have met three times in 2004 and once in 2005 and 2006. Although the headteachers of the district had some previous experiences of consultation and networking with the province, the main features of the first three conferences were, on the one hand, the efforts to define the identity of the conference itself as collective actor, the *position-practices* of the participants as well as the relations between them. On the other hand, the headteachers especially and the mayors looked at the conference as a place to express their problems while asking for solutions. The councillor opened the first conference with a rather long speech on the needs for the decision to institute the conferences.[4] She gave a quite detailed picture of the reforms occurring in the education system and the distribution of the functions. The reforms, she argued, made it necessary to find a way to coordinate the several interdependent actors in charge of governing the local educational system. In her words, the aim of the conference was to:

create moments of consultation in order to make decisions together, we hope shared decisions for the majority, to try to do our best for the governance of the system. … that is because we cannot accept that the province itself makes decisions alone in an authoritarian way.

(Provincia di Napoli 2003)

As it clearly states, the ambiguity about the purposes of the conference, shown above within the official documents and statements, still remained and she proposed conflicting meanings to the assembly, that is to say, the will to take decisions together but also the possibility for the province to decide by itself.

It is worth highlighting how the constraining character of the conference constitution with respect to the actions of the schools and the municipalities emerges quite clearly through her speech. The conference is presented as the means to shift from an individualistic way of thinking to a wider and collective logic in educational planning. Participating in the conference actually meant, she argued, having the possibility to be involved in the decision-making processes but also recognizing the supra-individualistic needs and, in certain ways, giving up part of one's own power in return for collective reasoning.

The democratization of the decision-making implied by the conference constitution appears immediately as contradictory: enacting and constraining at the same time. On the one hand it opens a space for possibilities for the participants to get involved in the governing of the system. On the other hand it exemplifies, in terms of power and norms, the asymmetries within their interaction. Furthermore, the councillor points out another relevant constraint emerging within the conference saying how the ministerial bureaucracy still controls some relevant resources that will affect any kind of decisions the conference makes. The councillor's speech also intends to identify the issue of the discussion within the conferences. On the basis of the experience of the other district conferences where all the participants tried to set the agenda on the issue of school buildings she pointed out that she was 'aware that the issue of the school buildings is relevant and that it is the duty of the province to provide appropriate structures and spaces' (Conference proceedings, 24 March 2004). Nonetheless she strongly invited all the participants to shift their attention to educational planning, which was what the conferences were created to discuss.

Actually most of the speeches by the headteachers and mayors implicitly challenged the councillor's agenda, proposing alternative meanings-norms and mobilizing their resources to support them. Despite the definition of the conference focus that the councillor gave, during the meetings they complained mainly about the problems of their schools, focusing especially on buildings. They asked for short-term solutions, seemingly more concerned with their own situations and refusing the requested shift towards the new collective logic. More generally, each category of participants mutually criticized the others for the slowness of their intervention in solving problems and the lack of predisposition towards cooperation and collaboration. The councillor and her staff intervened several times answering to single requests or complaints, mainly recalling the constraints that impeded their satisfaction but also criticizing the partisan view at the base of the participants' speeches.

The headteachers especially ignored the agenda, focusing on their school situation and 'virtually' enacting the resources they thought they had to influence the councillor in the dialectic of control (that are the public complaints). The councillor and her staff answered mainly by referring to some of the constraints coming from the different institutional levels that tie school autonomy: the budget limitations, the supra-district planning, the interdependence with the functions of other local authorities. They also tried again to return to the agenda, shifting attention from the issue of building to that of planning and guidance. Despite these efforts the resistance towards the proposed set of meanings and logic still remained. In this way, there was a rejection, or at least questioning, of the new 'social imaginary' proposed by the province's new policy of governance (Newman 2005).

Ruling the conference and asking for decentralization

Part of the discussion within the first two conferences was also dedicated to the rules for the organization of the conference as democratic body. The councillor and the provincial bureaucrats brought a regulation draft to the second meeting. The debate about the draft was long and heated since headteachers and mayors raised many objections. Most of them concerned the strong centralization of the conference organization. They asked for the possibility to call a meeting autonomously, to decentralize the conference, establishing a headquarter of the district itself in one of the municipalities and to make the rules through which decisions were made more clear. Provincial actors had to restate again the formal constraints in order to make the participants approve the regulation. Although the issue of decentralization was brought up by many of the participants, the councillor seemed in her answer to avoid it, dismissing the request as an act of mistrust. The regulation draft was approved without any substantial change, but the request of decentralization represented a break-point of the conferences experience since the councillor and her staff started a process of self-reflection that brought them to change, in part, their strategic conduct. Furthermore, it opened a new range of possible courses of action for some of the headteachers.

Making decisions?

In 2004, 2005 and 2006, after the approval of the organization rules, the conference met with the official intent of discussing the annual education plan which the province had to deliberate about (what was supposed to be the main objective of the conference itself). In Table 6.1, we compare the proposals about the educational plan and the content of the discussion within the conferences with the decisions made by the province as emerged from the plans approved by the Provincial Council.

Table 6.1 Proposals and decisions made in the conference compared with the annual educational plans 2004–2006

Year	Proposals made within the conferences	Decisions made within the conferences	Decisions made within the annual plan regarding the district
2004	Two proposals – *Head 1* asks for a new course in his school – *Mayor 1* asks for a new school in the municipality	Two decisions – *Head 1* proposal is accepted – *Mayor 1* proposal is refused	One decision – Establishment of a new school in the municipality of *Mayor 2*
2005	No proposals	No decisions	One decision – Opening of a new course in a school
2006	One proposal – *Head 2* makes the same request *Mayor 1* did in 2004	No decisions	No decisions

Three aspects of the data shown in Table 6.1 are worthy of close analysis. First of all, the conferences seem not to be decisional arenas. There is no link between what emerged during the discussions and the annual plans. The decision-making processes concerning educational planning continued to unfold following the 'old' bureaucratic routines based on the individual relationship between the councillor and the single headteachers and mayors. During our observations in the provincial department for education in 2004 and 2005 we were able to record several interactions between headteachers and the provincial bureaucrats following a *script with four steps.* First, a headteacher comes into the office affirming that he/she had a previous meeting with the councillor and her staff about a problem; she/he reports the problem and what the councillor said about the possibility of finding a solution; she/he proposes her/his solution. Second, the bureaucrat discusses the case with the headteacher, analysing data from databases and considering the possible solutions. The encounter always finished, third, with the commitment by the bureaucrats to bring to the attention of the councillor the different realistic solutions they were able to identify. In the case that the problem concerned a school building, the bureaucrat and the head could agree about the opportunity to make a survey before defining possible solutions. Decision-making thus continued outside the conference.

It is also relevant to notice that the proposals at the conference itself were few – only three in three years. Headteachers and mayors seemed not much concerned with any change in the educational plan, focusing mainly on the building issue. Although the headteachers, in particular, declared in many cases to be satisfied with the present situation, in 2005 and 2006 their inertia in making proposals was strongly influenced by two factors: the councillor agenda-setting and the actualization within the conference of external constraints. In the 2005 conference, the councillor opened the meeting announcing a suggestion by the region inviting the five provinces not to make any change in their plans (implicitly stating that they would not have been accepted). As she explained, the region's decision derived from the uncertainty of the national educational reform implementation and the conflict at national level between the right-wing government and the regional representatives. Furthermore, she recalled the impossibility of opening new schools or courses due also to the freeze on hiring teachers and headteachers decided by the ministry. Before the conference, she formally asked all participants to focus and think of proposals on the issue of school transport deficiencies, inviting another provincial bureaucrat in charge of public transport management to the meeting. Those limitations were recalled also by Bureaucrat 2 when he led the conference in 2006. Most of the participants at the meetings soon became aware of the impossibility of reaching any kind of decision and this was quite clear in the interviews conducted with most of the headteachers involved, all of whom described the conferences as un-useful public rituals, and a 'waste of time'.

The conference could thus not be established as an element of regional education policy-making in the way that it was originally conceived. The conferences did not decide anything and they could only be described as a ritualistic innovation or as a failed attempt to restructure the local educational arena. Position-practices regarding the planning activities and their relations apparently did not change in any relevant way; the main mode of regulation remained bureaucratic. Despite those limitations, the establishment of the conferences represented, for the district, an occasion for structuring new kinds of relations between the position-practices involved in the governing of the system. Those practice-relations were, at least until today, not fully established, but their unfolding has, in perspective, a relevant potential in the restructuration of the local government of education. The unfolding of the meetings made all the participants face some unintended consequences of the interactions. The provincial policy, in fact, was intended to set new forms of participation, but it could also provoke 'a constrained, managed and consensus-oriented political imaginary' (Newman 2005: 135) where the actors are constituted as *participative subjects*, even beyond their initial intentions. In this way, the councillor and the bureaucrats had to face a massive challenge to their agenda-setting as well as a resistance to the shift of logic they were asking for. The headteachers were not able to obtain what they wanted in the conference, and furthermore they were asked to give up some of their autonomy. However, the conferences were also a means of becoming more aware of the interdependencies and constraints and of focusing on the possible course of action that they could enact in order to accomplish their objectives and at least solve some of their problems.

Exchanging knowledge and decentralizing the network

One specific interactive sequence identified within the conference had a major impact on the implementation process. One mayor (1) and one headteacher (1) had a central role in developing this sequence. In the end, the headteachers position-practices and their relations changed. The process started during the second conference in 2004, after the councillor had set the agenda on the need for a stronger activity of vocational guidance. Mayor 1 presented to the assembly his experience in running three high schools in his municipality and their management of guidance. The high schools coordinated with the primary schools in the municipality, matching the data about the availability of places in the three schools and the number of pupils leaving primary school. Mayor 1 recognized that the experience was imperfect due to the narrow area in which it worked, but suggested that the adoption of such a practice between all the district schools would have helped to manage the flow of applications and avoid the need to change the educational plan itself. Mayor 1 was immediately followed by Head-teacher 1 – whose school was involved in the matching process – who reinforced the proposal:

> I believe that we need to think like a district and think about a policy for the district. We have to seek solutions that match the needs of our public with the resources available, before starting to ask for impossible things, like more classrooms, more schools, etc. I invite all my colleagues to participate as much as they can in informal meetings where we can organize discussions about our needs and identify possible solutions!
>
> (Conference proceedings, 4 October 2006)

With these statements, the conference suddenly became a collective arena of shared experiences and practices, although the proposal remained, at the beginning, unheeded. One year later, Mayor 1 and Headteacher 1 recalled again the experience in the conference, and at that time, the councillor seemed to be more sensible to the proposal. She accepted the proposal and invited Headteacher 1 to involve her colleagues in creating an informal board on vocational guidance. She highlighted the lack of horizontal connection between the schools in the district and wished that the 'board' could be the first step in building stabilized forms of horizontal networks between schools and municipalities. In late 2005, Head-teacher 1 accepted the role of coordinator of the district and many headteachers started to participate to the meetings she organized to discuss guidance.

In 2005 and 2006, the board met four times each year. The main activity of the board was to collect data about the student applications expected for the following school year. The data collected were, first, the numbers of pupils leaving the primary school that year, in the whole district and disaggregated per each school; second, the number of applications each high school could receive disaggregated by type of courses, in relation also to the building structures. Matching those data the headteachers tried to anticipate critical situations and imagine possible solutions mainly in terms of guidance activities to be implemented in the primary schools themselves.

In the 2006 conference, the activity of the board, the way to extend and improve it, became the central issue. The discussion itself led to the definition of a set of shared meanings regarding the scope of the conferences, the identities of the participants and the relations among them. The provincial staff reshaped the meanings they proposed at the beginning in a more decentralized way, asking for a more autonomous and active participation and invoking the constitution of horizontal networks. The necessity to develop such kinds of experience was in several provincial staff talks indirectly related to the limitations deriving from the hierarchical interdependences and constraints. The headteachers seemed to accept this way of thinking, and in their speeches the self-centred attitude shown at the beginning began to fade. A collective agreement implicitly emerged during the discussion. Due to the contextual constraints the only 'right thing to do' was to work within the interstices of the system developing a horizontal cooperation between schools and a '*networking culture*'. Headteacher 1, who runs the governing board, was identified as a key actor in promoting this process. The conferences' purpose itself changed and was defined in a more clear and shared way. Everybody appeared to be aware of the impossibility for the conferences to be real decision-making centres, but at the same time it was recognized that they could be the occasion for starting more continuous cooperative courses of action. The initiative of one mayor and, later, the intensive work of one headteacher had transformed the conference into a valuable and effective tool for a new form of governance in education. While the conference itself was initially seen as a 'waste of time', the additional time spent in the newly created governing board had a far-reaching impact on the overall governance structure in the district.

Moreover, it is worth noting here that this interactive sequence could also potentially be a real point of transformation for all the other districts. The provincial actors started to recognize in the district experience a possible example to follow, and the agendas of the other district conferences were reset, always opened by the councillor recalling the experience of the informal board. Moreover, the councillor and her staff identified one headteacher for each district, pressing them to take the same role of leadership that Headteacher 1 had. Although the results of these pressures are not yet clearly apparent, it is undeniable that the construction of horizontal networks has become one of the main themes of the conferences.

Conclusion

Presenting our case study we tried to show two main aspects. First, we illustrated the effects of the implementation of an instrument of integration and coordination such as the 'conference of district' in the Italian education system. We focused both on unintended consequences and re-structuring of the local system. Second, we showed the space for leadership and above all the role of policy entrepreneurs in this process. The following conclusions should be read as 'explanatory propositions of a generalizing type' (Giddens 1984: xviii). In essence, our aim is to highlight key aspects, critical nodes and possible outcomes of the implementation of such governing processes in contexts characterized by a relevant degree of complexity and diversity (Kooiman 2000).

The key findings of the research make evident that in a system such as the Italian one the establishment of locus of dialogue similar to the conferences of district could not be an effective way of providing integration and coordination in decentralized educational arenas, at least in the short term. First, several constraints limit their decisional power due to the fragmentation of administrative functions and resources. Second, the implementation of these governing institutions has some unintended consequences, such as a progressive disclosing of decision-making, a growth of mutual accountability and the increasing difficulty in answering to the challenges of integration.

Consequently, the conferences probably leave an increasing number of decisions to be explained, negotiated or justified. At least at the beginning, this could lead to a growth of conflicts due to the diversity (Kooiman 2000) of the actors involved. New governing bodies such as the conferences constitute, in fact, 'front regions' (Giddens 1984: 122) in which all the participants have to give up part of their autonomy, and their behaviour is subject to collective control and related sanctions. As in the case presented, the probable 'composite effect' is that the hierarchical-bureaucratic mode of coordination remains the most effective. Thus decision-making continues to take place within the 'back regions', hidden to intersubjective control in which relations among actors are based on particularism, self-interest and negotiation between the various vertical levels.

Nonetheless, the research shows how the overlapping of intended and unintended consequences of the establishment of such governing institutions leads to a complex trajectory of change, characterized by ambiguity and contradictions. On the one hand, it means the establishment of a new form of control that is an increase of the constraints on the agency of the actors involved. On the other hand, it implies a redistribution of resources and leadership, enabling and empowering those actors and supporting the constitution of horizontal networks. Furthermore, the institution of such a locus of coordination and a more general decentralization as governance strategy (Karlsen 2000) can represent a way of confining the same networks to self-controlling roles (Newman 2005), delegating problem-solving in particular to the headteachers.

The most relevant enabling outcome of the implementation process seems to relate to the development of reflectivity. In a certain way, such governing bodies constitute discursive arenas in which the awareness of the actors about the logic of the system (re)-production, the constraints and the mutual interdependencies, increases reasonably. As 'front regions', they can be locus of dialogue where the same actors enacting the bureaucratic scripts within the 'back regions' become able to imagine and lay the foundations for new opportunities (Newman 2005). In our case, for example, faced with the emergence of structural constraints and interdependences within the meetings the actors worked to identify the interstices and the 'zones of minor friction' of the system in order to solve problems with the available resources. The meetings became arenas in which future-oriented exchanges of knowledge about positively experienced practices to be shared took place. As in the case of the informal board, the reproduction of meanings and the re-mobilization of resources and norms in the unfolding of the conferences represent occasions for:

1   restructuring the relations among position-practices in a more decentralized way;
2   developing trust, cooperation and a networking culture.

Therefore, the production of a 'new imaginary' (Newman 2001) can be crucial in developing new modes of integration and coordination. As our case shows, this activity of 'imaginary' is supported, first, by the role of those policy entrepreneurs able to sustain this reflexivity making available not only meanings but also effective resources, that is to say shared knowledge, horizontal relations, modelling appropriate behaviour, means and tools, help and advice. Providing such an opportunity implies the awareness of several 'good' solutions to a given problem (Derouet 2000) and the ability to reflect on unintended consequences betraying the spirit of effective democratic-participative governance (Newman 2005). Second, it is also supported by the existence of a background of trustful and mutual relations as well as previous experiences of coordination among the actors involved in the implementation process of partnership-rich areas (Sterling 2005).

In conclusion, the establishment of governing bodies such as the conferences of districts could be interpreted as a way to move away from the 'Hierarchy Model' of governance 'characterised by bureaucratic power and vertical patterns of relationships', to an 'Open System Model ... oriented towards network forms of interaction and iterative processes of adaptation' (Newman 2001: 33–35). From a normative perspective, however, it can be said that in a 'decentralized centralism' (Karlsen 2000) where the devolving trajectories are still top-down planned, the hierarchical structure is too complicated and at the same time it leaves schools quite isolated, coping with the dilemmas of the educational public services. The establishment of governing institutions such as the conferences of district could certainly represent a relevant innovation, constituting an intermediary integrating and coordinating level between the administration and schools. However, they would be more useful if they were implemented and led starting from the awareness that it is pointless to expect schools to innovate and build networks by themselves. In order to allow them to make full use of the potentialities of autonomous schools' networking (decentralization) it is indispensable to enact chances of reflective monitoring. It also implies that the actors should be enabled to go beyond the surface of this monitoring and reveal the complex nature of their position-practices and their relations (Cohen 1989). In this way they would be encouraged to convert the logic of aggregation of self-interest with a logic of trust and effective integration. Our case shows also the important role of policy entrepreneurship as a necessary but not sufficient condition.

Notes

1 The reflections presented in the chapter are the outcome of the joint collaboration of both the authors. However, in order to ascribe responsibility, Roberto Serpieri wrote the introduction and the conclusion, while Emiliano Grimaldi is the author of the other paragraphs.
2 In Italy there are 20 regions, 109 provinces and 8,088 municipalities.
3 The district and the persons involved into the research will remain anonymous. We will refer to them in the following pages as the district, the councillor, Bureaucrat 1, Head-teacher 1, Mayor 1 etc.
4 She introduced all the district conferences in a very similar way.

References

Ball, S. (2006) *Educational Policy and Social Class*, London: Routledge.
Barley, S.R. and Tolbert, P. (1997) 'Institutionalization and structuration: studying the links between action and institution', *Organization Studies*, 18, 1: 93–117.
Börzel, T.J. (1998) 'Organising Babylon: on the different conceptions of policy networks', *Public Administration*, 76, 2: 253–273.
Bryson, J.M. and Crosby, B.C. (1993) 'Policy planning and the design and use of forums, arenas, and courts', *Environment and Planning B: Planning and Design*, 20, 2: 175–194.
Cohen, I.J. (1989) *Structuration Theory: Anthony Giddens and the Constitution of Social Life*, Basingstoke: Macmillan.
Derouet, J.L. (2000) 'School autonomy in a society with multi-faceted political references: the search for new ways of coordinating action', *Journal of Education Policy*, 15, 1: 61–69.
Fischer, F. and Forester, J. (eds) (1993) *The Argumentative Turn in Policy Analysis and Planning*, Durham: Duke University Press.
George, A.L. and Bennett, A. (2005) *Case Studies and Theory Development in the Social Sciences*, Cambridge: MIT Press.
Giddens, A. (1976) *New Rules of Sociological Method*, London: Hutchinson.
—— (1979) *Central Problems in Social Theory*, London: Macmillan.
—— (1984) *The Constitution of Society*, Berkeley: University of California Press.
Grimaldi, E., Landri, P. and Serpieri, R. (2006) 'Governance as it happens. The emergence of a practice of governance in educational arenas', paper presented at the 22nd EGOS Colloquium, Bergen.
Hay, C. (2002) *Political Analysis. A Critical Introduction*, Basingstoke: Palgrave.
Jessop, B. (1997) 'The governance of complexity and the complexity of governance: preliminary remarks on some problems and limits of economic guidance', in A. Amin and J. Hausner (eds) *Beyond Market and Hierarchy: Interactive Governance and Social Complexity*, Cheltenham: Edward Elgar, 95–108.
Karlsen, G.E. (2000) 'Decentralized centralism: framework for a better understanding of governance in the field of education', *Journal of Education Policy*, 15, 5: 525–538.
Kickert, W., Klijn, E.H. and Koppenjan, J.F.M. (1997) *Managing Complex Networks: Strategies for the Public Sectors*, London: Sage.
Kooiman, J. (ed.) (1993) *Modern Governance. New Government-Society Interactions*, London: Sage.
—— (2000) 'Societal governance: levels, modes and orders of social-political interaction', in J. Pierre (ed.) *Debating Governance*, Oxford: Oxford University Press, 138–164.

Newman, J. (2001) *Modernising Governance*, London: Sage.
—— (2005) (ed.) *Remaking Governance*, Bristol: Policy Press.
Peters, B.G. (1996) *The Future of Governing: Four Emerging Models*, Lawrence: University of Kansas Press.
Pierre, J. (ed.) (2000) *Debating Governance*, Oxford: Oxford University Press.
Pressman, J. and Wildavsky, A. (1973) *Implementation*, Berkeley: University of California Press.
Provincia di Napoli (2003) *Conferenze d'Ambito. Linee guida*, Napoli.
Rhodes, R.A.W. (1997) *Understanding Governance: Networks, Reflexivity, Accountability*, Buckingham: Open University Press.
—— (2000) 'Governance and public administration', in J. Pierre (ed.) *Debating Governance*, Oxford: Oxford University Press, 55–90.
Roberts, N.C. (1992) 'Public entrepreneurship and innovation', *Policy Studies Review*, 11, 1: 55–74.
Silverman, D. (2000) *Doing Qualitative Research. A Practical Guide*, London: Sage.
Sterling, R. (2005) 'Promoting democratic governance through partnership', in J. Newman (ed.) *Remaking Governance*, Bristol: Policy Press, 139–157.
Stones, R. (2005) *Structuration Theory*, Basingstoke: Palgrave Macmillan.

7 Bounded rationality in Finnish education policy-making

Pertti Ahonen

Introduction

This chapter explores a reform process of primary and secondary schools in Finland's capital city of Helsinki, inhabited by about 10 per cent of the national population. Since Finland's victories in the OECD PISA studies have accumulated, there have been analyses and study visits to the country by observers trying to discover its assumed secret roots of the success. This analysis entails the argument that learning from Finland can only be limited, because political goals are implemented in Finland in a no more unambiguous and rational manner than in other countries, and the particular constellations between the actors are unique to particular contexts and subject to incessant change. The chapter thus also focuses on obstacles that education policies may face when new ways of governance are to be implemented. In the case presented subsequently, Finnish school policy has changed towards a more demand-based model of administrating schools, including mergers and closures of schools in areas with a diminished number of pupils. The rather clear objective, however, turned out to be difficult to realize in the course of the policy process.

Such research also draws its rationale from the rarity of internationally disseminated studies that look under the surface of Finland's PISA success. During the 2005 launching of the first stage of the policy cycle studied, the City of Helsinki Office of Teaching announced the aim to adapt educational real estate volumes to statistical forecasts on decreasing student numbers. The cycle on the contrary came to entail efforts by many of the participants to eliminate the proposed measures as far as possible. To thoroughly investigate this policy process and to illustrate its development and conditions, the study is theoretically framed by James G. March's bounded rationality theory and supplemented selectively with some other theoretical elements. The case presented is a 2005–2007 policy process in Helsinki, literally called the 'school network revision', with special reference to Finnish-speaking schools of primary education and lower secondary education. The study also fills a gap linked to privatization studies and the scarcity of previous relevant studies on education in that context (Starke 2006; Basu 2004, 2007).

The discussion is structured as follows: the second section introduces March's theory and a necessary minimum of other relevant theories, the study methods and the study sources. The third section proceeds from a concise contextualization of the case study to the Office of Teaching's school network revision effort of 2005 and from there to the Office's launching of the 2006 external evaluation of the revision needs. The fourth section considers the ensuing evaluation including its recommendations. The fifth section analyses the last stages of the policy cycle including the final decision of the City Council in 2007. The last section consists of conclusions and evaluates the reach and implication of this study.

Theory, methods and sources

Basically, bounded rationality theories aim to better explain decision-making than theories with assumptions on unconstrained rationality (Gigerenzer and Selten 2001). Although not the only theory in this field, March's bounded rationality theory is an important approach applied in the analysis of policy persistence and change (thus confer Jones 1999; Weyland 2006). With regard to its focus on policy continuity, its proponents make frequent reference to theories of *path dependence*, originating from economies of scale considerations (Boas 2007; Peters *et al.* 2005). There are also resemblances between March's theory and approaches towards filling the gap between path dependence and punctuated equilibrium with accounts on how change accumulates from small events of organizational *conversion* to new functions and organizational *layering* with new structures and rules (Thelen 2003; Brunsson and Olsen 1993). Nonetheless, Marchian bounded rationality theorists still rarely carry out analyses of abrupt change resembling those pursued with such approaches as *punctuated equilibrium* models (Pierson 2005).

In early theoretical texts, Cyert and March (1963) formulated hypotheses on how goals and aspiration levels are selected, how expectations arise from information, how problems are defined and how decision-making rules regulate the consideration of alternatives. Organizations are, first, generally seen as *collections of conflicting interests* where solid consensus is rare, conflict is frequently resolved by 'local rationality' that entails splitting problems into sub-problems, and overall decisions arise as compromises between the local rationalities. Second, *uncertainty avoidance* entails short-termism, organizational negotiations with the action environment and hoarding of slack resources. Third, *problemistic search* is stimulated by the appearance of problems and tuned down at each problem solution with a simple-minded character: the simplest solutions are considered first, and there is a bias towards the goals, knowledge and values of the stakeholders and a tendency to look for solutions in the direction of the weakest opposition. Fourth, there is *learning*, which March's theory does not present as a necessary all-positive phenomenon, because as experience accumulates, goals and rules that regulate attention may tend towards cognitive myopia with search rules that focus attention where previous solutions were found.

Later, the *garbage-can model* of March's theory arose to analyse situations of 'organized anarchy' with 'problematic preferences', 'unclear technology' and 'fluid participation' by the stakeholders (Cohen *et al.* 1972; March and Olsen

1979). The organizational decision-makers have inconsistent and ill-defined preferences, processes are not well understood, the decision-makers operate by trial and error, internal and external boundaries are fluid, and the set of decision-makers may also change capriciously. Organizations produce solutions most of which are discarded in the absence of appropriate problems, but once new problems appear, search amongst the garbage may yield solutions.

The garbage-can model sees decisions as outcomes of relatively independent streams that meet where decisions happen, but, consistent with the earlier approaches, not necessarily as a product of rational problem searching and evaluation. The model has been applied in different fields of political science, for example in Kingdon's (1995: 87) version of the garbage-can model for the study of political and policy agenda-setting. There, he identifies a 'problem stream' of what may capture the attention of people as problems, a 'policy stream' of advice for the formulation of policy proposals the adequacy of which receives constant critical evaluation, and a 'political stream' of changes in electoral support, government, political causes and public opinion. Aligned to the streams, 'windows of opportunity' may open at major events such as crises and the formation of new alliances, resulting in changed political agendas.

Continuing the early studies, Levitt and March (1988) characterize bounded rationality as routine-based, history-dependent and target-oriented. Organizations learn by encoding inferences from their history into routines that guide the behaviour of their members, which threats to freeze in the status quo. Expanding the theory for the analysis of institutionalization and governance, March and Olsen (1989, 1995) see action in organizations driven not so much by mere rational calculation as interaction between two logics. The *logic of consequences* entails choices regulated by the anticipation of their impact. The *logic of appropriateness* entails the regulation of choices by what are perceived as the appropriate rules or the identity of which are carrying out the choices. Institutions no less than decisions and political and policy reform styles may arise as outcomes of bounded rationality decision-making. March's theory has also been deepened for the analysis of organizational rules (March *et al.* 2000; March and Olsen 1989, 1995).

Generally, March's theory is designed by its authors as hypotheses and working hypotheses to guide research. Applications of the theory allow for methods from what its proponents call 'samples less than one' or simulation, 'samples of one' or case studies, and studies with wider datasets. March's theory is in accordance with Yin (2003: 32–33) that although single case studies defy *statistical generalization*, they may allow *analytical generalization*. Even the 'sample of one' of a case may allow generalization to one or several 'theoretical populations' made up of previous studies or 'empirical populations' from which the case is drawn. This chapter is conceptualized in this tradition, presenting a case of policy development in local school governance. The sources of this study include the documentation of the 2005–2007 City of Helsinki school network revision policy cycle. They also include opinions of citizens and groups published on the website that the City Office of Teaching opened (City of Helsinki

2005, 2006, 2007a, 2007b, 2007c.) Published letters, news articles and leading articles in Finland's major newspaper *Helsingin Sanomat* were also utilized.

The 2005 school network revision in Helsinki

For concise contextualization of the case, let us utilize the policy theories taken up in the previous section. From such a perspective, the type of Finnish public sector reform has fundamentally changed from an earlier status quo to first exceptional symptoms and later into new routines. This took place as a process from an earlier path dependence interrupted with discontinuity that can be called a 'punctuated equilibrium' into a new path dependence: until 1991 Finland's welfare state, which bore features from the Nordic countries without being as 'social democratic' (see Esping-Andersen 1990), generally grew in terms of public budgets and public employment. Finland used to be ruled by changing multi-party government coalitions that constrained such determinate policies as many of those pursued in Britain and Sweden. In fact, Finland's 'moderate' welfare state in many respects resembled the welfare state in Britain and the Netherlands (Ahonen *et al.* 2006). A 'punctuated equilibrium' can be situated during the 1991–1995 rule of Finland's first all-bourgeois government since 1966. Once the government had ascended, the Soviet Union dissolved together with one-fifth of Finland's exports. In 1993–1995 the Prime Minister dragged the leading anti-EU party, which was his own Centre Party, to the EU and towards full membership in the euro zone with the support of the pro-EU parties, the Conservative coalition partner and the Social Democratic opposition (Ahonen and Wiberg 2004). It has been debated whether Finland's restrictive economic policies rather contributed to the fall of the gross domestic product by 13 per cent and the shooting of unemployment from 3 to 18 per cent rather than limited the catastrophe. Deep cutbacks were pursued in the public sector, but the corresponding policy-making style was not yet routinized.

During this economic crisis, a new path dependence started to stabilize, characterized by monetary and fiscal stringency, routinization of cutbacks and expanding. This can loosely be termed 'New Public Management' in this sole Nordic euro zone member-to-be. National planning – part of which was cost-sharing between national and local government – was abolished in key public services, also including education since 1993. Since that time, formula-based block grants are applied. For education, they represent a function of student numbers and student unit/student cost and marginally also population density and the school network structure. Presently, the national government covers a fixed percentage of the standard cost instead of its previous coverage of a fixed percentage of the real cost. This in effect punishes the local government for high unit costs and rewards it for low ones. Moreover, national primary and secondary education curricula were scrapped and replaced with separate curricular planning in each of the over 400 local governments. The national government pedagogical inspection of local governments, abolished in 1987, gradually turned into national government support of local educational development and evaluation.

Against that background, the legislation of the 1995–1998 Social Democrat-led coalition confirmed a statutory right of each student to attend a school that is close to her or his home. This does not prevent school principals from admitting a student who comes from far away, but parents can effectively choose their children's school by moving nearby. The legislation treated private non-profit schools the same way as local and national public schools but excluded for-profit education. Most private schools are so-called contract schools that are integrated to the local government educational system, whereas the approximately 70 Rudolf Steiner and Christian non-contract schools receive national and local government grants.

Studies on new public management in British and Swedish primary and secondary education may read as horror stories in Finland. There, resembling procedures are mostly applied only at the fringes, including real estate management, and the publication of 'league tables' of schools is ruled out. Since 2003, the two consecutive national governments led by the Centre, which has been the strongest political party in nearly 75 per cent of the around 400 local governments, pushed for reforms in local government funding, for local government mergers and for closer cooperation between the remaining local governments. While these developments are far-reaching, it is yet too early to see the implications for primary and secondary education (Moos and Møller 2003; Telhaug *et al.* 2006; Helgøy 2006; Wilson *et al.* 2006).

Finnish local school governance has nonetheless already faced many changes. The case presented here begins in October 2004, the start of a new four-year electoral period in Finland's local governments. In Helsinki, the already established political constellation remained nearly the same (see Table 7.1). A 29 per cent Conservative and a 25 per cent Social Democratic share of the City Council deputies are not unusual for a large Finnish city. However, Helsinki's unique political features include that it is the country's strongest Green and the weakest Centre

Table 7.1 Party membership in the city of Helsinki decision-making process, 2004–2008

	City council	*Executive board*	*Teaching council*	*Finnish-speaking section of the teaching council*	*Swedish-speaking section of the teaching council*
Conservative	26	5	4	3	1
SDP	21	4	2	2	2
Green	16	3	2	2	1
Left Alliance (ex-Communist)	8	1	1	1	0
Swedish People's Party	6	1	1	0	3
Centre	4	1	1	1	0
Christian Democratic	2	0	0	0	2
Finnish Communist Party	1	0	0	0	0
Basic Finns (populist)	1	0	0	0	0
Total	85	15	11	9	9

electoral region, the former accounting for one-fifth of the deputies, compared to their national 2.6 per cent share, and the latter 4.7 per cent, compared to a national share of 37 per cent. The new City Council elected the City Executive Board, the Teaching Council, its Finnish-speaking section, and its Swedish-speaking section.

In primary and secondary education, the current path dependence of Finnish national politics and policy-making has lately entailed the annual abolition of about 3 per cent of the 3,000 basic schools (AFLG 2006). Unlike organized opposition to privatization in other countries (Anderson 2001: 1064), opposition to school network revisions in Finnish cities has rarely prevented a large part of the proposed measures, although the opponents have won some limited shorter-term victories. In Helsinki, particular motivation for school network revisions has been derived from several arguments such as imbalances in costs, services, residential location and workplace location in relation to surrounding local governments, or national policies distributing wealth to remote areas and national reforms decreasing local government tax revenue, as well as a more elderly population than in some of the surrounding local governments. Furthermore, Helsinki's city politics and policies are nationally particularly exposed because of a strong concentration of national politicians and civil servants, key people of culture and research and most of the national media. Moreover, even though the national minority of Swedish-speakers – once a majority in Helsinki – nowadays make up only 5 per cent of the local inhabitants, their population is still larger than in any other Finnish city.

In April 2005, the City of Helsinki Office of Teaching published a school network revision plan (CoH 2005). The revision concerned all Finnish- and Swedish-speaking primary schools, lower secondary schools and upper secondary schools (*gymnasia*) covered by the city's educational policies, more specifically: the primary and the lower secondary schools for 7–16 year-olds and the city gymnasia, the private non-profit contract schools and gymnasia, the private non-profit non-contract schools and gymnasia, the national government schools and gymnasia operating in the city, and the city vocational schools. The only exceptions were the vocational schools run by other organizers than the city, covering 46 per cent of the city's vocational students.

The fiscal base to be improved was made up of the annual 200,000,000 euro of the city's budgeted educational expenditure. For reasons of delimitation and for the sake of a clearer focus on the policy cycle, let us only consider the Finnish-speaking primary and lower secondary education (see Table 7.2). In that context, the policy was declared as follows:

> The school network shall be revised as presupposed by decreasing student numbers. The resources vacated from more efficient utilization of space will be allocated to the gradual cancellation of the earlier cutback decisions on the teaching hour frame, starting from the youngest age groups. The unit student cost in each form of education will be drawn closer to the average of the five other cities next to Helsinki in population.

(CoH 2005)

Table 7.2 Primary schools and lower secondary schools in Helsinki, autumn 2006

	Schools	(%)	Students	(%)	Students per school
Finnish-speaking city schools	109	69	36.1	74	330
Swedish-speaking city schools	22	14	3.3	7	150
Private contract schools	14	9	5.4	11	390
National government schools	6	4	2.2	5	370
Private non-contract schools	6	4	1.7	4	290
Total	157	100	48.7	100	310

Source: City of Helsinki (2007a), rounded figures.

According to Helin (2006), in 2005 the average student cost was 7,200 euro per annum in schools operated by the City of Helsinki. After factoring out differences in accounting principles, Helin concluded that the Helsinki unit cost was higher than in any other of the eight largest cities and also above the national average of 6,100 euro.

The details of the 2005 proposal are presented in Table 7.3. The implied real estate costs encompass reductions until a full effect in 2010 and of 2,100,000 euro per annum. From these savings, the City Office of Teaching intended to use a part for taking back 1 per cent of earlier cutbacks in the so-called teaching hour frames. These are the actual hours of teaching available at each school with constraints on the minimal teaching hours of the compulsory subjects. The intended purpose was to restore part of the reduced student choice. In total, this measure would have shrunk the savings of the real estate reductions by 600,000 euro, but still net savings of 1,500,000 euro would have remained. The Office of Teaching suggested the closure of nine subsidiaries of schools, the merger of eight into four larger schools and downward revisions in the school building investment programme (CoH 2005). The sections of the Teaching Council and the Plenary Teaching Council considered and commented the proposal and acquired comments from the stakeholders, most of whom held a negative opinion. The proposal never proceeded to implementation.

From the viewpoint of March's theory, an implicit limitation of the entire 2005–2007 policy cycle necessitates commentary. Unlike in common notions (McKinley *et al.* 2000), only measures regarding school buildings were planned, while the personnel, mostly consisting of teachers and representing two-thirds of the city's educational cost, were not be touched. This may be explained by the fact that the Trade Union of Education is the largest union of the Finnish Confederation of Unions for Professional and Managerial Staff in Finland, representing 177,000 members. The influential confederation experienced the rapid membership growth of 50 per cent in 1993–2006 to almost half a million members, while blue-collar unionism generally weakened. Note also that there is an uninterrupted Finnish tradition of local public employment of teachers since the nineteenth century, unlike in other Nordic countries that have introduced it only more recently (Telhaug *et al.* 2006).

There was short-termist uncertainty avoidance by the Teaching Council, leading to inaction and the suffocation of the problemistic search because of the Council's inability to trace weak opposition and its cognitive myopia tending towards the status quo. Applying contrafactual inference, the Council lacked a garbage can of discarded policy proposals. For the policy opponents, the Council was what is called in March's theory a 'weak opponent', creating a window of opportunity to undo the policy at that time.

Once the 2005 policy had fallen, the Office fumbled in its garbage can, finding two potential elements for solution. First, corresponding to the 'problems' dimension in Kingdon's model of agenda-setting, the Office reintroduced a 2005 forecast on decreasing school population. Second, the Office decided to engage in outsourcing, by commissioning an external evaluation of the needs for school network revision in the light of these forecasts (CoH 2006).

The school network revision evaluation of 2006

Formally, the scope of the school network evaluation commissioned by the Office of Teaching was conceptualized comparably to that of the discarded 2005 policy. However, in actual practice the supervisory group, made up of Office representatives, conducted the evaluation mostly to focus upon Finnish-language city-operated schools of primary and lower secondary education. The evaluators were commissioned to calculate the savings implied by their proposals. Detailed data by individual schools in Finnish- and Swedish-speaking education were supplied by the Office, which presupposed the evaluators to utilize the Office's criteria in formulating their proposals. These included a standardized 'utility teaching square meters per student' measure that had the history of having turned in 1993 from a binding national norm to a mere technical and professional convention (NBE 2003; Nuikkinen 2005). The criteria also included the standardized measure multiplied by 1.15 to have an 'efficient use of utility teaching square meters' measure, and the standardized measure multiplied by 1.5 for the 'utility teaching square meter requirement per each special student' with problems requiring particular teacher attention. The evaluators were not to consider the use of the future redundant school real estate.

Over a period of six months, the evaluators gathered and analysed City raw data, carried out interviews and analysed their results, interacted with the Office's supervisory group and engaged in calculation and report writing. They submitted the report on 30 October 2006; the proposal is summarized in Table 7.3 below. Note that the projected annual savings since 2011 were to be more than four times larger than in the 2005 Office proposal: 9,900,000 Euro or 14 per cent of the total real estate cost in Finnish-language schools of primary and lower secondary education, 316,000 euro or 3 per cent in gymnasia, and 358,000 euro or 5 per cent in Swedish-speaking schools of primary and lower secondary education. Seven integrated schools with classes from one to nine were to be substituted by 14 schools with classes of one to six or seven to nine. The Office organized numerous occasions for the evaluators to explain the proposal for various audiences, as principals, representatives of parents and city area associations, and by the different types of education such as basic education, gymnasia and vocational education, and both in Finnish and Swedish.

From the viewpoint of March's theory, the Office split the general school network revision problem into sub-problems, leaving the overall decision a matter of compromises to be concluded in the separate domains. The guidance by the Office's supervisory group, which prompted the evaluators to focus on the Finnish-speaking schools of primary and lower secondary education can also be seen as a bounded rationality measure. Note that the evaluation came to share an implicit bounded rationality constraint of Helsinki educational politics and policy-making. There was no account of Finland's foremost concentration of foreign citizens or foreign-born naturalized Finnish citizens in Helsinki. They make 8 per cent of the city population or more than the city's Swedish-speakers, but they may not stand out as a politically important group because of their division into various national groups and the fact that only 10 per cent of those entitled to vote in local government elections used this right in 2004 as opposed to 57 per cent of all Helsinki voters.

In analysing the Office's outsourcing to evaluation consultants, March's theory can be spiced up with relevant other policy theories. The outsourcing of what was nothing but cost accounting indicates policy-making with *conversion* of a public agency from a provider into a purchaser that draws upon external providers and *layering* of policy-making with organizations of such provision (Thelen 2003). Policy theories of *symbolic legitimation* also shed light on the outsourcing with the Office, which channelled its data and its evaluation criteria through a professional commercial outsider organization (Weyland 2006: 30–68).

Against the background of March's theory, the Office did not only pay these consultants for expert services but also for assuming the role as a weak and even mute opponent to those who wanted to criticize the ensuing proposal. Indeed, even when made targets of outrageous allegations the consultants' integrity did not yield up to their revealing the Office as the source of the data and the criteria. The restriction for the evaluators not to consider the future redundant school real estate was a further instance of bounded rationality: to proceed to such considerations would also have been beyond the generic evaluation competence that the Office had commissioned in this case.

School network revision policies in 2006 and 2007

The school network revision proposal was first explained in special occasions arranged by the Office of Teaching; later, the office sent the report for comments to boards of the schools concerned, other educational institutions, student unions, umbrella associations of parents' associations and citizen associations in different city parts. It also published the proposal on its website to receive anonymous comments, an opportunity that was amply used (CoH 2006). Finland's leading newspaper *Helsingin Sanomat*, read daily by one-fourth of adult Finns, assumed an active role. It opened its section of letters sent to the editor to those who wanted to express their views, provided comprehensive news coverage and ran leading articles. The letters were mostly emotional; the news articles conveyed the views of students, parents, teachers and politicians, whereas the leading articles focused more on facts with a more neutral tone.

Five months after the evaluators' report the Office published its school network revision proposal on 27 March 2007 and announced another round of comments and citizen feedback. The document package made available by the Office over the web consisted of a proposal text and its motivation in ten annexes. The proposal summarized in Table 7.3 implied savings of 4,170,000 million euro per annum from 2010 on, which was less than half of what the evaluators had proposed but twice above the 2005 Office proposal (CoH 2007b).

The 2007 proposal was the most detailed the proposals mentioned so far. As shown in Table 7.3, some elements of the 2005 proposal had been implemented by 2007. The 2007 proposal introduced 'value added' elements dealt with in the 2005 proposal but excluded from the consultants' commission: Finnish-speaking 'applicability test classes' in certain subjects; 'language bath teaching'; and the voluntary tenth class. The Office proposal also touched upon aspects of special education, a field the consultants had not been commissioned to consider, and it included fewer proposals on gymnasia but more on vocational education.

In a leading article of 29 March 2007 *Helsingin Sanomat* received the Office's proposal with mild satisfaction but with a more critical attitude than in its leading article of 23 November 2006 on the consultants' proposal. The 29 March editor wrote that instead of the 'formalistic consultant proposal built upon square meters and population forecasts', pedagogical aspects, the safety of the student's trip to school and the statutory 'near school' principle had been better observed.

After the decisions of the Sections of the Teaching Council on 29 May 2007, the plenary Teaching Council decision ensued. The City Executive Board made its decision on 11 June 2007, deleting some items, and in its ultimate 20 June 2007 decision, the City Council fully accepted the Executive Board proposal. In its decision the City Council referred to the forecasted decrease of 4,500 children aged seven to 15 years in the years 2006–2010. It estimated a corresponding decrease of 1,750 student places in city-operated schools as a consequence of its decision, constituting 40 per cent of the expected student number decrease. The City Council decision also encompassed the merging of four schools with years one–six or seven–nine into two schools with classes one–nine, as well as the merger of four gymnasia into two, both changes to be implemented in August 2009. It further determined the merger of four further schools with classes one–six or seven–nine into two schools with classes one–nine, to be implemented by August 2010. The decision also announced 27 school network revision measures at the remaining schools to carry out by 2010. Finally, the City Council also announced future consideration of further measures, and it obliged the Office of Teaching to prepare a revision of the network of special teaching, the network of applicability test classes and the student recruitment areas of Finnish-speaking primary and lower secondary schools (CoH 2007c).

Table 7.3 The 2005–2007 Helsinki school network proposals

Proposal	Number of targets in proposal		
	2005 Office of Teaching	*2006 evaluation consultants for the Office of Teaching*	*2007 Office of Teaching*
Focus			
Finnish-speaking primary and lower secondary schools	24	39, of which 20 among the 24 of 2005	38; 20 of the 24 of 2005, some of which completed by 2007, 29 of the 39 of 2006, and 9 others
Finnish-speaking 'value added' education	5	1; none of the 5 of 2005	10; including 3 of the 5 of 2005 and the sole target of 2006
Swedish-speaking primary and lower secondary schools	Reference to these not included in the 2007 Office of Teaching proposal Annexes		9, and 2 of a lower order
Swedish-speaking gymnasia			1
Special education	22	2, the other of which was one of the 2005 targets	24; 17 of the 22 of 2005 including some completed by 2007, and the sole new target of 2006
Finnish-speaking gymnasia	1	8, including the single 2005 target	4; 2 presented with 2–3 options; includes the single 2005 target and 4 of the 8 of 2006
Vocational education	Not covered in 2005	1	2, the other of which was the single 2006 target
Total number of targets in proposal	52, and reference to conceivable proposals on Swedish-speaking education	50	85
Total cost reduction in euro per annum	2,100,000	10,600,000	4,200,000

Comparing the measures over time, the number of targets of revision had been 52 in the Office proposal 2005, 50 in the consultants' proposal 2006 and 88 in the final Office proposal 2007. They were, in effect, reduced to 44 in the City Council decision. While the evaluators' proposals of 2006 would have reduced student places by 3,500 and the Office proposal of 2007 by 2,600, the reduction implied by the City Council decision was only 1,750, and the savings ensuing from that decision were estimated to be 1,800,000 euro, which is only a little less than in the Office proposal of 2005.

Turning to interpretation, further evidence for the legitimatory and symbolic role of the evaluators suggested in the previous section can be obtained from an analysis of two letters published in *Helsingin Sanomat*, in which facts were obviously misunderstood. The allowance of such venting of emotions without anybody trying to correct the factual misconceptions further suggest a role of the evaluators in the support of the legitimacy of the city decision-making organizations through 'outsourcing the blame'. The success of this process is suggested by the absence of any critique towards the City organization despite the emotional public debate.

The Office's structuring of its March 2007 proposal entails 'ambiguity' in the sense of March's theory. There, the division of the overall problem into subproblems indicates an Office measure pushing other stakeholders towards applying bounded rationality. Yet the later stages of the policy process suggest that the 'ambiguation' may not have been enough, especially as it was impossible to decompose the 69 per cent of the number of schools and the 74 per cent of the number of students made up by the Finnish-speaking primary and lower secondary schools operated by the city.

Moreover, the Office's proposal from March 2007 contained in its annex a section on additional 'qualitative perspectives', in which it was argued that the Office had taken into account 'environmental risks in different city regions', 'safety of the trip to school', 'functionality of buildings as schools' and 'the condition of school buildings and their cultural-historical value'. In terms of March's theory, this section indicates Office steps towards a 'logic of appropriateness', intending to water down the 'logic of consequences' of the consultants' proposal. The leading *Helsingin Sanomat* article of 29 March 2007 cited above suggests that the Office's adjustment was not without credibility, but we have seen that such activity could not prevent considerable eliminations from the Office's proposal in later decision-making. In particular, the 'logic of consequences' of the Office's real estate management measures drowned amongst the emotionally spiced 'logic of appropriateness' of the opponents.

The 20 June 2007 City Council decision spells out the ultimate result of the struggle between the 'logic of appropriateness' and the 'logic of consequences': the reduction of student places corresponding to only one-fourth of the expected reduction in student numbers. Note also the final but vain 'logic of consequences' of the dissenting opinion to the City Executive Board rendered by the Deputy City Manager, under whose responsibility the Office and the Teaching Council operates, and who argued that the proposal should have been carried out as it stood after the Teaching Council consideration.

From the viewpoint of March's theory the March 2006–June 2007 Helsinki school network revision politics and policy show evidence of a particular kind of learning. It was a learning process by those – the Teaching Council Section and Plenum members, the City Executive Board members and the City Council members – who may first have opposed only the closure or merger of a given, single school, but ended up in political cooperation with others in eliminating closures and mergers, resulting in a broad coalition against political change. The minutes of the City Council debates reveal many council members becoming 'city-part politicians', taking up nostalgic memories of their school days and fighting for their own old school (CoH 2007c). The bounded rationality learning thus supported the deletion of ever further closure and merger measures, bringing about tendencies towards the preservation of the status quo.

Despite the numerous eliminations, several mergers, closures and other measures were decided upon anyway. Supplementing March's theory with Kahneman's (2002) related approach, Kahneman's notion of 'framing' sheds light on aspects of the case. As we could see, the external evaluators proposed cost reductions of ten million euro in 2006, while, one year later, the city politicians were content with reductions of about two million, which happened to be approximately the same magnitude as proposed by the Office of Education in 2005. The question arises whether, in the end, the Office did not just have its way and whether the consultants' proposal work as a deterrent increased the appeal of more moderate mergers and closures.

Conclusions

As the analysis has shown, establishing new ways of governing schools is far from easy, even in a country that is famous for its school policies and their success. Analysing the different proposals and the outcome suggest that people prefer tangible things such as buildings utilized by organizations identifiable as schools to the abstract cancellation of previous cutbacks to restore student choice. The case therewith also joins decades of policy analyses on the difficulty of redistribution (Baumgartner *et al.* 2006) with a special emphasis of March's theory on the cognitive myopia of people who will themselves ultimately turn elderly from having been students, parents or politicians struggling for votes.

Also the argument of attending a 'near school', representing a statutory right, could in fact only be used as in a restrictive way for opposing school closure or merger. Calculating from raw data obtained by the City of Helsinki statistics, we can find that on the average only two-thirds of the students in classes one–six attend their statutory 'near school', with a range by schools of 35–86 per cent, and that an average of about one half of those in classes seven–nine attend the near school, ranging from 25–79 per cent across the schools. Comparing this fact to the cutback in student choice reveals again the interaction between March's 'logic of appropriateness' and 'logic of consequences'. It is unlikely that many of the opponents were defending a given school, but instead they waged a principled struggle against changes to the status quo. This is one of the well allowable options available in a political democracy.

In sum, the chapter illustrates that the internationally renowned achievements of Finnish education policies are not only results of rationalistic implementation of determinate school policies, but also influenced by other variables and, moreover, constrained by bounded rationality. Besides, Finland's shining results in the OECD PISA studies make it not only a conceivable benchmark to be studied by education policy-makers of other countries, but they also reduce the possibilities of the Finns themselves to learn from experiences gained in other countries. By focusing on the policy process and its constraints, this chapter did not elaborate on other important variables in Finnish school policies. Such variables to be taken into account in other studies include the traditionally close distance between the Finnish local governments and the teachers or the relative weakness of new public management in Finnish primary and lower secondary education. Related studies on school management, reforming educational systems, and developing indicators to measure educational achievement and penultimate effects of education have their legitimate place. However, as this chapter intended to show, there is more to the policies and politics of education, including that not all educational policies have been and should not be rationalized up to their full de-politicization. Analysing local politics and policies of education with a framework of March's bounded rationality theory is one, although only one suggestive option in order to pinpoint, to clarify and to analyse the very political elements that constitute such an evidently successful national system of education as the Finnish one of primary and lower secondary education. In this way political science can work towards enabling the prevention of taking other countries naively as examples for policy learning.

The analysis has definite limits that derive from the characteristics of the educational sector in general and from its particular shape in Finland in particular. A different analysis would have resulted if the Finnish higher education or Finnish vocational education would have been inquired upon, as they are fields that lack the shine of the country's primary and lower secondary education. Moreover, the results are hardly generalizable across different policy sectors. Analysing healthcare, the other one of Finland's two best established welfare sectors, would have shown substantially more privatization to take into account, more applications of the newest technological innovations, the prospect of an increasing demand of services as the population ages, and a wide amplitude of managerialist tools applied.

References

AFLG (Association for Finnish Local Governments) (2006) 'Peruskoulut 1990–2006', Helsinki: AFLG.

Ahonen, P. and Wiberg, M. (2004) 'Il percorso della Finlandia in Europa: dalla periferia nord-orientale al centro continentale', in Ariane Landuyt (ed.) *Storia Federalismo e Dell'Integrazione Europea*, Bologna: Il Mulino, 451–504.

Ahonen, P., Hyyryläinen, E. and Salminen, A. (2006) 'Looking for governance configurations of European welfare states', *Journal of European Social Policy*, 16, 2: 173–184.

Anderson, K.M. (2001) 'The politics of retrenchment in a social democratic welfare state: reform of Swedish pensions and unemployment insurance', *Comparative Political Studies*, 34, 9: 1063–1091.

Basu, R. (2004) 'The rationalization of neoliberalism in Ontario's public education system, 1995–2000', *Geoforum*, 35: 621–634.

—— (2007) 'Negotiating acts of citizenship in an era of neoliberal reform: the game of school closures', *International Journal or Urban and Regional Research*, 31, 1: 109–127.

Baumgartner, F.R., Green-Pedersen, C. and Jones, B.D. (2006) 'Comparative studies of policy agendas', *Journal of European Public Policy*, 13, 7: 959–974.

Boas, T.C. (2007) 'Conceptualizing continuity and change: the composite standard model of path dependence', *Journal of Theoretical Politics*, 19, 1: 33–54.

Brunsson, N. and Olsen, J.P. (1993) *The Reforming Organization*, London: Routledge.

City of Helsinki (CoH) (2005) 'Kouluverkoston tarkistaminen', Helsinki: City Office of Teaching.

—— (2006) 'Kouluverkoston tarkistaminen', Helsinki: City Office of Teaching.

—— (2007a) 'Perusopetuksen opiskelijat', Helsinki: City Office of Teaching.

—— (2007b) 'Kouluverkoston tarkistaminen', Helsinki: City Office of Teaching.

—— (2007c) 'Kouluverkoston tarkistaminen', Helsinki City Council, 20 June 2007, Helsinki: City Council.

Cohen, M.D., March, J.G. and Olsen, J.P. (1972) 'A garbage can model of organizational choice', *Administrative Science Quarterly*, 17, 1: 1–25.

Cyert, R.M. and March, J.M. (1963) *A Behavioral Theory of the Firm*, Oxford: Blackwell.

Esping-Andersen, G. (1990) *Three Worlds of Welfare Capitalism*, Cambridge: Cambridge University Press.

Gigerenzer, G. and Selten, R. (eds) (2001) *Bounded Rationality: The Adaptive Toolbox*, Cambridge: MIT Press.

Helgøy, I. (2006) 'Rhetoric and action in regulating the public schools in Norway and Sweden', *Scandinavian Political Studies*, 29, 2: 89–110.

Helin, H. (2006) 'Palvelujen kapea rahoituspohja', *City of Helsinki Urban Facts*, 37.

Jones, B.D. (1999) 'Bounded rationality', *Annual Review of Political Science*, 2: 297–321.

Kahneman, D. (2002) *Maps of Bounded Rationality*, Stockholm: The Nobel Foundation.

Kingdon, J.W. (1995) *Agendas, Alternatives, and Public Policy*, New York: Harper Collins.

Levitt, B. and March, J.G. (1988) 'Organizational learning', *Annual Review of Sociology*, 14: 319–340.

McKinley, W., Zhao, J. and Rust, K.G. (2000) 'A sociocognitive interpretation of organizational downsizing', *Academy of Management Review*, 25, 1: 227–243.

March, J.G. and Olsen, J.P. (1979) *Ambiguity and Choice in Organizations*, Bergen: Universitetsforlaget.

—— (1989) *Rediscovering Institutions: the Organizational Basis of Politics*, New York: Free Press.

—— (1995) *Democratic Governance*, New York: Free Press.

March, J.G., Schultz, M. and Zhou, X. (2000) *The Dynamics of Rules: Change in Written Organizational Codes*, Stanford: Stanford University Press.

Moos, L. and Møller, J. (2003) 'Schools and leadership in transition: the case of Scandinavia', *Cambridge Journal of Education*, 33, 3: 353–370.

NBE (National Board of Education) (2003) 'Koulurakennusten mitoitusnormit', Helsinki: NBE.

Nuikkinen, K. (2005) *Terveellinen ja turvallinen koulurakennus*, Saarijärvi: National Board of Education.

Peters, B.G., Pierre, J. and King, D.S. (2005) 'The politics of path dependency: political conflict in historical institutionalism', *The Journal of Politics*, 67, 4: 1275–1300.

Pierson, P. (2005) 'The study of policy development', *The Journal of Policy History*, 17, 1: 34–51.

Starke, P. (2006) 'The politics of welfare state retrenchment: a literature review', *Social Policy & Administration*, 40, 1: 104–120.

Telhaug, A.O., Mediås, O.A. and Aasen, P. (2006) 'The Nordic model in education: education as part of the political system in the last 50 years', *Scandinavian Journal of Educational Research*, 50, 3: 245–283.

Thelen, K. (2003) 'How institutions evolve: insights from comparative historical analysis', in J. Mahoney and D. Rueschemeyer (eds) *Comparative Historical Analysis in the Social Sciences*, New York: Cambridge University Press, 208–240.

Weyland, K. (2006) *Bounded Rationality and Policy Diffusion: Social Sector Reform in Latin America*, Princeton: Princeton University Press.

Wilson, D., Croxson, B. and Atkinson, A. (2006) '"What gets measured gets done": headteachers' responses to the English Secondary School Performance Management System', *Policy Studies*, 27, 2: 153–171.

Yin, R.K. (2003) *Case Study Research*, London: Sage.

Part III

Education in international relations

An emerging multi-level setting

8 The role of ideas in GATS education negotiations

Evidence from Argentina and Chile

Antoni Verger

Introduction

The General Agreement on Trade in Services (GATS) introduces complexity into the international governance of education: it creates a new international arena for negotiation concerned with national education governance, and it realizes a comprehensive economic perspective on education. Since this agreement was created in the framework of the World Trade Organization (WTO) in 1995, new non-conventional actors and extra-educational rationales are introduced into the international regulation of education activities. The system of rules of GATS pushes for a progressive trade liberalization of education all over the world and, consequently, for the transnationalization and privatization of education systems. Education liberalization under GATS, however, is also a contested process (Scherrer 2007). Teachers' unions, non-governmental organizations (NGOs) in the field of development, associations of public universities and other education stakeholders have opposed and campaigned against GATS in different countries and at a range of levels from the local to the global (Verger and Bonal 2008).

In this chapter, I explore the influence of these actors on GATS outcomes in the education field. My hypothesis is that domestic contestation to GATS and the ideas (for and against) the liberalization of trade in education services are able to shape the preferences and behavior of state actors in the negotiation process. I explore the explanatory power of these elements through a constructivist approach. My arguments are based on intensive fieldwork involving country studies on Argentina and Chile, which are analyzed by means of a comparative strategy.[1] Argentina and Chile are countries with similar characteristics – both are developing countries, with a similar social structure and located in the same region – but they demonstrate very different behavior in trade policies and, specifically, in the introduction of education in trade agreements. This makes it especially pertinent for the comparison of both cases. The similarity in the main features of the cases and the differences manifested in the independent variable provide the appropriate conditions to create knowledge through comparison (Green 2002).

The chapter is divided in four main sections. The first section introduces the role of ideas in politics. In the second section I briefly explain GATS and justify the pertinence of analyzing GATS negotiations in education through a constructivist approach. In the third section I explore the process of preference-shaping in relation to GATS and education in the two selected countries, Argentina and Chile. Finally, I conclude by contrasting the empirical case study observations with the constructivist theoretical framework.

The role of ideas in international politics

Constructivism can be defined as an approach to social and political analysis that deals with the role of human consciousness and the embeddedness of actors in their social context. This approach 'focuses on the role of ideas, norms, knowledge, culture, and argument in politics, stressing in particular the role of collectively held or "intersubjective" ideas and understandings on social life' (Finnemore and Sikkink 2001: 392). Constructivism is an epistemological current and a framework of thinking about the nature of politics, social life and social interaction. A core assumption in constructivist research is that interests and preferences are social constructions that are not objectively given (Haas 2004; Hay 2002). Constructivists also emphasize the role of non-state actors in politics as a consequence of giving importance to the role of ideas. Non-state actors do not have as much material power as state actors, but they can hold 'powerful ideas' that are independent of economic and military capacities (Keck and Sikkink 1998). To a great extent, the strength and legitimacy of non-state actors depends on their beliefs, scientific evidence and moral principles (Korzeniewicz and Smith 2003). That is the reason why *persuasion* is one of the principal tactics of civil-society organizations to influence political outcomes.

In International Relations, constructivism has been applied to a broad range of issues such as the study of social movements and transnational advocacy coalitions (Keck and Sikkink 1998), the political impact of epistemic communities (Haas 2004) or the construction of international regimes (Arts 2000). The constructivist research question is not *whether* ideas matter, because it is assumed that human interpretation and ideas are key variables for political outcomes; rather, the questions are *how* and *when* do ideas matter more (Wendt 1999)? Are they autonomous sources of power (Walsh 2000)? And, what kind of ideas (worldviews, principled beliefs or causal beliefs) matter more (Goldstein and Keohane 1993)?

Nevertheless, constructivism is not a monolithic current. There is not a common understanding on the level of autonomy that can be attributed to ideas as explanatory factors of political processes and outcomes, as constructivists differ in the extent to which ideas matter. Some assert that ideas can influence politics when they become *institutionalized*. This means that ideas exert influence as elements that are embedded in institutions, regimes or policy paradigms.[2] For weak constructivists, ideas can also exert influence as *lenses* that focus on the best option for policymakers to maximize their interests or as *coalitional glue* to facilitate the cohesion of particular groups. In this way, ideas just alleviate coordination problems in those situations without a unique possible equilibrium (Goldstein and Keohane 1993).

It is also feasible to attribute a more 'protagonist' character to ideas and consider that they can work as *road maps*. In these cases, ideas act more clearly as explanatory variables to define the preferences of the actors 'by stipulating causal patterns or by providing compelling ethical or moral motivations for action' (Goldstein and Keohane 1993: 16). Ideas have more possibilities to act in this way in periods of crisis or when policy-makers have to face new and complex problems in the political agenda that generate uncertainity (Finnemore and Sikkink 2001; Richardson 1996). A further group of constructivists, finally, considers ideas as being more than simple instruments of human action; they have constitutive power and intrinsic forces and, consequently, are able to become weapons in political struggles (Blyth 2004). These authors do not deny that ideas can act embedded in institutions, but they are interested in the processes by which ideas that were initially held by a minority become widely held and institutionalized (Hasenclever *et al.* 1996). Their research focuses on the role of persuasive arguments and communicative action as independent causes of social behavior and political change (Risse 2000, 2004).

The constructivist approach and, specifically, the latter more comprehensive assumptions on the role of ideas as explanatory factors, seem suitable for the analysis of GATS due to its technical complexity and the uncertainities it generates in the education field. In the following sections, I justify this theoretical choice and I explore how ideas, and which ideas, matter in the context of GATS and education negotiations. Specifically, my research aims to find out if arguments for and against GATS, and the actors that sustain them, have the capacity to influence the outcomes of the negotiation.

Arguments for and against GATS in the education field

The GATS promotes the elimination of barriers to trade in services by the member states of the WTO. The most significant thing about this process is that the barriers that GATS seeks to eliminate are not strictly of a conventional tariff nature, as with trade in goods. Rather, they are concerned with the rules and regulations of government systems that hinder the transnationalization of service companies. In the area of education, these barrier rules might be taxes on the repatriation of the profits of education companies, stipulations as to what type of judicial personality educational centers must adopt, measures for controlling the guarantee of the quality of educational services, tests of financial need, systems of scholarships or subsidies to specific educational centers, and so forth (Verger 2008). On the other hand, to inculcate the principle of predictability, GATS 'freezes' the commitments made by countries, making it extremely difficult to withdraw from or reduce commitments once they are made (see article XXI of the agreement).

This regulatory power of GATS, together with the sanctioning capabilities of the WTO (Jackson 2002), have turned the Agreement into a key element in the global educational governance scenario (Robertson *et al.* 2002). Therefore, the regime for education that GATS promotes is not ideologically neutral, rather the opposite: it seeks to institute a commercial regime of disembedded liberalism that contradicts the Keynesian proposal of embedded liberalism instituted by the original GATT (General Agreement on Tariffs and Trade). Then, it breaks the balance between global free trade and the capacity of states to deliver their legitimate social purpose in favor of the former. This reflects a more general ideological shift between the GATT'47 and the WTO'95 regimes, as has been stated by Ford (2002) and Ruggie (1994).

Concerning the education sector, GATS generates much uncertainity and the resulting public debate has been very intense. Based on broad documentary analysis, I identified the main topics that appear in the debate and the different meaning repertoires concerning each topic, summarized in the Table 8.1.[3] As can be observed, the GATS and education debate has seen plenty of ideas that, very often, are totally opposing. It allows for the identification of two clear interpretation lines: one that is against the interference of GATS in the education field,

Table 8.1 The GATS and education debate

Topics	Interpretative repertoires	
	GATS Critics (The GATS…)	Pro-GATS (The GATS…)
1 Right to regulate of the states	1.1. … restricts the *policy space* of countries and its capacity to regulate education	1.2. … respects the regulation capacity of the States
2 Effects in developing countries	2.1. … promotes an unequal exchange between North and South in education services	2.2. … favors the development of the education systems in Southern countries
3 Education equity	3.1. … privatize the funding to education and the access becomes more restricted	3.2. … creates larger offer and investment in education
4 Education quality	4.1. … undermines education quality	4.2. … favors education quality through competition
5 Traditional functions of education	5.1. … alters traditional functions of education (social cohesion, nation building, etc.). Education becomes an *end* itself	5.2. … strengthens and complements the traditional functions of education
6 Labor conditions of teachers	6.1. … damages labor conditions	6.2. … improves labor conditions and creates new jobs in the education field
7 Prognostic	7.1. Rupture (education out of GATS) 7.2. Reform (education in GATS but subordinated to education policies and priorities)	7.3. Continuity (deepening liberalization commitments is positive for education)

and the other that advocates GATS. Therefore, there is a broad 'market of ideas' for policy-making on the topic.

Most of the ideas in the GATS and education debate are constructed through and with a hypothetic-deductive procedure. They are statements on the potential effects, positive or negative, of GATS on education systems. Two clear epistemic communities are identified in this debate, one of which is critical of the GATS, while the other defends it. The critical epistemic community is made up of educational scientists, researchers of education unions, non-governmental organizations in the development sector, associations of public universities and the staff of the United Nations Educational, Scientific and Cultural Organization (UNESCO). The pro-GATS epistemic community is made up of experts on trade and researchers associated with the World Bank or the Trade Department of the Organization for Economic Co-operation and Development (OECD). Other actors, such as the educational research institute of the OECD, have assumed the role of brokers between these two big groups. Following Critical Discourse Analysis, it is possible to identify two semiotic orders (Fairclough 2003) directly linked to two different social and institutional orders: one made up of education representatives and the other of pro-free trade advocates. This partially explains the polarization of the debate because the social and semiotic orders act as systems of internal logic that condition activities such as interpretation, explanation and policy recommendation. Therefore, the critical repertoires of GATS are built on moral principles based on pro public education and they highlight the dangers of GATS and minimize its possible positive implications. Instead, the pro-GATS sector applies the same trade theory and principles to the liberalization of education that they would apply to the analyses of trade liberalization in other sectors of the economy. These observations also show that most of the actors that are involved in the GATS and education debate are not only looking for validity claims in a communicative action context. Rather, they are pushing for the particular interests or the core principles of the social group or institutions they remain part of.

Case studies: GATS in Chile and Argentina

Both Argentina and Chile did not make commitments for the education sector during the services negotiations of the Uruguay Round that ended 1994, but they are behaving differently in the current 'Doha Round' of negotiations, ongoing since 2001. This round has not finished, but it is almost certain that Argentina will not introduce education into the GATS agreement since the Ministry of Education has repeatedly stated that it is not going to commit education to free trade: it has fixed its preferences against GATS in its last Education Act (2006), and it signed two related international declarations, the Brasilia and the Montevideo declarations. The first one was signed by the ministries of education of Brazil and Argentina, and the main teacher unions of both countries. The second one was promoted by a platform of unions of the Common Market of the South (MERCO-SUR) and signed by the ministries of education of its member countries.

Chile has a more liberal position on this topic. It did not make commitments for education and most of the other services sectors in the Uruguay Round, because the topic was very new and there were a lot of uncertainties. At that time, therefore, the country opted to remain cautious. However, in the later Doha Round it has been prepared to commit education to free trade if the liberalization results of the negotiations are high. In consequence, education could be treated by this country as a bargaining chip during the negotiation process. Moreover, Chile has already liberalized education in the framework of multiple free-trade agreements with the main education exporters of the planet. Argentina also participates in plurilateral trade agreements, but instead of signing them with the main global players, its geopolitical priorities are the regional space and south–south relations, such as the MERCOSUR.

Tracing back the negotiation process

Most of the WTO member countries design their negotiation strategy and establish their preferences on services liberalization at the national level.[4] To do that, negotiators usually consult the main exporters, the domestic industry and the regulators of each service sector. The Ministry of Trade coordinates this consultation process, but it is not necessarily a neutral coordinator. Trade ministries are political actors that try to pursue a specific political agenda that normally consists in opening markets abroad and does not necessarily match the preferences of the regulators and other stakeholders of the sector. To better reach their aims, the trade negotiators can try to persuade the stakeholders to frame their preferences or to hide some information. To some extent, this is what happened in the negotiations of the education sector in Argentina and Chile. Trade representatives in both countries support the introduction of education under GATS and actively advocate opening education to trade, above all when it enables them to obtain concessions from other countries during the trade negotiations. Morevoer, they are skeptical of the critics of GATS and they think that their respective countries could identify offensive interests in education exports. Chilean trade negotiators also believe that GATS could improve education quality (Interview Argentina #02, 2006; Interview Argentina #03, 2006; Interview Chile #01, 2006; Interview Chile #02, 2006; Interview Chile #04, 2006).

In spite of trade representatives preferences, the regulator of the education sector in both countries, the Education Ministry, should have the formal capacity to veto any decision in the area – above all when the establishment of commitments means having to change any education regulation. To understand the negotiation's outcomes, it is therefore necessary to analyze the position and preferences of education stakeholders. As we will see, they have very different positions in each analyzed country. Moreover, their role in the negotiation process of GATS has also been very different. This process, which will be explored in the following pages, is represented in Table 8.2 where the main facts and events of the negotiations in each country from 1986 to 2006 are presented.

Table 8.2 GATS and education negotiation process in Argentina and Chile

Dates and general events	Argentina	Chile
1986–1994: Uruguay Round	Argentina does not establish liberalization commitments in education	Chile does not commit education [1996: Education commitments in FTA with Canada]
2000: Services negotiations start		
2001: Services are incorporated to the Doha Round		
2002: First Doha Round services demands ['Porto Alegre Declaration' signed by Latin American public universities]	Korea makes a demand on education to Argentina Trade Ministry consults education stakeholders. All of them are opposed to make an offer in education	[Education commitments in FTAs with El Salvador and Costa Rica]
2003: First Doha Round services offers	First services offer is published. It does not include education	First services offer is published. It does not include education [Education commitments in FTAs with Korea and USA]
2004: Countries carry on with the negotiations	Brasilia Declaration is signed Debate on GATS in education in the Argentinean Congress	
2005: WTO Ministerial Conference in Hong Kong: Plurilateral demands are allowed	Montevideo Declaration is signed Argentina does not present revised offer in services	Revised offer: does not include education [Education commitments in FTA with N. Zealand, Singapore, Brunei]
2006: Plurilateral negotiations start	Argentina receives plurilateral demand on education coordinated by N. Zealand The HE Division is consulted. They respond appealing to the Montevideo Declaration New Education Act establishes that Argentina will not commit education in trade agreements	Chile receives plurilateral demand on education coordinated by N. Zealand Chile will commit education depending on the evolution of Doha Round

In the Doha Round, the Argentinean Ministry of Trade has organized two rounds of consultations with education stakeholders. The *first consultations* took place in 2002, coinciding with the start of the GATS negotiations. The stakeholders summoned were the Public Universities Council, the Private Universities Council and the Higher Education Division of the Ministry of Education. All of them declared their opposition to the establishment of liberalization commitments in education, but for different reasons. The private universities were against GATS to avoid competition with foreign universities, fearing a lack of competitiveness in comparison to universities from richer countries (Interview Argentina #17, 2006). Public universities maintained a more politically committed position: at the time of the consultation, they had recently signed a declaration, la *Carta de Porto Alegre*, in the framework of a Summit of Public Universities of Iberoamerica. Therein, they stated that GATS contradicts the conception of education as a public good and that the Agreement can have harmful consequences for education. It was added that the governments have to be pressured to avoid subscribing any kind of commitments in the framework of the agreement. The Argentinean public universities council, guided by the content of the *Carta*, strongly rejected the possibility of introducing education in the GATS. For its part, the Higher Education Division did not have much information on the topic at that moment, but decided to support the position of the public and private universities and expressed that they share the conception of education as a public good and their worry about the fact that GATS could undermine this (Interview Argentina #07, 2006).

The *second consultation* was organized in the year 2006, in the framework of the plurilateral negotiations round. By then, Argentina was faced with plurilateral demands with regard to education, which were coordinated by New Zealand. The Ministry of Trade decided to inquire again about the preference of the education sector on the possibility of offering education. For that purpose, only the ministerial Higher Education Division was invited. Their representatives stated that it was not possible to subscribe liberalization commitments in education because the Ministry of Education had publicly declared (in the Montevideo Declaration and in the Brasilia Declaration) that Argentina would not introduce its education services in free-trade agreements. Based on this document, the Division stated that a *red line* had been drawn on the education sector and that it was not negotiable. This strict stance created some tensions between the trade and the education representatives. The trade negotiator was keen on obtaining a concession from the education regulator, and told the education representative that the Trade Minister would 'solve this problem with the Education Minister at the political level' (Interview Argentina #08, 2006). In the end the position of the Ministry of Education prevailed.

It is important to state that the debate on GATS and education has assumed an unusual degree of centrality in the political arena in Argentina. It is one of the few known countries where the congress has debated this specific topic. Moreover, in the 2003 presidential elections, the candidate and former President Carlos S. Menem proposed to introduce education to GATS as one of the solutions to solve the economic crisis of the country (Schugurensky and Davidson-Harden 2003).

The negotiation process in Chile has been very different from the Argentinean one. In Chile, education stakeholders have not been systematically consulted and the definition of preferences has been much more centralized in the Ministry of Trade. The latter has only consulted the representatives of the education quality assurance agencies in the framework of Free Trade Agrements with Europe and the USA. Unlike in the Argentinean case, the purpose of these consultations was not to ask for permission for education liberalization, but to adjust some technical aspects of the liberalization process. Specifically, the factor that unleashed the consultations was the concern expressed by Europe and the United States with regard to the value and quality of Chilean education certificates, but not the aim of making the negotiation process more participatory and inclusive. For that reason, only the country's education quality assurance agency was contacted (Interview Chile #12, 2006). On the other hand, Chile also received the plurilateral demand of New Zealand, but it did not initiate any consultations. Currently, the trade negotiators from Chile feel free to offer education in the GATS context and they will do so if the level of ambition of the Doha Round is high enough (Interview Chile #01, 2006).

Nevertheless, the secrecy and the centralization of the definition of preferences on GATS in the Ministry of Trade are not the only elements that explain the pro free-trade position adopted by Chile in the education field. Another important factor is that there is a significant correlation of the ideas on the topic between the trade representatives and the education representatives. In Chile, education stakeholders do not subscribe to the widely established perception about the dangers of GATS within the international education comunity. The Ministry of Education, the quality assurance agencies and the education providers generally agree on the opportunities of education liberalization and, to some extent, they participate actively in the trade strategy of their country. For instance, several Chilean universities, both private and traditional,[5] participate in the University Services Exports Committee created by the Ministry of Trade in 1998 to promote education exports from the country. The teachers' unions are the only key stakeholders that have raised their voice against GATS and the commodification of education that it favors.

This 'uncritical' position of education stakeholders in Chile contrasts with the regulation necessities, weakness and potentialities of the sector in this country. The higher education system in Chile is unequal, unstable and unpredictable (Goic-Goic 2004). The education regulation is very soft and very permissive toward private providers. For instance, quality evaluation is not compulsory for these universities (Lemaitre 2005). The system almost works as a pure market and the role of the state in higher education is only secondary. The state focuses on providing information to students as a basis for choosing the best option in the higher education market, and it finances private and public universities based on market criteria (Brunner and Uribe 2007). The GATS could accentuate the current regulatory problems and weakness of the Chilean education system.

Nevertheless, these potential dangers are not perceived as such by the education ministry and other stakeholders. This contradicts the assumption that the countries take commitments on education in GATS depending on the actual needs and potentialities of their education systems – see for instance (Sauvé 2002).

Table 8.3 summarizes the preferences and interpretations on the topic of the actors involved, more or less actively, in GATS and education negotiations both in Argentina and in Chile.

Table 8.3 The stakeholders approach to GATS and education in Argentina and Chile

Actor	Country	Position/preferences	Interpretative repertoires
Trade Ministry	Argentina	PRO-GATS: • Education as a bargaining chip	• GATS Respects the regulation capacity of the states • Increases the exportation opportunities for the country
	Chile	PRO-GATS: • Education as a bargaining chip • Free Trade can benefit education	• GATS Respects the regulation capacity of the States • Increases the exportation opportunities for the country • Creates more offer and investment in education and favors education quality
Education Ministry	Argentina	AGAINST GATS: • Education is not a commodity	• Alters traditional functions of education
	Chile	PRO-GATS: • Free Trade can benefit education	• Liberalization is positive if quality can be assured
Universities	Argentina	AGAINST GATS: • Education is not a commodity (public universities) • Defensive interests (private universities)	• Alters traditional functions of education (public universities) • Unequal exchange in education (private universities)
	Chile	PRO-GATS: • Free Trade can benefit education	• Increases the export opportunities for the country and the available resources for universities
Teacher Unions	Argentina	AGAINST GATS: • Education is not a commodity	• Restricts *policy space* • Unequal exchange in education • Privatization of education • Alters traditional functions of education • Damages labor conditions
	Chile	AGAINST GATS: • Education is not a commodity	
Quality Assurance Agencies	Argentina	*[no defined preferences]*	*[no defined discourse on the topic]*
	Chile	PRO-GATS: • Free Trade can benefit education	• Liberalization is positive if quality can be assured

The role of teachers' unions

Table 8.3 clearly shows that education stakeholders in Argentina and Chile have a very different opinion on the topic of GATS and education. The only education stakeholders with a common position in both countries are the teachers' unions. The main teachers' union in Chile (*Colegio de Profesores*) and the principal teachers' union in Argentina (*Central de Trabajadores de la Educación de la República Argentina*) are very critical of GATS. These actors have been systematically ignored by the trade ministries of their respective countries during the GATS negotiations at the state level. Nevertheless, the Argentinean union has had the capacity to influence indirectly the development of preferences and, consequently, it has influenced the position that the Argentinean trade negotiators have to defend at the global level. The union started its campaign against GATS after attending the Tri-annual Conference of Education International, the world's biggest confederation of teachers, in 2004. The GATS issue constituted an important part of the agenda of that meeting, and the Argentinean union decided to introduce this topic to their domestic agenda (Interview Argentina #16, 2006).

Asking the contrafactual question on the political influence of this union – thus whether the *outcome of the negotiation process would be different in Argentina if the union had not intervened* – I deduce that it has been a key actor in understanding the official position of Argentina in the GATS negotiations on the education sector.[6] Probably, Argentina would have had a critical position on the negotiation for liberalization of education anyway, given that the public and private education providers were also critical with GATS, but it would not have drawn a red line on the education sector so clearly. The union has been an active promoter of the Brasilia and Montevideo Declarations, as well as of the article in the *Ley de Educación Nacional* where it is stated that Argentina will not make commitments on education in free-trade agreements.

The Chilean teachers' union, however, has not been influential at all, even though it has promoted similar repertoires for action, has invested a similar level of resources and has used a similar discourse on the topic as the Argentinean union. These unequal outcomes are less related to the intrinsic capacities of the unions or their strategies and more to contextual factors. As Colin Hay states, the context is strategically selective, which means that the context favors certain strategies, actors and discourses and is against others. Subsequently, not all the outcomes are possible for everybody, for every strategy and at every moment (Hay 2002).

The Argentinean union benefited from the political conjuncture generated in the country after the deep economic crisis that exploded in 2001. The post-crisis government is trying to break with the neoliberal policies of the 1990s which they are conceived are the main cause of the deep crisis suffered by the country. In this context, the government's refusal of GATS fits perfectly into the current governmental strategy of breaking with the policies of liberalization and privatization of education in the 1990s. It also coincides with the government's attitude, sometimes theatrical, against neoliberal international organizations. On the other hand, the current Argentinean government has been very active in establishing alliances with progressive social movements as a way of achieving social peace after several years of political instability. Making some concessions towards the teachers' union, which is a key actor in the socio-political arena, can benefit this civil society–state alliance strategy and make overall policy-making much smoother in the education field that traditionally has been highly contested. Obviously, this political context has opened various windows of political opportunity to the union. Moreover, its power of influence has become larger because other actors such as the public or private universities have not acted contrary to its interests. Rather, they have pressured the government in the same direction as the teachers' union.

However, in Chile, the rules of free trade have been hegemonic since the 1970s. In this country, the free-trade policies were introduced by General Pinochet after a long period of economic nationalism (Agosin 1999). They have demonstrated a clear continuity in the democratic period that started in 1990 and economic liberalism guides most of the political decisions in nearly all sectors (Angell 1999). As one of the interviewed trade negotiators stated:

> Chile feels much closer to the free trade model: an open economy, predomination of the private sector, non-state intervention, or a state that intervenes as little as possible, the regulation must be as pro-market as possible … These conceptions are deeply-rooted and have consensus, a strong consensus … you can find coherence between the different public or private institutions; they talk the same language. Some years ago, some public institutions had a different approach to the Treasury or to the Central Bank. But today, there is strong coherence between all the institutions … we speak the same language.
>
> (Interview Chile #04, 2006)

This established consensus in Chile makes it very difficult to establish critical ideas toward free trade and for actors to trigger change in the political system. For that reason, the Chilean union, although it has opposed GATS, has not been able to succeed at a level comparable to the Argentinean union.

Comparison

The case studies contributed to a better understanding of the role that ideas concerning GATS and education have played in the development of preferences of the WTO member countries and, consequently, in the GATS negotiations outcomes. The negotiations for education liberalization in the GATS context meet some of the main conditions for the influence of ideas: it is a new, constantly changing and technically complex process that generates uncertainty. Nonetheless, causal beliefs about GATS and education do not act as the only explanatory variables for the results of the negotiations in the analyzed countries. And, by contrast, decisions were taken on the basis of an argumented and reasoned consensus according to which all the interested parties were satisfied with the results. This lack of common understanding could be stressed due to the fact that there is not a policy consensus between the international scientific community on the effects of GATS in the education field. Causal theories are more influential when there is a clear scientific consensus (Walsh 2000) and, currently, policy choices on GATS and education could be both supported or rejected by the existing theories.

Nevertheless, other elements make it difficult not to conceive ideas as autonomous explanatory factors. In the case studies presented, ideas about GATS and education did not mainly act as roadmaps or as weapons of political struggles at the national level because their influence has been strongly subordinated to the ideational, historical and institutional context of each country. In Chile, the neoliberal ideology dominates the arguments of the trade actors, but also the rationale of the education representatives. This country defines its negotiation preferences on education based on *path dependences* originating from GATT, and on pro-free trade ideas that are embedded in an institutional context where free trade is a hegemonic idea. Therefore, the debate on GATS and education has not served to open up new paths in Chile. Rather, the development of preferences has followed the known path of free trade. In this country, the trade negotiations are very much centralized in the Ministry of Trade. This explains partially this pro-free trade bias. Nevertheless, most of the education stakeholders are aligned with the preferences of the trade representatives. To explain this alignment process between the discourses and preferences of the trade and education representatives in Chile the concept of policy paradigm becomes useful. In this country, a monetarist-neoliberal policy paradigm clearly prevails. The core ideas of this paradigm reflect a certain mode of regulation, a fixed accumulation regime and a system of production and exchange of commodities and services. Hence, the link between ideas and material factors is very strong and is coherently structured and institutionalized. This ideational structuration process has important effects. On the one hand, in those contexts where a policy paradigm is hegemonic, the role of ideas is more subtle. It does not mean that ideas are not important, but certain fixed ideas become natural and its influence is less evident (Hay 2002). This way, policy paradigms are also sources of inculcation of ideas and policy actors that have been socialized in a fixed paradigm act in a routine way according to these ideas.

On the other hand, the structuration of certain core ideas delimits the parameters of what is required and acceptable in terms of political power. In this context, those actors that reproduce the core ideas of the paradigm are awarded – such as the universities that participate in the University Services Exports Committee – and those actors with contradictory ideas are penalized, such as the Chilean teachers' union and its demands to exclude education from free-trade agreements. Therefore, it is more difficult to influence politics for political actors, although their objective power capacities are high.

The core ideas of a policy paradigm are questioned in periods of crisis. This is the case in Argentina. During the 1990s, the neoliberal and monetarist policy paradigm was also dominant there, but the deep economic crisis in 2001 made this paradigm teeter, and a process of redefinition of some of its core ideas started. The crisis opened new windows of opportunity for new policy elements. Consequently, some ideas and actors, which were outsiders in the 1990s, have penetrated the current network of governance. The economic nationalism, the third-worldism, the redistribution of wealth and the direct intervention of the state in the provision of basic services gained centrality on the Argentinean political agenda and in official discourse. The opposition to introducing education into GATS fits perfectly into this broader set of ideas and the arguments against GATS resound positively in the new dominant ideological framework. Therefore, although the Argentinean union has used similar resources and discourses as its Chilean counterpart, it has been much more successful. This reinforces the idea that the same actors with similar cognitive and material capabilities will become more or less influential depending on the political and ideational context in which they are embedded.

In Argentina, there is a clear correlation between the official position of the government and the critical ideas on GATS and education disseminated by the teachers' union and other stakeholders. But it does not mean that these ideas are the *cause* of the government behavior in the negotiations. Rather, ideas have acted as lenses and coalitional glue that helped Argentinean policy-makers to reaffirm their ideology and to embed their preferences on the topic in a broader political program.

Conclusions

In this chapter, I have argued that ideas matter most when they can be linked to specific material and institutional background factors. As we have seen, the same idea – and the same strategic action based on this idea – put in different contexts can result in very different outcomes. Moreover, the effects of the international debate on GATS and education are contingent on domestic factors. In order to be internalized, new ideas need to be congruent with historically formed ideologies and the dominant political discourse in a country. The results obtained support the shift towards a critical constructivist understanding of the role of ideas in politics. This shift implies both the recognition that ideational and material factors interact in a dialectical way and also that the influence of ideas is tightly linked to already existing power relations. It also supports the necessity of conceiving of ideas as knowledge structures, and not only as elements that people 'hold in their heads' (Gofas and Hay 2008: 11).

Finally, the results reaffirm the necessitiy of challenging 'methodological statism' when analyzing education policies and politics in the global governance scenario as stated by Dale and Robertson (2007). First, the clash of preferences in relation to the GATS negotiations between the Education Ministry and the Trade Ministry, which I have observed very clearly in the Argentinean case, shows that the state cannot be conceived as a static unit. Therefore, it is more appropriate to consider the state as a field made up of different units that can act in autonomous and sometimes contradictory ways. Second, the GATS negotiations introduce complexity to the coordination of state activities as well as new power relations within statehood. This is due to the fact that the internationalization of the state normally means that only specific factions of the state become effectively internationalized. The part of the state that participates more directly in international organizations and other supra-state processes becomes more powerful because it has better control over the information, the norms, the procedures and the processes themselves. In the GATS/WTO context, the Trade Ministry has the main control over the negotiations. As a consequence, it can use such international instruments to alter the national agenda and priorities in a range of policy fields, such as education. The last observation that challenges methodological statism is that non-state actors are also able to play an active role in governance activities. In the GATS negotiations, non-state actors do not act as decision-makers, but they have the capacity to contribute to the development of preferences of the governments and to generate new path dependences that will shape the process and results of future negotiations. Therefore, in the global governance scenario, states do not have a monopoly over political action, neither in education nor in other policy fields. Instead, governance is shared among several actors and institutions, creating complexity and new interdependencies.

Notes

1 The fieldwork also includes interviews with international actors involved in the negotiation subsystem of GATS. Specifically, I have conducted 29 interviews at the international level (trade negotiatiors in the WTO, WTO staff, UNESCO staff, UNCTAD staff and international NGOs representatives), and 30 interviews with trade and education representatives in Argentina and Chile.
2 A *policy paradigm* is an ideational framework that specifies the goals of policy and the kind of instruments that can be used to attain them, as well as the nature of the problems they are meant to be addressing. Policy paradigms have a solid economic base and a clear orientation to policy-making. That is the reason why they are conceived as guidelines for policies (Hall 1993).
3 Specifically, I have analyzed 86 documents that deal with the GATS and education debate.
4 The least developed countries do not fulfil this rule. These countries usually define their preferences at the global level and do not have a strong mandate from their nation state when they face international trade negotiations (Curzon and Curzon 1972; Verger 2009).
5 The concept of public university is not used in Chile. They refer to traditional universities, which are the older universities of the country that were considered state universities until the beginning of the 1980s.
6 The adoption of the contrafactual strategy to analyze the political influence of different actors is recommended by: Korzeniewicz and Smith (2003); Blyth (1997); Guzzini (2005); Ekstrom and Danermark (2002).

References

Agosin, M.R. (1999) 'Comercio y crecimiento en Chile', *Revista de la CEPAL*, 68 (August 1999): 79–100.

Angell, A. (1999) 'La descentralización en Chile', *Instituciones y Desarrollo*, 3: 131–172.

Arts, B. (2000) 'Regimes, non-state actors and the state system: a "structurational" regime model', *European Journal of International Relations*, 6, 4: 513–542.

Blyth, M.M. (1997) '"Any more bright ideas?" The ideational turn of comparative political economy', *Comparative Politics*, 29, 2: 229–250.

—— (2004) 'Structures do not come with an instruction sheet: interests, ideas, and progress in political science', *Perspectives on Politics*, 1, 4: 695–706.

Brunner, J.J. and Uribe, D. (2007). *Mercados universitarios: el nuevo escenario de la educación superior*, Santiago: Ediciones Universidad Diego Portales.

Curzon, G. and Curzon, V. (1972) 'GATT: Traders' Club', in R.W. Cox and H.K. Jacobson (eds) *The Anatomy of Influence: Decision Making in International Organization*, New Haven: Yale University Press, 298–333.

Dale, R. and Robertson, S. (2007), 'Beyond methodological "isms" in comparative education in an era of globalisation', in A. Kazamias and R. Cowan (eds) *Handbook on Comparative Education*, Dordrecht: Springer, 19–32.

Ekstrom, M. and Danermark, B. (2002) *Explaining Society: An Introduction to Critical Realism in the Social Sciences*, London: Routledge.

Fairclough, N. (2003) *Analysing Discourse*, London: Routledge.

Finnemore, M. and Sikkink, K. (2001) 'Taking stock: the constructivist research program in international relations and comparative politics', *Annual Review of Political Science*, 4: 391–416.

Ford, J. (2002) 'A social theory of trade regime change: GATT to WTO', *International Studies Review*, 4, 3: 115–138.

Gofas, A. and Hay, C. (2008) 'The ideas debate in international studies: towards a cartography and critical assessment', *IBEI Working Paper* No. 2008/11: 1–42. Online, available at: http://ssrn.com/abstract=1086060 (accessed 2 November 2008).

Goic-Goic, A. (2004) 'Descripción y Análisis Crítico del Actual Sistema de Educación Superior en Chile', *Anales del Instituto de Chile*, 24, 2: 83–125.

Goldstein, J. and Keohane, R.O. (1993) *Ideas and Foreign Policy: Beliefs, Institutions and Political Change*, New York: Cornell University Press.

Green, A. (2002) 'Education, globalisation and the role of comparative research', *London Review of Education*, 1, 2: 84–97.

Guzzini, S. (2005) 'The concept of power: a constructivist analysis', *Millenium: Journal of International Studies*, 33, 3: 495–521.

Haas, P.M. (2004) 'When does power listen to truth? A constructivist approach to the policy process?', *Journal of European Public Policy*, 11, 4: 569–592.

Hall, P. (1993) 'Policy paradigms, social learning and the state. the case of economic policymaking in Britain', *Comparative Politics*, 25, 3: 275–296.

Hasenclever, A., Mayer, P. and Rittberger, V. (1996) 'Interests, power, knowledge: the study of international regimes', *Mershon International Studies Review*, 40, 2: 177–228.

Hay, C. (2002) *Political Analysis. A Critical Introduction*, New York: Palgrave.

Jackson, J. H. (2002) *The World Trading System: Law and Policy of International Economic Relations*, London: MIT Press.

Keck, M.E. and Sikkink, K. (1998) *Activists Beyond Borders. Advocacy Networks in International Politics*, New York: Cornell University Press.

Korzeniewicz, R.P. and Smith, W.C. (2003) 'Redes Transnacionales de la Sociedad Civil', in D. Tussie and M. Botto (eds) *El ALCA y las Cumbres de las Américas: ¿Una Nueva Relación Público-Privado?*, Buenos Aires: Biblos, 47–75.

Lemaitre, M.J. (2005) *Between Privatization and State Control: Chile's Experience of Regulating a Widely Privatized System through Quality Assurance*, Paris: IIPE-UNESCO.

Richardson, J. (1996) 'Policy-making in the EU interests, ideas and garbage cans of primeval soup', in J. Richardson (ed.) *European Union: Power and Policy-Making*, London: Routledge, 3–26.

Risse, T. (2000) '"Let's argue!": communicative action in world politics', *International Organization*, 54, 1: 1–39.

—— (2004) 'Global governance and communicative action', *Government and Opposition*, 39, 2: 288–313.

Robertson, S., Bonal, X. and Dale, R. (2002) 'GATS and the education services industry: the politics of scale and global reterritorialization', *Comparative Education Review*, 46, 4: 472–496.

Ruggie, J.G. (1994) 'Trade, protectionism and the future of welfare capitalism', *Journal of International Affairs*, 48, 1: 1–11.

Sauvé, P. (2002) 'Trade, education and the GATS: what's in, what's out, what's all the fuss about?', *Higher Education Management and Policy*, 14, 3: 47–76.

Scherrer, C. (2007) 'GATS: commodifying education via trade treaties', in K. Martens, A. Rusconi and K. Leuze (eds) *New Arenas of Education Governance: The Impact of International Organizations and Markets on Educational Policy Making*, London: Palgrave, 117–135.

Schugurensky, D. and Davidson-Harden, A. (2003) 'From Córdoba to Washington: WTO/GATS and Latin American education', *Globalisation, Societies and Education*, 1, 3: 321–357.

Verger, A. (2008) 'The constitution of a new global regime: higher education in the GATS/WTO framework', in D. Epstein, R. Boden, R. Deem, F. Rizvi and S. Wright (eds) *World Yearbook of Education 2008: Geographies of Knowledge, Geometries of Power: Framing the Future of Higher Education*, London: Routledge, 111–127.

—— (2009) *WTO/GATS and the Global Politics of Higher Education*, London: Routledge.

Verger, A. and Bonal, X. (2008) 'Education vs trade: global struggles challenging WTO/GATS', in D. Hill and E. Rosskam (eds) *Contesting Neoliberal Education: Public Resistance and Collective Advance*, New York: Routledge, 181–201.

Walsh, J.I. (2000) 'When do ideas matter? Explaining the successes and failures of Thatcherite ideas', *Comparative Political Studies*, 33, 4: 483–516.

Wendt, A. (1999) *Social Theory of International Politics*, Cambridge: Cambridge University Press.

9 Multilateral surveillance in education by the OMC

Rik de Ruiter

Introduction

Since tools such as international benchmarking, stocktaking and rankings have become more prominent in recent years, scholars are increasingly interested in studying policy instruments based on multilateral surveillance of national policies (Zeitlin 2005; Schäfer 2006a, 2006b; Kohler-Koch and Rittberger 2006; Martens 2007). This chapter will focus on one of the more elaborate multilateral surveillance tools applied in the EU context – the Open Method of Coordination (OMC) – and will examine its application in the field of education, a domain only marginally exposed to Europeanization in the last decades. As the chapter shows, the OMC created a new level for education governance, constituting an important internationalization process in this field.

In 2000 the heads of state and government of the EU member states codified the OMC by including four elements in the Lisbon presidency conclusions,[1] together forming the *infrastructure* of an OMC (European Council 2000). The complete infrastructure of the OMC consists of guidelines or objectives, indicators and benchmarks, National Action Plans (NAPs), as well as peer review. In the subsequent years these four elements came to function as a template for implementing OMCs on various policy fields, including education policy. Due to the use of this template, national governments play the central role in all OMCs. They approve by qualified majority in the Council the guidelines, indicators and benchmarks on which the different national policies are scored, and formulate NAPs in which it is specified how they plan to improve their policies. The ranking of member states from best performing to worst performing is done by the European Commission. Experts identify the factors that cause a national policy to perform best and review the National Action Plans of the member states.

Although the initial enthusiasm about the OMC as a way to speed up the policy-making process diminished in the last years (De Ruiter 2007: 150), it remains an interesting case to study for answering the question of how policy tools based on the multilateral surveillance of national policies gain presence on the international level. Due to the marginal attention dedicated to the OMC education in the 'new modes of governance' literature (Alexiadou 2007), the need to address this question for the education field is even more pressing. Scholars writing about the OMC education define it as a 'nascent' OMC (Szyszczak 2006: 494) and consider it as part of a broader development on the international level towards 'a solid state of politics' (Novoa and deJong-Lambert 2003: 55; see also Chapter 8, this volume), whereas not much attention is paid to the impact of the OMC on national education policies (except Alexiadou 2007).

This chapter aims at contributing to this emerging field of research in a different way, by explaining the degree of development of the infrastructure of the OMC in education; that is the presence, respectively absence, of guidelines or objectives, indicators and benchmarks, reporting via NAPs, and peer reviews. Hence, this chapter will not focus on the process of development, but instead on the outcome of the development of the infrastructure of the OMC in education. It is rather striking that this aspect has not yet been analysed given that the presence of guidelines, indicators and benchmarks and reporting requirements facilitate mutual learning processes between member states, with policy adjustments on the national level being a possible result. This contribution seeks to fill this gap.

It is claimed in this chapter that an explanation for the presence of a full-blown OMC on the education field has to include two, at first sight contra-intuitive, factors:

1   the incentives pushing member states to act on the EU level; and
2   the reluctance of member states to act on the EU level: national governments can have various reasons to act on the EU level *and at the same time* be reluctant to shift competences from the national to the European level.

These factors explain the reason for EU activity of member states on the education field, and the choice for a non-binding policy instrument to structure this activity.

Official documents of European institutional actors were studied to gain insights with regard to the dependent variable, which is the presence or absence of guidelines, indicators and benchmarks, NAPs and peer review in the OMC education. Second, the positions of member states towards the OMC education were assessed through the extensive coding of articles published in Agence Europe bulletins during the period 1999–2005. These bulletins provided a wealth of information on Council reactions to Commission communications, priorities of member states during their Council presidencies, as well as agendas of sectoral Council meetings, summaries of discussions, discussions or press releases afterwards, and summaries of related plenary debates in the European Parliament. The insights obtained were cross-checked by interviewing Commission officials who were present in the meetings of member-state representatives in which the initiatives related to the infrastructure of the OMC education were discussed. To further understand the general policy context, Agence Europe bulletin articles and European Voice articles on the Lisbon strategy were also coded (see also De Ruiter 2007 for more details on the methodological approach).

After a theoretical approach on the infrastructure of the OMC is formulated, it will be tested in the context of the OMC education. In the third section of this chapter empirical findings will be presented on the incentive and reluctance to act of member states, the OMC education as a compromise instrument, and the reasons for its degree of development. In the concluding section the implications for the international governance of education policies will be discussed, and the question will be addressed what we can learn about education policy when analysed from the perspective of political science.

Explaining the development of the infrastructure of OMCs

Although the template along which an OMC is envisaged to develop is specified in the Lisbon presidency conclusions, the degree in which this template is applied to policy fields differs in practice. Table 9.1 shows the variety of OMCs in place, scored against the core elements of the European Employment Strategy (EES), the most elaborate OMC applied on the EU level. As can be seen, there are considerable differences between the degrees of development of OMCs, especially with regard to the institutionalization of the reporting on national policies. Reporting via NAPs can take place every year – in the case of the EES – biannually (for example social inclusion, education) or in a less elaborate way as part of the general reporting on the Lisbon strategy (as R&D, e-Europe) (see

Table 9.1 The infrastructure of the Open Method of Coordination in different policy areas[2]

Elements OMC	Guidelines/objectives/ indicators	Benchmarking	Reporting structure	Recommendations
EES	Yes: guidelines and indicators	Yes	Yes: one-yearly NAP-process and specific reviews	Yes
Education	Yes: objectives and indicators	Yes	Yes: two-yearly NAP-process	No
Social inclusion*	Yes: objectives and indicators	Yes	Yes: two-yearly NAP-process	No
Pensions*	Yes: objectives and indicators	Yes	Yes: National strategy reports	No
R&D	Yes: objectives and indicators	Yes	Partial, but in context of National Reform Programmes	No
e-Europe	No**	Yes	Partial, but in context of National Reform Programmes	No

Notes
* Since 2005 a streamlining process has taken place, leading to the incorporation of the OMC social inclusion and pensions into the social protection agenda.
** Short-term objectives and indicators are present in the e-Europe Action Plans and i2010, but form only a weak basis for the OMC e-Europe.

Chalmers and Lodge 2003; De La Porte 2002; Radaelli 2003; Lange and Alexiadou 2007, Alexiadou 2007). Because the requirement of reporting is one of the main instruments through which mutual learning can be facilitated, these differences are crucial to take into account and an explanation for the observed variety should be given.

A second point that follows from this survey is that national governments choose to adopt an OMC with elaborate reporting requirements on policy fields that lie at the core of the competences of the member states. Eurobarometer data show that the public in the member states defines various issues as 'important problems' that should remain an exclusive competence of the member states (e.g. housing, social policy, education, pensions). Moreover, political parties in the member states pay abundant attention to these problems in their party manifestos and propose solutions to be implemented on the *national* level (De Ruiter 2007). Examples of OMCs addressing this type of 'important problems' are the EES, the OMC education – which is of particular interest in this chapter – and social policy OMCs such as the OMC social inclusion and OMC pensions. But why do national governments choose to adopt an OMC with elaborate reporting requirements on policy fields that are at the core of the competences of the member states?

I claim that national governments only choose an OMC with a developed infrastructure when they have an incentive to act on an issue on the European level, and at the same time are highly reluctant to shift competences from the national to the European level. This claim corresponds with two strands in the literature on the EES – the oldest and most elaborate OMC applied on the EU level. Both strands present the OMC as a compromise instrument to solve the conflict between an incentive and reluctance to act. The first strand views the OMC as a problem-solving tool and shows similarities with a traditional functionalist account of European integration. In this account, I claim that national governments opt for the OMC in relation to the capacity of the OMC to generate solutions that are less vulnerable to the legal and economic challenges of the European Monetary Union (EMU), whilst still maintaining the legitimate diversity of existing welfare state institutions at the national level (Scharpf 2001: 17; Scharpf 2002). The second strand claims that the OMC is backed up by a 'winning coalition' of actors whose strategic interests are served by the introduction of this multilateral surveillance tool (Gornitzka 2005: 14). This coalition consisted mainly of national governments dominated by social-democratic parties (Schäfer 2004; Ladrech 2003), who wanted to emphasize the importance of job creation – one of the main selling points in their electoral profile – and at the same time remain in control over employment policies on the national level.

In line with the two strands in the literature on the EES, it is expected in this chapter that, when confronted with a conflict between an incentive and reluctance to act, national governments will in general be unwilling to transfer sovereignty to the EU level and, hence, an alternative governance mode needs to be chosen and developed to structure EU activities. This mode will be considered appropriate by both member states with an incentive to act and member states with reluctance to act on the EU level, as long as it has a compromise character; that is, allows for EU activity, without risking a shift of competences from the national to the European level. An OMC with a developed infrastructure is thus expected to be judged in this situation as the most appropriate policy tool because it is 'European' enough to address the incentive to act of member states – for example to discuss possible solutions for problems member states are confronted with on the national level – and sufficiently 'national' – which means non-binding – to prevent a shift of competences. Moreover, it is assumed that the member states with an incentive to act will *push* the development of the infrastructure of the OMC forward, whereas member states more reluctant to act *pull* the more enthusiastic member states back and restrict the choice for a policy tool to the OMC. This dynamic will be referred to as the 'push–pull dynamic'.

Furthermore, I assume that in policy fields that lie close to the core competences of the member states, such as education, conflict is more likely to occur between an incentive and reluctance to act. In these policy fields national politicians are likely to have a preference for keeping control at the national level. The resulting reluctance to act on the EU level can be related to various factors, including concerns over national or cultural identity, as well as electoral strategies of political parties on the national level. On the other hand, politicians are expected to be more willing to act on issues that are part of the core of the competences of the member states because the public expects politicians to show policy results on these issues (Carrubba 2001; Lahav 2004; Manza and Cook 2002).

While I investigate the general reasons for OMC development elsewhere (De Ruiter 2008), this chapter will elaborate more closely on the presence of guidelines/objectives, indicators and benchmarks, NAPs and peer reviews in the OMC education, based on the above developed assumptions. Through this assessment it will become clear whether a conflict between an incentive and reluctance to act on the EU level with regard to education issues can explain the corresponding OMC adoption, including objectives, indicators and benchmarks, reporting requirements and peer review.

The OMC education

At the Lisbon summit of March 2000, the heads of state and government explicitly asked the education ministers to begin an in-depth reflection on the future of national education systems. Subsequently, the infrastructure of the OMC education developed along the lines of the OMC template included in the Lisbon presidency conclusions. To understand whether the outcome of this development is in line with the theoretical assumptions outlined before, it is necessary to look at the incentive and reluctance of national governments to act on the EU level and analyse push–pull factors and their consequences.

An incentive to act on the EU level

The main driving force behind the decision of member states to act on the European level in the context of education issues was the need to collect information on how to address common challenges related to national education policies. One of the new challenges identified was how education policy can contribute to increasing the social cohesion of societies. By continuously enhancing the skills of the population it would be possible to allow people – immigrants and non-immigrants alike – to take active part in the labour market and in the democratic process. Especially France (Agence Europe 1999b, 2000h), Germany (Agence Europe 1999a), and Portugal (Agence Europe 2000a, 2000d) emphasized the link between education, job creation and social cohesion.

A second common challenge for EU member states with regard to education policies is related to the EMU. Because of the focus of the EMU on strict budget deficits, member states are limited in their use of macro-economic instruments on the national level to stimulate demand. As a result, national governments are searching for alternative ways to influence socio-economic developments. One of the alternatives discussed by politicians and policy-makers is the reinforcement of the supply-side of the economy through investments in education (Interview European Commission #1 2005). Third, the ageing of the population creates a necessity to raise the participation levels in the labour market. The latter can be achieved by making the demand and supply of labour match better through investing in the education of the labour force (Interview European Commission #2 2005; Munk 2003; Van der Wende 2000: 308).

Although member states mainly focus their attention on the national level when addressing the specified challenges, it became commonly accepted at the end of the 1990s that the EU could function as a platform to exchange information on how other member states are dealing with these issues (Interview European Commission #2 2005). In the words of an official working in the Directorate-General (DG) education:

> The member states see that they have common problems, common issues that they are confronted with, and because of this they see an advantage in being able to exchange information and experiences on how other countries are tackling more or less the same problems. They think that through this exchange they can enhance their own policy practices.
>
> (Interview European Commission #1 2005)

Reluctance to act

The supportive measures on the European level had to be organized in a specific way in order to take into account the reluctance of member states to act on the EU level with regard to education issues. Various scholars claim that national governments are reluctant to act on the EU level with regard to education policy (De Wit 2003: 166–167; Lawn 2003; Mitter 2004b; Novoa and deJong-Lambert 2003: 49). Moreover, Eurobarometer data show that the public has a preference for leaving the formulation of educational policies at the level of the member states (see Figure 9.1).

146 R. de Ruiter

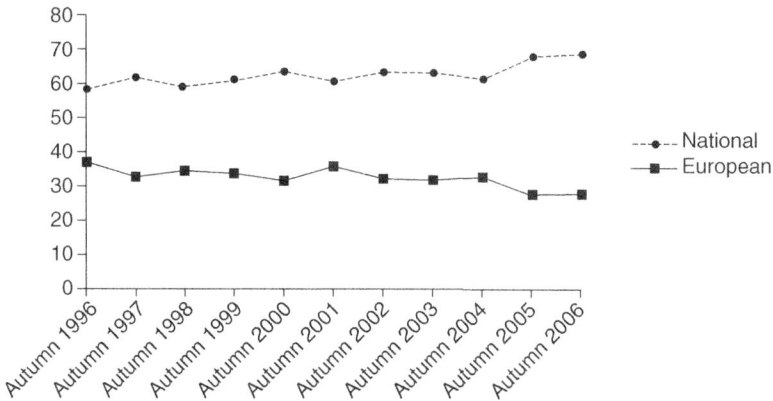

Figure 9.1 Education policy, national competence or joint competence on EU level? (source: based on Eurobarometer 46, 48, 50, 52, 54, 56, 58, 60, 62, 64, 66; EU-15).[3]

In addition, the fact that EU member states spent between 5 and 8 per cent of their GDP on education and training provides an additional reason why governments, policy-makers and political parties consider it an important national issue (Interview European Commission #1 2005).

The reluctance to act on the EU level with regard to education issues manifests itself in various ways. First, articles 149 and 150 of the Treaty establishing the European Community (as amended by the Treaty of Amsterdam) codify a hands-off approach with regard to education issues and only allow room for the use of non-binding legal instruments. Second, the principle of subsidiarity guides EU initiatives in the education field, which in practice excludes all forms of harmonization (Van der Wende 2000: 307) and leaves the OMC as one of the few viable options (Agence Europe 2000b, 2000d, 2000e, 2000f, 2003c).

Third, the reluctance to act on the EU level is also reflected on the subnational level (Mitter 2004a). The German Länder, for example, do not want the federal government to use the European level to take on competences that the Länder have acquired (Interview European Commission #1 2005, I; Interview European Commission #2 2005; Agence Europe 2000g; Obinger *et al.* 2005: 567; see also Chapter 5, this volume). Commissioner Vivianne Reding stated on this: 'Germany, with its Länder for education policy, does not wish to be excluded from international comparisons. But the Länder believe there is a problem when comparison entails decisions. What Germany fears here is EU interference with regard to education' (Agence Europe 2003a).

Can the OMC education strike a compromise?

From the previous two sections it became clear that national governments did have reasons to act on the EU level with regard to education policies, whilst also having reasons to be reluctant to act. The empirical findings presented below indicate that soon after its introduction, the OMC education was viewed as a middle way between EU cooperation and independent action of national state authorities.

After the heads of state and government present at the Lisbon summit asked for the implementation of the OMC education, it was up to the ministers of education and the Commission (i.e. DG education) to interpret the rather broadly defined OMC template. The Education Council and DG education soon came to view the OMC as an appropriate instrument to structure their EU activities. According to an official working in the DG education this view is related with the compromise character of the OMC:

> The OMC is a good instrument in terms of creating a balance in sensitive policy areas between a European wish of going forward and Member State wishes to get help with structural problems, but at the same time keeping the political initiatives in their own hands.
>
> (Interview European Commission #3 2005)

In other words, the OMC education provided a way out of an impasse (Novoa and deJong-Lambert 2003: 55; Livingston 2003: 590–591), through which a balance was created between European convergence and national diversity (Dion 2005). This hints at the presence of a push–pull dynamic in which member states limit EU activities on the education field to the OMC, whilst at the same time maximizing the cooperation through adopting objectives, indicators and benchmarks, NAPs and joint reports with the Commission.

The development of the infrastructure of the OMC education

As we have seen, the OMC education was viewed as a compromise instrument to solve the conflict between an incentive and reluctance to act of member states. It will be assessed whether – as assumed – the presence of this view triggers a push–pull dynamic through which a full-blown OMC gets adopted on the education field. As a first step, the degree of development of the infrastructure of the OMC education will be described.

The empirical findings indicate that the infrastructure of the OMC education reached a degree of development close to the upper limit of the OMC template included in the Lisbon presidency conclusions. The first step in the development of the infrastructure of the OMC education was the mandate from the Lisbon Council to the ministers of education and the Commission to draw up an objectives framework. Subsequently, the Commission proposed a detailed work programme, which was swiftly adopted by the Education Council. The key objectives of the plan consist in improving the quality and efficiency of education systems, facilitating access to education for everyone and opening up the EU educational establishment to the outside world. In the work programme these three key objectives are split into more detailed objectives and key issues. For every concrete objective it is indicated how follow-up activities are organized, what the indicators for measuring the progress are (see Table 9.2), and the

Table 9.2 Indicators used in the OMC education

Indicators, key issues	*Description indicators*
Teachers and trainers	1 Age distribution of teachers together with upper and lower retirement age.
	2 Number of young people in the 0–14 and 15–19 age groups and as a percentage of the total population.
	3 Ratio of pupils to teaching staff by education level.
Skills for the knowledge society	4 Percentage of those aged 22 who have successfully completed at least upper secondary education.
	5 Percentage of pupils with reading literacy proficiency "level 1" and lower on the PISA reading literacy scale.
	6 Distribution and mean performance of students, per country, on the PISA reading literacy scale.
	7 Distribution and mean performance of students, per country, on the PISA mathematical literacy scale.
	8 Distribution and mean performance of students, per country, on the PISA science literacy scale.
	9 Percentage of adults with less than upper secondary education who have participated in any form of education or training, in the last four weeks by age group (25–34, 35–54 and 55–64).
Mathematics, science and technology	10 Students enrolled in mathematics, science and technology as a proportion of all students in tertiary education.
	11 Graduates in mathematics, science and technology as a percentage of all graduates.
	12 Total number of tertiary graduates from mathematics, science and technology fields.
	13 Number of tertiary graduates in mathematics, science and technology per 1,000 inhabitants aged 20–29.
Investments in education and training	14 Public expenditure on education as a percentage of GDP.
	15 Private expenditure on educational institutions as a percentage of GDP.
	16 Enterprise expenditure on continuing vocational training courses as a percentage of total labour costs.
	17 Total expenditure on education per pupil/student, by level of education.
	18 Total expenditure on education per pupil/student.
Open learning environment	19 Percentage of population aged 25–64 participating in education and training four weeks prior to the survey by level of educational attainment.
Making learning more attractive	20 Hours in continuing vocational training courses per 1,000 working hours.
	21 Hours in continuing vocational training courses per 1,000 working hours.
	22 Participation rates in education by age and by level of education.
	23 Share of the population aged 18–24 with only lower secondary education and not in education or training.

Table 9.2 contd.

Indicators, key issues	Description indicators
Foreign Language Learning	24 Distribution of lower/upper secondary pupils learning foreign languages. 25 Average number of foreign languages learned per pupil in upper secondary education.
Mobility	26 Inward and outward mobility of teachers and trainers within the Socrates and Leonardo da Vinci programmes. 27 Inward and outward mobility of Erasmus students and Leonardo da Vinci trainees. 28 Foreign students enrolled in tertiary education as a percentage of all students enrolled in the country of destination, by nationality (European country or other countries). 29 Percentage of students of the country of origin enrolled abroad (in a European country or other countries).

Source: European Commission 2004.

themes and benchmarks for exchanging experience and good practice (European Commission and European Council 2002: 43). In 2004, five benchmarks were defined – with a time schedule running until 2010 – touching upon the following themes:

1   early school leavers;
2   young people with upper secondary education;
3   low-achieving 15-year-olds in reading;
4   graduates in mathematics;
5   participation in lifelong learning (European Commission 2004).

For the implementation of the work programme 'objective groups' were created, each working on one specific objective. The participants in these groups are experts of the member states, with the Commission as the organizer, initiator of proposals and source of expertise. The mandate of each objective group was to make an inventory of activities in their area, contribute to the development of policy objectives, formulate opinions concerning suitable indicators and benchmarks, and organize the mutual learning exercise (European Commission and European Council 2002; European Commission Standing Group on Indicators and Benchmarks 2003). More recently peer learning is gaining a role in the OMC education, which resulted in a shift in focus from the objective groups to countries, their specific interests and the concrete implementation of new policies (Interview European Commission #1 2005). This shift was institutionalized through the introduction of 'clusters'; that is 'groupings of countries around a specific theme on which they expressed a desire to learn from other interested countries, or to share with others their successful or unsuccessful experiences' (European Commission 2006).

Although more and more elements of the OMC template are present, the infrastructure of the OMC education is still not on the level of the EES. First, the introduction of NAPs and the drawing up of joint reports is fairly recent. Based on the national reports of member states, a first joint report was published in November 2005. In this report, the Commission indicated which countries performed best, and discussed best practices (European Commission 2005). This reporting structure has remained intact after the revision of the Lisbon strategy; the crucial role of education in the Lisbon strategy justifies – according to the (Education) Council – a parallel reporting process for education next to the reporting taking place in the context of the National Reform Programmes of the revised Lisbon strategy. However, the joint report does not go very much into detail for specific countries and did not identify what the bad policy practices are. Reporting activities in the context of the OMC education are likely to continue with the publication of the second joint report in 2008. Second, the recent shift from the objectives groups to clusters of countries is likely to facilitate mutual learning between member states and the identification of best practices. However, the cluster activities are voluntary for member states to participate in, and there is no monitoring of the performance or participation of member states in the clusters (Alexiadou 2007).

Explaining the development of the infrastructure of the OMC education

After having *described* the infrastructure of the OMC education, the next question that needs to be addressed is what can *explain* this degree of development. A first point to be mentioned is that there was a considerable amount of overlap between the interests and wishes of the heads of government and the ministers of education. Both parties viewed the OMC as an instrument to trace underperformance of national education policies and address common challenges, without risking a shift of competences from the national to the European level (Interview European Commission #3 2005). Second, the ministers of education were searching in the 1990s for ways to prevent the general themes on the agenda of the Education Council from changing drastically each time the presidency of the Council would rotate (Gornitzka 2005: 22, 32). An OMC with a developed infrastructure could grant this long-term wish for more coherence (Interview European Commission #1 2005). Third, the Commission was motivated to contribute to the development of the infrastructure of the OMC education. Through the OMC the Commission was allowed to play a role on a policy field for which it considers EU action important but does not have competences (Agence Europe 2000c, 2001, 2003b, 2005).

In sum, the fit between the interests and wishes of the Commission and the Education Council and the way the OMC functions, opened the way for the development of the OMC education along the timetable that was set by the heads of government. Without the shared view on the added value of the OMC, the Commission would not have made a serious effort to come up with proposals to put in practice the mandate of the heads of government, and the Education Council would not have agreed with these proposals. Hence, the two institutions form – in the words of an official of the DG education – 'a dynamic duo', sharing the responsibility for the development of the infrastructure of the OMC education (Interview European Commission #3 2005).

Although many elements of the OMC education are inspired by the EES, the latter did not function as a blueprint for developing the infrastructure of the OMC education; the OMC education lacks Commission-based country-specific offices to make evaluations of individual countries' policies and give country-specific recommendations. According to an official working in the DG education: 'The OMC employment (i.e. the EES) is much stronger and much heavier than ours. If we would make a reference to employment, then we would say, in a sense, that this process is going to be more heavy than it is' (Interview European Commission #1 2005). According to another Commission official, member states learned that the infrastructure of the OMC can lead to too much interference by the Commission in national policy practices, and wanted to prevent this interference in the OMC education (Interview European Commission #3 2005). As a result, and in line with the push–pull dynamic, the infrastructure of the OMC education remained close to the lighter OMC template codified in the Lisbon presidency conclusions.

Conclusion

It was assumed that for an OMC to develop to a high degree, there must be a need for an instrument that can strike a compromise between an incentive and reluctance to act on the EU level. This conflict would especially be present in policy fields that lie at the core of the competences of the member states. The empirical findings on the OMC education presented in this chapter confirm these assumptions and show that national governments are pushed to participate in international comparisons and stocktaking in order to deal with challenges on the national level. The push–pull dynamic proved central in explaining the presence in the OMC education of objectives, indicators and benchmarks, and NAPs. First, the reluctance to act on the EU level of member states prevented a different governance mode than the OMC template codified in the Lisbon presidency conclusions from being chosen; the (sectoral) Council considered all other governance modes as too binding (i.e. the Community method or an EES-like OMC). Second, the wish to create a coherent framework on the EU level to discuss solutions to common challenges fosters an interest on the side of the member states to develop the infrastructure of the OMC education. In sum, while member states with an incentive to act pushed the development of the infrastructure of the OMC education forward, other member states were reluctant to act and pulled the more enthusiastic member states back. This push–pull dynamic limits the choice for a governance mode in the education field to the OMC template codified in the Lisbon presidency conclusions, while being a driving force behind the development of objectives, indicators and benchmarks, and reporting via NAPs.

To answer the question 'what we can learn about education policy when analysed from the perspective of political science?', it is insightful to analyse the findings presented in this chapter in light of some of the main European integration theories. First, from the previous section it became clear that the OMC education is viewed by the member states and the Commission as a problem-solving tool, in line with a traditional functionalist account of European integration. However, this has an intergovernmental twist: member states act on the EU level to solve a problem for which an exclusive focus on the national level is not sufficient, but all competences need to remain national. Second, one of the empirical findings for the education case was not accounted for by the approach developed above and hints at the relevance of neofunctionalist theorizing. The active role of the Commission in the development of the OMC education indicates that the conflict between an incentive and reluctance to act on the side of national governments is a necessary but not sufficient condition for the development of the infrastructure of OMCs. A second necessary condition is the identification by the Commission of a need to adopt the OMC. This shows parallels with neofunctionalist reasoning, with the 'high authority' that is appointed to oversee the operations leading to European integration – which is the Commission – as one of the key sponsors of further regional integration (Rosamond 2000: 58). However, instead of aiming for further regional integration, the empirical findings indicate that the Commission plays a catalytic role in the adoption of a full-blown OMC for the education field, without aiming at transferring member state sovereignty with regard to education policy to the EU level.

Besides the usefulness of European integration theories for analysing developments in the education field, it also became clear from the findings presented in this chapter that the choice for an EU policy tool in a policy field that is a core competence of the member states is highly restrictive. A further comparison between policy fields is necessary to assess whether this restriction in the choice for policy tools is also present in other domains that belong to the core competences of nation states. This lesson from the education case for analyses in political science directs our attention to another question: what can the analysis of education policy teach us concerning the transformation of the state?

By opening up to the multilateral surveillance of their national education policies, states allow international organizations such as the EU to become active in a policy field that lies at the core of their sovereignty. However, this change in attitude of states and the resulting choice for a 'new mode of governance' in the education field does not lead to the undermining of internal or external state sovereignty, but – at most – can have consequences for the autonomy of European states vis-à-vis international organizations. As we saw from the case of the EES, the participation of states in the multilateral surveillance of their national policies can occasionally lead to annoyances among the member states over the interference of the European Commission with national affairs, thus restricting the freedom of the state vis-à-vis the EU. In sum, the room to manoeuvre of states is circumscribed even if no formal transfer of sovereign authority occurred (Rosamond 2000: 155). The empirical findings on the OMC education indicate that these restrictions in the autonomy of states are less present for OMCs that are developed on the basis of the Lisbon presidency conclusions. It remains an open question whether these findings are particular to the multilateral surveillance policy tools in function in the EU, or whether similar dynamics also come into play in other international organizations.

Notes

1 The OMC was strongly inspired by the Luxembourg process, designed in 1997 to establish the European Employment Strategy (EES).
2 This table is based on a study of Commission and Council documents published in the period 1999–2007.
3 There are no large differences between member states in the public support for education policy as an exclusively national competence or as a joint competence on the EU level.

References

Agence Europe (1999a) 'On Monday, ministers will hold first exchange of views on implementation of results of Cologne summit and will take stock of situation for Socrates II and Leonardo II', 7479 04/06/1999, Brussels.

—— (1999b) 'Guidelines for Socrates II and Leonardo II programmes, which must be more transparent and simpler – education, essential element in the fight against unemployment', 7481 07/06/1999, Brussels.

—— (2000a) 'President of Education Council, Oliveira Martins sets up European charter on basic skill, that will enable a same language to be spoken in the field of education', 7644 28/01/2000, Brussels.

—— (2000b) 'The three-stage plan proposed by Spain provides for total liberalization of electricity, oil, gas and telecommunications markets and reduction in state aid by 2004', 7662 23/02/2000, Brussels.

—— (2000c) 'Viviane Reding launched an e-learning initiative that emphasises the educational side of the "e-europe" initiative while awaiting Lisbon summit "a helping hand" to push forward issues in this field', 7673 09/03/2000, Brussels.

—— (2000d) 'Introduction of educational dimension in Luxembourg process and importance of lifelong training subjects of broad consensus', 7680 20/03/2000, Brussels.

—— (2000e) 'Ministers to review on Thursday the many challenges facing education in the new information society', 7732 06/06/2000, Brussels.

—— (2000f) 'According to Council president, education must remain Member States responsibility but convergence must be sought in educational policies – results of Council – "European software" for our schools', 7736 13/06/2000, Brussels.

—— (2000g) '12 to 18 June 2000, brief items for which space was lacking in earlier editions', 7740 20/06/2000, Brussels.

—— (2000h) 'Approving "mobility" package, education ministers facilitate and encourage mobility in the young – a "historic symbol" believe Viviane Reding and Jack Lang', 7839 09/11/2000, Brussels.

—— (2001) 'Commission adopts its communication on future objectives for educational systems (to be handed to Stockholm summit)', 7839 31/01/2001, Brussels.

—— (2003a) 'Towards structured dialogue between education council and European social partners', 8396 07/02/2003, Brussels.

—— (2003b) 'Viviane Reding calls for title on "education, training, youth, culture and sport" in future treaty – articles proposed', 8400 13/02/2003, Brussels.

—— (2003c) 'Action against failure at school and investment in human capital – Viviane

Reding welcomes collective awareness of need for Community policy in education',
8593 26/11/2003, Brussels.

—— (2005) 'Jan Figel says that relaunch of Lisbon strategy will require creation of
knowledge-based society', 8890 16/02/2005, Brussels.

Alexiadou, N. (2007) 'The Europeanisation of education policy: researching changing
governance and "new" modes of coordination', *Research in Comparative and International Education*, 2, 2: 102–116.

Carrubba, C.J. (2001) 'The electoral connection in European Union politics', *Journal of
Politics*, 63, 1: 141–158.

Chalmers, D. and Lodge, M. (2003) *The Open Method of Co-ordination and the European Welfare State*, London: London School of Economics and Political Science.

De La Porte, C. (2002) 'Is the Open Method of Coordination appropriate for organising
activities at European level in sensitive policy areas?', *European Law Journal*, 8, 1:
38–58.

De Ruiter, R. (2007) 'To prevent a shift of competences. Developing the Open Method of
Coordination: education, research and development, social inclusion and e-Europe',
unpublished thesis, Florence: European University Institute.

—— (2008) 'Developing multilateral surveillance tools in the EU', *West European Politics*, 31, 5: 896–914.

De Wit, K. (2003) 'The consequences of European integration for higher education',
Higher Education Policy, 16, 2: 161–178.

Dion, D.P. (2005) 'The Lisbon process: a European odyssey', *European Journal of Education*, 40, 3: 295–313.

European Commission (2004) 'Progress towards the common objectives in education and
training: indicators and benchmarks', Brussels.

—— (2005) 'Joint progress report of the Council and the Commission on the implementation of the Education and Training 2010 work programme', Brussels.

—— (2006) 'Operational guide for clusters and Peer Learning Activities (PLAs) in the
context of the Education and Training 2010 work programme', Brussels.

European Commission and European Council (2002) 'Detailed work programme on the
follow-up of the objectives of education and training systems in Europe', Brussels.

European Commission Standing Group on Indicators and Benchmarks (2003) 'Implementation of "Education and Training 2010" work programme. Final list of indicators to
support the implementation of the work programme on the future objectives of the education and training systems', Brussels.

European Council (2000) 'Presidency conclusions Lisbon European Council, 23–24
March', Brussels.

Gornitzka, A. (2005) *Coordinating Policies for a 'Europe of Knowledge'. Emerging
Practices of the 'Open Method of Coordination' in Education and Research*, Centre for
European Studies, University of Oslo, Oslo: ARENA.

Kohler-Koch, B. and Rittberger, B. (2006) 'The "Governance Turn" in EU studies',
Journal of Common Market Studies, 44, s1: 27–49.

Ladrech, R. (2003) 'The Left and the European Union', *Parliamentary Affairs*, 56, 1:
112–124.

Lahav, G. (2004) *Immigration and Politics in the New Europe: Reinventing Borders*,
Cambridge: Cambridge University Press.

Lange, B. and Alexiadou, N. (2007) 'New forms of European Union governance in the
education sector? A preliminary analysis of the Open Method of Coordination', *European Education Research Journal*, 6, 4: 321–335.

Lawn, M. (2003) 'The "usefulness" of learning: the struggle over governance, meaning and the European education space', *Discourse: Studies in the Cultural Politics of Education*, 24, 3: 325–336.

Livingston, K. (2003) 'What is the future for national policy Making in education in the context of an enlarged European Union?', *Policy Futures in Education*, 1, 3: 586–600.

Manza, J. and Cook, F.L. (2002) 'A democratic polity? Three views of policy responsiveness to public opinion in the United States', *American Politics Research*, 30, 6: 630–667.

Martens, Kerstin (2007) 'How to become an influential actor – the "Comparative Turn" in OECD education policy', in K. Martens, A. Rusconi and K. Leuze (eds) *New Arenas of Education Governance – The Impact of International Organisations and Markets on Education Policy Making*, Basingstoke: Palgrave Macmillan, 40–56.

Mitter, W. (2004a) 'Nation-states versus regions in European education', *European Education*, 36, 3: 5–18.

—— (2004b) 'Rise and decline of education systems: a contribution to the history of the modern state', *Compare*, 34, 4: 351–369.

Munk, D. (2003) 'Impact of the European Union on the vocational training system in Germany', *Vocational Training*, 30, 3: 40–52.

Novoa, A. and deJong-Lambert, W. (2003) 'Educating Europe: an analysis of EU educational policies', in D. Phillips and H. Ertl (eds) *Implementing European Union Education and Training Policy*, Dordrecht: Kluwer, 41–72.

Obinger, H., Leibfried, S. and Castles, F.G. (2005) 'Bypasses to a social Europe? Lessons from federal experience', *Journal of European Public Policy*, 12, 3: 545–571.

Radaelli, C.M. (2003) *The Open Method of Coordination: A New Governance Architecture for the European Union?*, Stockholm: Swedish Institute for European Policy Studies.

Rosamond, B. (2000) *Theories of European Integration*, Basingstoke: Palgrave Macmillan.

Schäfer, A (2004) 'Beyond the Community Method: why the Open Method of Coordination was introduced to EU policy-making', *European Integration online Papers*. Online, available at: http://eiop.or.at/eiop/texte/2004–013a.htm (accessed 27 October 2008), p. 8.

—— (2006a) 'A new form of governance? Comparing the Open Method of Co-ordination to multilateral surveillance by the IMF and the OECD', *Journal of European Public Policy*, 13, 1: 70–88.

—— (2006b) 'Resolving deadlock: why international organisations introduce soft law', *European Law Journal*, 12, 2: 194–208.

Scharpf, F.W. (2001) *European Governance: Common Concerns vs. the Challenge of Diversity*, New York: New York University School of Law.

—— (2002) 'The European social model: coping with the challenges of diversity', *Journal of Common Market Studies*, 40, 4: 645–670.

Szyszczak, E. (2006) 'Experimental governance: the Open Method of Coordination', *European Law Journal*, 12, 4: 486–502.

Van der Wende, M. (2000) 'The Bologna Declaration: enhancing the transparency and competitiveness of European higher education', *Higher Education in Europe*, 25, 3: 305–310.

Zeitlin, J. (2005) 'Introduction', in J. Zeitlin, P. Pochet and L. Magnusson (eds) *The Open Method of Co-ordination in Action: The European Employment and Social Inclusion Strategies*, Oxford: Peter Lang, 19–36.

10 International networks in education politics

Alexander-Kenneth Nagel

Introduction

Within the general research on the transformation of the state in political science (Hurrelmann *et al.* 2007) the field of education policy has received attention primarily from the actor-centred perspective of a shift from the state to international organizations. The internationalization of education politics, manifested in the increasing engagement and interference of international organizations, such as the European Union (EU) or the Organization for Economic Co-operation and Development (OECD) (Weymann and Martens 2005), has created an astonishing analytical puzzle because education policy is so closely intertwined with the sovereignty of nation states. After international organizations had been identified as central promoters of the internationalization of education politics, special attention was given to their specific modes of governance (Leuze *et al.* 2007) as well as to the strategic interaction between national and international actors (Martens and Wolf 2008).

I will complement these actor-centred approaches with a more structural view. Focusing on the Bologna Process to create a European Higher Education Area, I will investigate the structures of an international network in education politics. My aim is to propose both the heuristic value of a network perspective on global governance as well as network analysis as a methodological means for making valuable contributions to education politics as an emerging field of study. The Bologna Process is particularly well suited for such an enterprise due to its clear specification in thematic (policy issues) and temporal terms (policy events). Moreover, it is a paradigmatic example of multi-level governance due to its hybrid nature as a forum for intergovernmental interactions between 46 nation states, from Albania to the United Kingdom, and as a platform for interactions between these states and international or supranational organizations, such as the EU Commission or UNESCO.

With reference to the goal set out above, the analytical aim of this chapter is to explore the Bologna Process as an international policy network with regard to several types of relations, which have been specified in some earlier work (Nagel 2006, 2007b). I use network-analytical coefficients to pursue a structural analysis of power, i.e. to identify prominent senders or receivers of material (money), immaterial (information) and symbolical resources (legitimacy) in the network. My general focus of research is to provide a systematic description of the power-setting within the network. The more specific research question is whether there is a more vertical (national–international) or horizontal (public–private) division of power.

The elaboration of this exchange-theoretical concept of power is presented in the following theoretical part, embedded into general considerations about the role networks play in multi-level governance. This section also contains some remarks as to the methods and sources of data used in this chapter. The third and main part exhibits a systematic description of the transaction-, information- and legitimacy-network of the Bologna Process regarding the respective network as a whole, as well as prominent single actors. Concluding in the fourth part, I sum up the main results with regard to the vertical or horizontal fragmentation of power in the network and embed them in the current debate on multi-level and network governance.

Background: a network perspective on education politics

The following theoretical considerations are meant to embed my network approach in a broader framework of international relations theory as well as to elaborate on the relational dimensions, with a particular focus on an exchange-theoretical notion of power in networks.

In international relations, policy networks are primarily discussed in the context of multi-level governance. When international organizations or supranational entities become involved in policy fields which were formerly regarded as national domains (such as education politics), new modes of political communication and decision-making have to be established. The main reason for the involvement of international actors in national issues is their factual potential to promote political developments, such as expert knowledge, by coordination of the stakeholders involved or simply due to their role as external mediators (Martens *et al.* 2004).

In such a multi-level constellation of international organizations (or supranational entities) and national governments the latter are, however, anything but weak or incapable of action. In contrast, national decision-makers may try to instrumentalize the 'transcendent' international sphere to promote their own interests at the domestic level. Moreover, the formal competency of decision-making in most cases thoroughly remains in the hands of national legislative actors, as is certainly the case in the policy field of education. Scholars of multi-level governance suggest that such a fluent setting cannot entirely be grasped by classical concepts of (national) governance. Following Gamble (2004), policy networks therefore are an important means to conceptualize multi-level governance more appropriately.

Besides the vertical structuration of politics, either in the form of sub-nationalization or internationalization, there is a second trend within the transformation of the state which can also well be accounted for by a policy network perspective: the increasing involvement of societal actors into the decision making process (Bache and Flinders 2004: 3). It is exactly this blurring of the public and the private sphere that both network governance as a conceptual tool and network analysis as a method have been designed for. While network analysis has already been successfully applied to national policy domains such as labour (Knoke *et al.* 1996), energy and environment (Laumann and Knoke 1987), a comparable application in a setting of multi-level governance, in this case applied to education policy, is still lacking.

As a matter of fact, the theoretical perspectives on network analysis taken in political sociology and in the study of international relations are quite disparate, especially as to the underlying conception of power and legitimacy. With respect to network governance, scholars of international relations tend to focus on *normative* problems that may be connected with the lack of transparency and democratic legitimacy, as Noelke's qualitative comparative case study on 'The relevance of transnational policy networks' suggests (Noelke 2003). This perspective conceives power and legitimacy as normative concepts based on theories of democracy. In contrast, the network approach in political sociology pursues an *empirical* approach to power and rests on an exchange-theoretical understanding of legitimacy (for a related approach in international relations see Hurrelmann *et al.* 2005: 2).

In political sociology there is a twofold notion of power: *power-networks and power in networks*. According to Knoke *et al.*, power networks are political configurations in which 'the content of relations linking network actors can be interpreted as a power measure' (Knoke *et al.* 1996: 189) while power may also be regarded as a 'latent dimension of all networks or at least of those with asymmetric or directed relations' (Knoke *et al.* 1996: 190). In the first case, the ties between two actors are meant to represent *explicit* power relations, such as formal mandates and directives. I concentrate on power as a *latent* dimension of networks represented in the flow of resources (ties) between actors (nodes). As to the nodes, I focus on corporate actors of public and private as well as national and international provenience. As to the ties I present three networks of resource exchange: information, transaction and legitimacy. All networks are asymmetric, directed and weighted.[1] The information-network of the Bologna Process is based on flows of knowledge and expertise objectivated in studies, reports or surveys. The transaction-network covers flows of money and services with an obvious monetary value (e.g. certain forms of technical assistance). Finally, the legitimacy-network reflects transfers of legitimacy in two dimensions: legitimizing speech acts, such as statements of programmatic affirmation or promises of support and the formal inclusion into a given institution, such as granting membership to the Bologna Process.

The selection of these networks is not arbitrary, but guided both empirically (Nagel 2006: 106–114) and theoretically (Knoke and Kuklinski 1982; Knoke *et al.* 1996). Along with different modes of governance it may well be assumed that different 'forums' of a decision-making process involve different resources or 'currencies'. These resources, be they tangible or non-tangible, may have an influence on the way power is stratified in the policy network. The categorization of the relational content rests on recent theories of 'neocapital', that is an integrated approach regarding both tangible and non-tangible forms of capital (Storberg 2002). Here, relations of information and transaction are related to Bourdieu's notion of (objectivated) cultural and economic capital (Bourdieu 1986) whereas legitimacy as a network resource refers to his concept of symbolic capital (Bourdieu 1984) in its first dimension of legitimizing speech acts. The second dimension of legitimacy as a resource in policy networks (institutional access) is based on Esser's understanding of institutional capital as the 'cooperative outcomes of a successful institutionalization' (Esser 2000: 232, author's translation).

If power is conceived to be an implicit dimension in networks of information, transaction and legitimacy, it becomes a function of an actor's management of these resources and thus a question of exchange-theory (Coleman 1974; Esser 2000). For an empirical evaluation of powerful actors in these networks there are two contesting perceptions as to the relation between actors and resources: from a *classical Weberian* perspective an actor can be called powerful if he manages to prompt other actors to act in his own favour (Weber 2002: 711). In connection with an exchange-theoretical perspective an actor within a policy network would therefore strive to accumulate material and immaterial resources from other actors. Consequently, those actors would be regarded as powerful, who manage to give little (low outdegree) and to gain much (high indegree). From a *neo-institutionalist* point of view, however, an organizational field is structured by those actors who posses scarce resources sought for by other actors, or: 'The greater the centralization of organization A's resource supply, the greater the extent to which organization A will change isomorphically to resemble the organizations on which it depends for resources' (DiMaggio and Powell 1991: 74). The tension between 'to have' and 'want to have' thus forces marginal actors to conform to the holders of scarce resources (coercive isomorphism). In this sense an actor would be regarded as powerful who manages to (be able to) give much (high outdegree) and to (have to) receive little (low indegree). In the following investigation I apply the latter understanding, as the limitation to three types of resources in the policy network makes it difficult to assess whether a prominent receiver has or has not given anything in return that cannot be grasped by information, money or legitimacy.

The evidence I present rests on a network analysis of content-analytical relational data. The principal sources of data are therefore policy documents connected to the Bologna Process. The content-analytical collection of network data combines advantages of both analytical strategies: content analysis is non-reactive and allows an *ex post* extrapolation of change, network analysis is apt to cover the inherent complexity of international political processes with respect to the variety of actors, national and international, public and private. Altogether, a set of N=291 documents with 3,929 pages has been coded for actors and relations, which covers the years 1997–2006. A deeper insight to my coding procedure and sampling issues as well as to methodological questions can be gained from Nagel (2008).

Findings: a double hybrid setting

Having originally started as an intergovernmental initiative, interactions within the Bologna Process should mainly be accounted for by ministers or ministerial representatives. Yet, empirically there is a considerable variation in the actor-set. As I showed in an earlier analysis of the participation lists of the Bologna follow-up conferences in Berlin (2003) and in Bergen (2005), there are also representatives of national rectors' conferences, student unions or single universities (Nagel 2006: 2–3). At the conference in Berlin, one-third of all delegations consisted of three or more different types of actors while at the Bergen conference 87 per cent of the delegations were in this sense heterogeneous.

Table 10.1 displays the share of actors over all networks (information, transaction and legitimacy) with regard to their total network degree. The degree of an actor is a basic measure in network analysis and calculated as the sum of all its ties, which means the sum of all its relations, be they incoming or outgoing (Brinkmeier and Schank 2005: 294). In the right column the share of an actor in all dyads (N = 2,104) is presented as a measure for its overall prevalence in the actor-set.

Unsurprisingly, the – what I call – 'Bologna actors' prove most present, being either sender or receiver in more than one-fifth of all dyads. This category comprises core actors of the Bologna Process, such as the Follow-up Group, Board and Secretariat.[2] An interesting result with regard to the intergovernmental nature of the process is the equally high prevalence of supranational administrative actors (such as the European Commission) and national or regional actors (such as ministers or ministerial representatives) each of whom forms part in at least one out of eight dyads. This evidence may well be interpreted in the sense of a structural Europeanization of the Bologna Process. However, the high prev-

Table 10.1 Prevalence of actors

Actor	Share
Bologna actors (BOL)	0.22
Supranational administrative actors (EU-ADMIN)	0.14
National and regional actors (NAT)	0.14
University interest representation (UNI)	0.11
Accreditation agencies (ACR)	0.09
International organizations (IOS)	0.07
Expert networks (EXP)	0.06
Student interest representation (STU)	0.05
Supranational political actors (EU-POL)	0.04
Third countries (NA3)	0.03
Labor unions (LAB)	0.03
Trade associations (TRA)	0.02
Professional bodies (PRO)	0.01
Total (N = 2,104)	1.00

alence of both national (NAT) and intergovernmental actors (BOL) alludes to a rather hybrid setting on the vertical (territorial) axis. Among the special interest groups, universities as represented by the European University Association (EUA) prove to be most prominent as they are senders or receivers in almost one out of ten transactions of information, money or legitimacy. Similarly, Accreditations Agencies as organized in the European Association for Quality Assurance in Higher Education (ENQA) make up 9 per cent of all dyads, which underlines the importance of quality assurance as a central policy issue and challenge within the Bologna Process. To make the multi-level setting even more complex, international organizations, such as the United Nations Educational, Scientific and Cultural Organization (UNESCO) and OECD are half as prevalent as national and supranational actors. In contrast, expert networks, such as the Information Network on Education in Europe (Eurydice), and students' interest representation such as The National Unions of Students in Europe (ESIB), prove to be less prevalent than expected: the relatively low prevalence of expert networks is not consistent with the theorem of epistemic communities forming an integral part in international policy-making (Haas 1992), whereas the low prevalence of student unions is not in line with the political claim to further involve students as major stakeholders in the Bologna Process heard at least since the Prague Conference in 2001. Supranational political actors as a category mainly refer to the European Council, whereas third countries are a residual category for national states that are not yet part of the EU. In the actor-set both are of rather marginal relevance. The same refers to corporate societal actors, such as Labour and Trade Unions (e.g. the European Trade Union Committee for Education (ETUCE) and the Union of Industrial and Employers' Confederation of Europe (UNICE) on the European level) and professional bodies, such as the European Society for Engineering Education (SEFI). Despite the large variety of different organizations in this segment their overall share is surprisingly small. It would, however, be too early to generalize this evidence in the sense of a stronger vertical than horizontal structuration in the Bologna Process as these actors may play a particular role that is not very well grasped by relations of information, transaction or legitimacy. In the following sub-sections the single networks are presented in more detail.

Information network – structures and actors

Figure 10.1 shows the network of *information-flows* in the Bologna Process. The actors are represented by nodes, while the relations are represented by lines, the direction of which is marked by an arrow. At first glance, the network seems to be quite loosely coupled and there is neither an outstanding actor (a formation ideal typically labeled as 'star' (Jansen 2003: 130)), nor a completely symmetric structure of exchange ('ring'). In extension of the so-called 'double star' model (Jansen 2003: 130) the configuration may rather be characterized as a poly-star. These structural features are also represented by established coefficients. The density Δ of a network is defined as the share of the factual in all possible

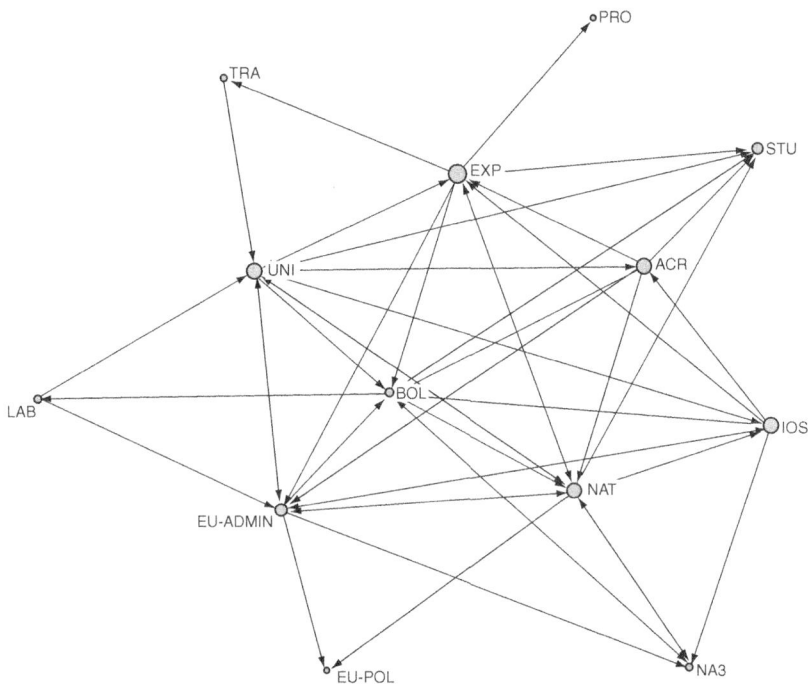

Figure 10.1 Information network.

relations (Kosub 2005). The first impression of a loose coupling is mirrored by a relatively low density of 0.269.[3] Depending on the symmetry or asymmetry of the network, different measures of centralization can be applied. These measures differ with reference to the underlying formal concept of a central actor. Here, I operationalize the above made reflections on exchange and power by calculating the so-called outdegree-centralization of the network. The outdegree *od* of an actor is defined as the sum of all outgoing relations (here: the provision of information). The outdegree-centralization of a network will therefore be higher, the bigger the difference between all actors with regard to their outdegree is. In the information network the prima facie notion of its polyarchic structure is reflected in a medium centralization of 0.373. Thus, there is quite some asymmetry, but the network is far from being monocratic. Instead there are several prominent senders of information that are interlinked with each other and additionally serving some clients at the margin.

For further insights into the latent power structure, the degree-centrality can be calculated for each actor with regard to both incoming (indegree) and outgoing (outdegree) information flows.

Table 10.2 specifies the in- and outdegree for each actor as well as the respective balance of these degrees (the three highest values in each row have been

Table 10.2 Information actor centrality

Actor	ACR	EU-ADMIN	EXP	BOL	UNI	NAT	IOS	STU	NA3	LAB	TRA	PRO	EU-POL
Indegree (*id*)	3	26	2	152	36	102	4	5	11	2	1	1	34
Outdegree (*od*)	86	61	54	52	38	29	28	17	11	2	1	0	0
Balance bl=*id-od*	-83	-35	-52	100	-2	73	-24	-12	0	0	0	1	34

marked). According to the concept of power outlined above, a corporate actor is regarded powerful if it manages to (be able to) give a lot and to (have to) gain little information. Here, Accreditation Agencies (above all ENQA) appear to be the biggest *net-sender* as they exhibit a balance of –83. Similar evidence can be given for expert networks (–52) and supranational administrative actors (–35). The most prominent *net-receivers* of information are Bologna actors (100), as well as national and regional actors (73). The emerging pattern of information exchange is clearly marked by the multi-level setting, that is the fragmented or hybrid nature of the Bologna Process on the vertical (territorial) axis. All net-senders of information can be attributed to the supranational level: as an umbrella organization for national accreditation agencies ENQA has taken on many surveys and reporting activities in the Bologna Process and collaborates closely with the EU Commission. Most of the expert networks are also international in style or directly affiliated with the supranational administration, such as Eurydice. In contrast, the net-receivers are situated either on the intergovernmental (BOL) or national (NAT) level.[4] With regard to the latent power setting in the network of information, we can thus account for a structural dominance of supranational actors.

Transaction network – structures and actors

If the information network was loosely coupled, the network of *monetary transactions* seems to be even more so, as a first look at Figure 10.2 shows. This observation is confirmed by a low density of 0.1978. On the other hand the

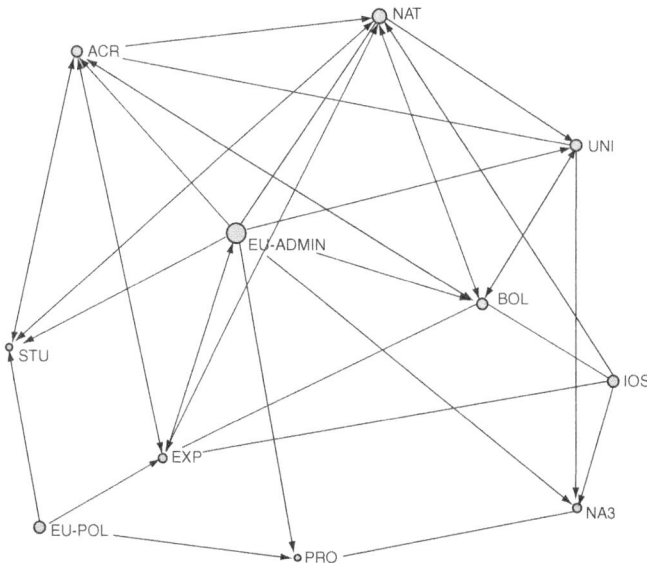

Figure 10.2 Transaction network.

Table 10.3 Transaction actor centrality

Actor	ACR	EU-ADMIN	EXP	BOL	UNI	NAT	IOS	STU	NA3	LAB	TRA	PRO	EU-POL
Indegree	42	4	43	47	70	16	0	15	19	0	0	4	0
Outdegree	4	147	2	9	11	52	32	1	1	0	0	0	4
Balance	38	−143	41	38	59	−36	−32	14	18	0	0	4	−4

network appears to be more clearly structured as far as prominent senders and receivers of monetary flows are concerned. In fact, the outdegree-centralization (0.532) proves to be significantly higher than in the network of information while at the same time the indegree-centralization turns out to be lower (0.284). Thus, the structural asymmetry in the network of transaction is larger among the senders than among the receivers or, to put it straight, the needy are more equal than the big spenders. Yet, despite its more centralized nature, the network is far from being strongly hierarchical. Without being as polycentric as the information network, the monetary flows in the Bologna Process might rather be labelled 'aristocratic' with supranational administrative bodies as the sovereign and some other corporative actors as its vessels.

Table 10.3 presents the in- and outdegrees of all actors in the transaction networks as well as the balance between the two. Again, an actor is regarded powerful if it manages to (be able to) provide a lot of money and technical assistance of monetary value and at the same time manages to (have to) receive little. In this sense, supranational administrative actors prove to be the most powerful actors in the network of transaction (–143). This result is perfectly in line with earlier observations of the European Commission being like the literal 'spider in its web' (Nagel 2008). Other less salient net-senders are the nation states (–36) and international organizations (–32), whereas the former rather provide cash and the latter technical assistance. The most prevalent net-receivers are universities (59) and expert networks (41), which reflects the decentralized implementation of the Bologna reforms with additional funds being allocated to the university level to create coordinative positions and increase performance of accompanying research. After all there is one big cluster of state actors (EU-ADMIN, NAT) who provide the money and another big cluster of hybrid performers (UNI, EXP, BOL, ACR) who take care of monitoring and implementation.[5] Thus, there is more of a structuration on the horizontal (public–private) axis than on the vertical one.

Legitimacy network – structures and actors

Figure 10.3 provides visual evidence of flows of *symbolical and institutional* capital in the Bologna Process. The first impression is that there is no convincing *prima facie* observation except that this network comprises many more interactions than the former, which is reflected in a high density of 0.637. At the same time, there are hardly any systematic asymmetries to be seen. Instead, the network appears like a diffuse ball of wool. Yet, centralization measures speak a different language: while the outdegree-centralization (0.391) is bigger than in the network of information, the indegree-centralization is considerably lower (0.225). Thus, the legitimacy network is complementary to the network of transaction with regard to its structural nature: the former is (rather) dense and non-hierarchical while the latter is (rather) loosely coupled and hierarchical. As the image provides no insights into the prevalence of single actors, again, actor-based centrality measures have to be consulted (Table 10.4).

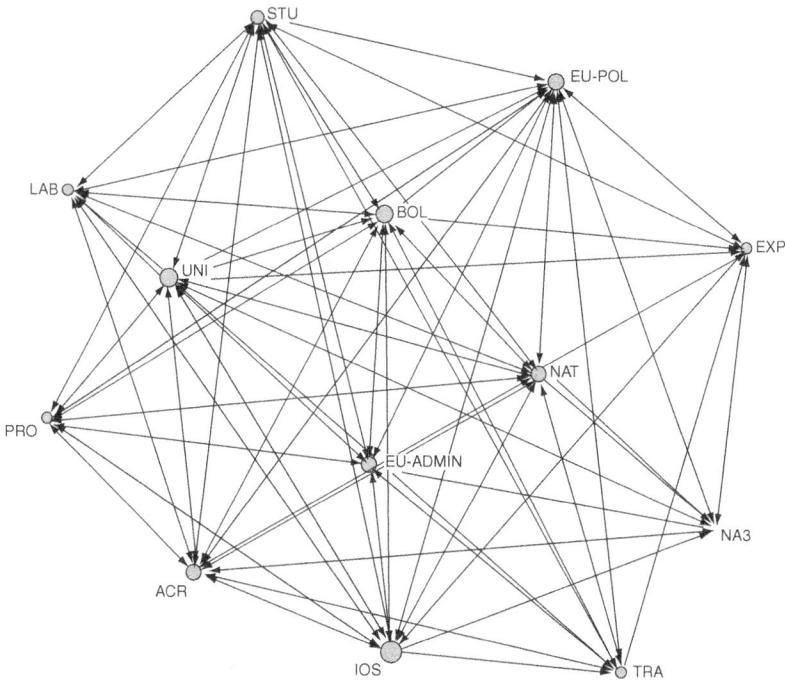

Figure 10.3 Legitimacy network.

Table 10.4 comes up with the weighted in- and outdegrees of all actors in the legitimacy network and with their respective balance. It has to be mentioned, though, that for symbolical resources the power-hypothesis 'being a big net-sender reflects a position of power' may be less appropriate. Nevertheless the most prominent absolute senders of symbolical and institutional capital coincide with the most prominent net-senders: similar to the transaction-network there is one salient type actor, Bologna core actors (–285), followed by universities (–13) and national states (–6). In contrast to the other networks studied, however, two of the main senders are also among the main receivers: national states (113) and universities (92).[6] The high net-outdegree of Bologna actors is due to their mediating role that implies both announcing and granting membership (institutional capital) and encouraging all stakeholders to continue their efforts by means of affirmative statements (symbolical capital).

Surprisingly, there is no systematic variation on the vertical axis. In line with theories of democratic deficits on the supra- and international level (Grunauer 2002) EU actors and international organizations should have turned out as prominent net-receivers of legitimacy while national public actors and/or societal actors should have appeared as prominent net-senders of legitimacy (Nagel 2007a). As a matter of fact, EU actors *are* the most prominent receivers

Table 10.4 Legitimacy actor centrality

Actor	ACR	EU-ADMIN	EXP	BOL	UNI	NAT	IOS	STU	NA3	LAB	TRA	PRO	EU-POL
Indegree	64	100	74	54	92	113	82	79	39	42	48	13	35
Outdegree	56	74	14	339	105	119	37	23	0	23	7	16	25
Balance	8	26	60	−285	−13	−6	45	56	39	19	41	−3	10

Table 10.5 Multi-level legitimacy transfers – partial matrix

Sender	Receiver			
	EU-ADMIN	NAT	UNI	Od
EU-ADMIN	0	3	3	6
NAT	7	0	17	24
UNI	25	11	0	36
Id	32	14	20	N = 66

(id = 100 + 35). Yet national (NAT) and local bodies (UNI) themselves appear to be processors rather than producers of legitimizing speech acts. Unlike monetary transactions and more than the transfer of information legitimacy, relations obviously are not a simple zero-sum game. From the perspective of multi-level governance the triadic relationship between supranational administrative actors, national actors and local interests represented by the universities deserves special attention. The resulting matrix as well as in- and outdegrees are presented in Table 10.5.

In contrast to the tables above Table 10.5 does not only show the degrees, but the whole matrix of the legitimacy triad. Thus, the most prevalent single relation consisted of legitimizing speech acts from the representation of university interests towards supranational administrative actors (25).[7] If the balance of in- and outdegree is calculated for each actor ($bl = id–od$) actors representing university interests appear to be the most prominent net-sender (–16) followed by national actors (–10), and in contrast to supranational actors (26). From this perspective there is a clear tendency with regard to a bottom-up supply of legitimacy in the multi-level setting of the Bologna Process. While some systematic variation on the vertical axis can be extrapolated in the legitimacy network by such means, the impression with regard to the horizontal axis (public–private) remains inconsistent.

A structural comparison

Some of the network-analytical measures used above yield more insights when put in a comparative perspective. Table 10.6 provides a synopsis of these mea-

Table 10.6 Measurements from a comparative perspective

	Information	Transaction	Legitimacy
Density (Δ)	0.2692	0.1978	0.6374
Structuration	Vertical	Horizontal	Vertical
Centralization (od)	37.278%	53.254%	39.053%
Centralization (id)	37.278%	28.402%	22.485%
NCI (betweenness)	18.72%	9.66%	8.07%

sures and illustrates differences and commonalities between networks of information, transaction and legitimacy.

As to the *density* it shows that the information- and transaction-network of the Bologna Process are far more loosely coupled than the network of legitimacy. The prevalence of symbolical capital over cultural and economical capital is certainly due to the double hybrid position of the Bologna Process itself as well as to the nature of data studied, that is political communication: having started as an intergovernmental process, the transnational network beyond the agenda for a European Higher Education Area has become betwixt and between supranational, national and local as well as public, semi-public (e.g. accreditation agencies) and private interests. In this precarious setting political decision-making is marked by symbolic interaction rather than material transaction or technical assistance. The transnational education policy network of the Bologna Process is in a situation of brokerage between the national 'cannot', a lack of appropriate governance capacities, and the supranational 'must not', a lack of formal decision-making competency.

Yet, the shadow of hierarchy is reflected in the structural patterns of *structuration* and centralization: an analysis of central and peripheral actors provides evidence for a vertical structuration in the networks of information and legitimacy and for a horizontal structuration in the network of monetary transaction. While there is an unequal distribution of non-tangible resources between local, national and supranational actors, there is a disparity between the public and the private sphere with respect to economic capital: in the network of information supranational actors have proved to be the most prominent senders whereas intergovernmental and national actors appeared to be the most prominent receivers. In the legitimacy network there was a complementary situation with the local, national and intergovernmental level being important senders and supranational actors being important receivers. In contrast, the transaction network was not structured along the territorial axis at all, but brought to light a cluster of state or state-like actors (supranational and national) as prominent senders and a cluster of societal actors as prominent receivers. These findings suggest that when it comes to budgetary responsibility, national and supranational bureaucracies as public actors form part of an 'Internationale' of hierarchy. *Outdegree-centralization* points to a similar direction. The measure reflects the relation between the most important sender of information, money or legitimacy and all other senders, i.e. the concentration of power in an exchange-theoretical sense (Jansen 2003: 138). As Table 10.6 shows, the outdegree-centralization of the transaction network is distinctly higher than of the two other networks. Thus, when it comes to money, polyarchy turns into oligarchy, which alludes to a connection between the tangibility of resources and the structures of exchange. When, in complement, the *indegree-centralization* is calculated, the network of information proves to be significantly more centralized than both the transaction and the legitimacy network. Thus, for knowledge and expertise the concentration of receivers is relatively higher than for economic capital and legitimizing speech acts. The latter networks are more centralized with regard to the senders than to the receivers as indicated in Table 10.6.

Thus, different to the network of information, the transfer of economic and symbolical capital is bound to one important sender whereas the concentration of receivers is considerably less prevalent, which alludes to these resources being more monopolized than cultural capital, that is, information. If, however, a less monocratic concept of power concentration is applied, there appears to be a meta-power structure in the network of information. The Network Centralization Index is calculated on the basis of the so-called *betweenness-centrality*. Here, an actor is regarded central not in terms of its mere number of ties to other actors, but with regard to its taking a mediating role between two other actors. As the last column of Table 10.6 reveals, betweenness-centralization is distinctly higher in the information-network. Therefore, although the networks of transaction and legitimacy are more clearly structured in a sense of power being based on (the capacity of) resource provision, the information network of the Bologna Process exhibits a higher concentration of brokerage positions in a sense of power being based on the capacity to bridge structural holes.

Conclusions

The aim of this chapter was to explore the transnational network of the Bologna Process for a Higher European Education Area as an example of a double hybrid multi-level setting in international policy-making. Particular attention was paid to the identification of powerful actors, with the notion of power being an empirical rather than a normative one. Following exchange-theoretical assumptions from sociological institutionalism, a corporate actor was regarded powerful if it can provide scarce resources desired by others and may thus cause coercive isomorphism (DiMaggio and Powell 1991). Based on considerations about both tangible and non-tangible resources underlying political processes, the policy network of the Bologna Process has been examined in three dimensions: information, transaction and legitimacy.

Unsurprisingly, there was no consistent picture as to the involvement of local, national and supranational or public, semi-public and private actors. As a matter of fact, the network of information proved to be structured along the territorial axis rather than horizontally. A similar observation could be made for the legitimacy network, whereas the network of monetary transaction revealed a public–private divide that bridged the territorial provenience. Thus, as a first result, processes of internationalization or privatization are by no means 'absolute', but connected to the character of resource, which is at stake in the decision-making process. Here, supra- and international actors are in an advantageous situation to produce, collect and spread *information*, which becomes eminently political when put into a comparative context as several trends and progress reports on the implementation of the Bologna Process (as well as the PISA indicator programme of the OECD) demonstrate. When it comes to the delegation of *legitimacy*, in contrast, local and national actors assign parts of their democratic mandate to some intergovernmental core actors of the Bologna Process. These 'Bologna actors' may now confer – or refuse – legitimacy, for example by means of programmatic affirmation or granting membership, which is in line with the debate on democratic deficits in international policy-making. In the network of transaction, finally, the European Commission proves to be the literal spider in the web as it is by far the most prominent net-sender of money and technical assistance. Therefore, economic capital is considerably more concentrated and the power structure is oligarchic rather than polyarchic.

Finally, what lesson can be learned for the study of multi-level figurations in education politics and for the study of multi-level governance in general? The dense network of legitimacy suggests that education policy-making is still a national issue, which is solved by the delegation of legitimacy to a transnational entity, the core actors of the Bologna Process. While nation states are obviously reluctant to cut the cord with respect to symbolical capital they seem to be quite willing to externalize costs and consult exterior expertise. Thus, the multi-level figuration of the Bologna Process reflects neither an expropriation of the national sphere nor any resorption of the process back into national sovereignty, but rather a sophisticated division of labour between national and supranational, public and societal actors. For a general perspective of multi-level governance the chapter demonstrated that both the conceptualization of politics as networks of resource exchange and their network-analytical description can yield detailed insights as to the complex structural grounding of political processes, which are fragmented in a vertical (territorial) as well as in a horizontal way (public–private divide). After all, the Bologna Process for a European Higher Education Area provides an example of a *double hybrid* setting and thus, as it were, for *poly-multi-level* governance.

Notes

1 For example, actor A may supply information, money or legitimacy to actor B who need not give him any of these in return.
2 For further information about the coding procedure and specification of categories see Nagel (2008, 2006).
3 Network density ranges from 0 to 1. If network density is 1 all actors are respectively interconnected, i.e. there are no structural holes. With reference to international policy networks where actors are generally more disparate, a network with a density of 0.3 or lower can be called loosely coupled, while a density between 0.4 and 0.6 is already considerable and a value above 0.7 yields to considerable cohesion and institutionalization.
4 Degrees can also be calculated with non-weighted (dichotomized) data to minimize biases of intentionality or hyperprevalence in political communication. Such a procedure leads to similar results with slight shifts in the order of actors, but without any revision of the general pattern.
5 If degrees are calculated with non-weighted data professional bodies and student unions appear to be 'hybrid performers' as well whereas universities appear to be less important as a net-sender. These results underline the interpretation of a public–private divide in the transaction network.
6 If the degrees are calculated with non-weighted (dichotomized) data, the quantitative differences are diminished without major changes in the general pattern. One important difference is, however, that students become more visible as important net-senders of

legitimacy, a result that is disguised by a hyperprevalence-bias of the big players when using weighted data.
7 The kind of statements behind this number may be illustrated as follows: 'Our institutions fully embrace the view expressed in the EU Commission memorandum on Lifelong Learning' (EURASHE 2002: 2).

References

Bache, I. and Flinders, M. (2004) 'Themes and issues in multi-level governance', in I. Bache and M. Flinders (eds) *Multi-Level Governance*, Oxford: Oxford University Press, 1–11.
Bourdieu, P. (1984) *Distinction*, London: Routledge.
—— (1986) 'The forms of capital', in J.G. Richardson (ed.) *Handbook of Theory and Research for the Sociology of Education*, New York: Greenwood, 241–258.
Brinkmeier, M. and Schank, T. (2005) 'Network statistics', in U. Brandes and T. Erlebach (eds) *Network Analysis. Methodological Foundations*, Berlin: Springer, 293–317.
Coleman, J. (1974) *Power and the Structure of Society*, New York: Norton.
DiMaggio, P.J. and Powell, W.W. (1991) 'The iron cage revisited: institutional isomorphism and collective rationality', in P.J. DiMaggio and W.W. Powell (eds) *The New Institutionalism in Organizational Analysis*, Chicago: Chicago University Press, 63–82.
Esser, H. (2000) *Opportunitäten und Restriktionen*, Frankfurt am Main: Campus.
EURASHE (2002) *EURASHE Policy Statement on the Bologna-Prague-Berlin Process*, Galway. Online, available at: www.bologna-berlin2003.de/pdf/Eurashe_Policy_Statement_Declaration.pdf (accessed 25 October 2008).
Gamble, A. (2004) 'Foreword', in I. Bache and M. Flinders (eds) *Multi-Level Governance*, Oxford: Oxford University Press, v–vii.
Grunauer, A. (2002) *Demokratie und Legitimation – Die Achillesferse der europäischen Union. Eine Studie zum Europäischen Parlament*, PhD Dissertation, Zürich: Universität Zürich.
Haas, P.M. (ed.) (1992) *Knowledge, Power, and International Policy Coordination*, Cambridge: MIT Press.
Hurrelmann, A., Krell-Laluhová, Z. and Schneider, St. (2005) *Mapping Legitimacy Discourses in Democratic Nation States: Great Britain, Switzerland, and the Unites States Compared*, Bremen: Sonderforschungsbereich 597 'Staatlichkeit im Wandel', Universität Bremen.
Hurrelmann, A., Leibfried, St., Martens, K. and Mayer, P. (2007) 'Transformation of the Golden-Age state: findings and perspectives', in A. Hurrelmann, Sr. Leibfried, K. Martens and P. Mayer (eds) *Transforming the Golden-Age Nation State*, Houndmills: Palgrave, 193–204.
Jansen, D. (2003) *Einführung in die Netzwerkanalyse*, Opladen: Leske & Budrich.
Knoke, D. and Kuklinski, J. (1982) *Network Analysis*, Beverly Hills: Sage.
Knoke, D., Pappi, F., Broadbent, J. and Tsujinaka, Y. (1996) *Comparing Policy Networks. Labor Politics in the U.S., Germany, and Japan*, Cambridge: Cambridge University Press.
Kosub, S. (2005) 'Local density', in U. Brandes and T. Erlebach (eds) *Network Analysis. Methodological Foundations*, Berlin: Springer, 112–142.
Laumann, E.O. and Knoke, D. (1987) *The Organizational State. Social Change in National Policy Domains*, Madison: Wisconsin University Press.

Leuze, K., Martens, K. and Rusconi, A. (2007) 'New arenas in education governance – the impact of international organizations and markets on education policy making', in K. Martens, A. Rusconi and K. Leuze (eds) *New Arenas of Education Governance – The Impact of International Organizations and Markets on Educational Policy Making*, Houndmills: Palgrave, 3–15.

Martens, K. and Wolf, K.D. (2008) 'Boomerangs and Trojan horses – the unintended consequences of internationalizing education policy through the EU and the OECD', in P. Massen, A. Gornitzka, A. Amaral and C. Musslin (eds) *European Integration and the Governance of Higher Education and Research – The Challenges and Complexities of an Emerging Multi-level Governance System*, Berlin: Springer.

Martens, K., Balzer, C., Sackmann, R. and Wexmann, A. (2004) *Comparing Governance of International Organisations – The EU, the OECD and Educational Policy*, Bremen: Sonderforschungsbereich 597 'Staatlichkeit im Wandel', Universität Bremen.

Nagel, A.-K. (2006) *Der Bologna-Prozess als Politiknetzwerk. Akteure, Beziehungen, Perspektiven*, Wiesbaden: DUV.

—— (2007a) *Analysing Change in Transnational Policy Networks. Legitimacy-transfers in the Bologna Process*, Bremen: Sonderforschungsbereich 597 'Staatlichkeit im Wandel', Universität Bremen.

—— (2007b) *Network-Governance in European Education Policy – Actors, Relations and Perspectives in the Bologna-Process*. Online, available at: http://keelingruth.googlepages.com/onlineworkingpapers (accessed 25 October 2008).

—— (2008) *Towards a Semiotic Method of Structural Connotation*, Bremen: Sonderforschungsbereich 597 'Staatlichkeit im Wandel', Universität Bremen.

Noelke, A. (2003) 'The relevance of transnational policy networks: some examples from the European Commission and the Bretton Woods institution', *Journal of International Relations and Development*, 6, 3: 276–298.

Storberg, J. (2002) 'The evolution of capital theory: a critique of a theory of social capital and implications for HRD', *Human Resources Development Review*, 1, 4: 468–499.

Weber, M. (2002) 'Soziologische Grundbegriffe', in D. Kaesler (ed.) *Schriften 1894–1922. Ausgewählt von Dirk Kaesler*, Stuttgart: Kröner, 653–716.

Weymann, A. and Martens, K. (2005) 'Bildungspolitik durch internationale Organisationen – Entwicklung, Strategien und Bedeutung der OECD', *Österreichische Zeitschrift für Soziologie*, 30, 4: 68–86.

Part IV

Meta-reflections on education and political science

Where to go and for whose good?

Normative dimensions of reforms
in higher education

Klaus Dieter Wolf

Introduction

The Bologna Process is too complex and too challenging for political science to leave it only to policy researchers. There was more at stake in the Europeanization of higher education policy than policy itself; Bologna is also about actors' strategies to strengthen their power and competencies in the field of higher education. Policy-oriented governance studies often miss this power dimension. Rather than analyzing and evaluating the reform of higher education in its policy dimension, I will question the supposed 'naturalness' of such an approach by identifying it as one of two general paradigmatic perspectives with which political science can take on the concept of reform: one represented by the mainstream of policy analysis, the other one based on normative political theory. Only by taking into account both approaches can we properly analyze the reform of higher education in Europe as part of a more comprehensive reform project which is characterized by a fundamental shift from appropriateness criteria of normative political theory to those of mainstream policy analysis in the political as well as the academic discourse. My conceptual approach (the second section) combines:

1   the perspectives of policy analysis and normative political theory, with:
2   first-order, second-order and meta-governing as three different levels of reform.

Embedded in this framework, the German case in the third section will illustrate the analytical value added by applying the perspective of normative political theory to the Bologna Process. From this perspective reform is primarily evaluated in terms of the democratic legitimacy of the reform process itself and of the (re-)distribution of power resulting from it, i.e. in terms of normative criteria which seem to have disappeared from the current academic and political reform discourse which evaluates the quality and success of reform solely by the effectiveness of its contributions to sectoral problem-solving.

How to evaluate a political reform process

If only result-oriented output or effectiveness criteria were applied to evaluating the Bologna Process, other important dimensions would disappear from the screen. Among these, the politics behind the Europeanization of educational reform deserve particular attention. National governments did not turn to the European level in a joint effort to search for better programs in education policy. Rather, it was in their strategic interest to use the intergovernmental policy arena to outmaneuver domestic opposition to educational policy goals which they already had on their list, but for which they did not have domestic support or the necessary legal competence (see Martens and Wolf 2008). Evaluation criteria for the Bologna reforms should relate to both dimensions – the programmatic one concerned with reforming the substance of education *policy*, and the strategic dimension concerned with the power and interests expressed in the *politics* involved.

By distinguishing between first-order, second-order and third-order or 'meta'-governing, Jan Kooiman (2000: 154–161; see also Chapter 1, this volume) offers a conceptual framework for the study of reform processes at three different layers of reform which are of equal significance for an evaluation of the Bologna Process: the generation and implementation of new and 'better' educational policies (first-order governing), the re-distribution of institutional competencies (second-order governing) in order to create favorable structural conditions for the introduction of such new educational policies; and the re-framing of the standards of appropriateness by which these policies can be measured (meta-governing). This typology also allows us to evaluate the policy, politics as well as polity aspects of reforms in higher education. However, its analytical potential cannot be exhausted by merely filling it with the evaluation criteria that can be derived from mainstream policy analysis which, at least in the German debate, is overly preoccupied with the outputs of concrete reform policies while neglecting the input (participation) and throughput (transparency and accountability) dimensions of reform processes which become more important the higher we climb up the analytical ladder from first-order to meta-governing.

In search of normative criteria for the evaluation of reform processes

A critical self-reflection of the current output-oriented 'framing' of the reform concept in political science reveals a paradigmatic shift from normative political theory to a *policy*-oriented perspective, which is also indicative of a creeping change in our discipline. This shift of research interests away from the normative foundations of traditional political science as a 'science of democracy' has marginalized the former in-house provider of belief systems: normative political theory. When dealing with 'modern governance' (Kooiman 1993), mainstream political science seems to have lost interest in matters of participation, self-determination, or the checks and balances to control political power in the public interest. The democratic quality of the political system is taken for granted.

Therefore, the focus is on goal attainment rather than on the democratic legitimacy of reform processes and their results.

This shift reveals the existence of two different approaches within the theoretical debates about reform which do not only differ with regard to what they mean by reform and how to evaluate it, but also in their basic understanding of political science and politics as such: is it about exerting power, or is it about solving problems? When political science turned into the 'science of political steering' or, more recently, the new 'governance science' (see Mayntz 1996, 2006), its original interest, rooted in normative political theory, in the impact of reform measures on the distribution of political power relations and the democratic quality *of* the political system gave way to a new 'technical' understanding of reform (Glotz and Schultze 2005: 836). From this new and still prevailing perspective, the same changes nowadays appear as a re-arrangement of actor constellations which become interesting because they affect problem-solving capabilities *within* the political system. This new focus is generally perceived – and perceives itself – as being far less value-loaded. Reforms are measures for improving the quality of the practical day-to-day results of the political process. This shift of perspective is of crucial importance for reflections about normative demands on the appropriateness of how reforms should take place, which goals they should have, and how their success should be measured.

Return to normative.

The perspective of normative political theory on reform: democratic legitimacy

Since the nineteenth century and until the 1970s 'reform or revolution' has always been the terminological dichotomy with reference to which the meaning of reform was defined (see Greiffenhagen 1978: 8; Krockow 1976: 82). In this context reform was characterized as a change of the present shape of the political order *within* the rules prescribed by this very order. Obviously not just any change could count as a reform, rather only structural changes of existing institutions which, directly or indirectly, implied a redistribution of power (see Krockow 1976: 12). The existing distribution of power can thus be identified as the classical frame of reference for the traditional reform discourse. Accordingly, the legitimacy of reform has always been judged in terms of the normative criteria of democratic theory. *Democratic* reforms require a comprehensive inclusion of those affected in the decision-making process concerning these reforms. In other words, the legitimacy of reform increases with the convergence of the subjects and objects of reform in the political process (see Greiffenhagen 1978: 20–21).

The perspective of policy analysis on reform: effective problem-solving

In the reform discourse in mainstream political science today, neither this traditional coordinate system, nor the criteria of democratic legitimacy derived from normative political theory seem to be of any direct relevance. References to the overall structures of the political system are rare, and – rather than the reform of the whole – reforms of the parts are at stake, which relate to demands at the level of first-order governing in the sense of addressing collective action problems in given issue areas. At the same time, the notion of the political has shifted to a more technical understanding of politics 'not as the use of power in one's own interest or in the interest of a class, but as acting in the public interest for solving the problems of a society' (Mayntz 2006: 12, author's translation). Politics is about regulation and political steering, its main objectives are proper solutions to concrete questions regarding concrete subject matters.

When power comes in again, it has mutated from its original nature as a threat to self-determination which had to be balanced, to a functional necessity for securing effective compliance and problem-solving. The former bottom-up per-spective – based on the assumption of certain rights of those governed vis-à-vis those who govern – has thus given way to the top-down demands of political steering. In other words, Dahl's often quoted democratic dilemma between system effectiveness and citizen participation (Dahl 1994) is solved by giving priority to the former and looking at the latter as being instrumental.

Within political science, the sub-discipline of *policy analysis* takes responsi-bility for re-defining what politics is all about: the effective organization of col-lectively binding decisions in order to solve sectoral problems efficiently. For this perspective, the original normative criteria, rooted in democratic theory and provided by normative political theory, were of little use. Instead, new and more technical standards for evaluating the success of reform(s) were borrowed from a neighboring discipline: economics. As a result of this normative outsourcing, all sub-units of the political system have gradually become 'like' units in that all reform measures are evaluated by the same output-oriented criteria of effective-ness and efficiency (see Nullmeier 2005). For example, reforms of the social systems are measured according to their contribution to the productivity and competitiveness of the national economy on the world market; reforms of the educational systems have to increase the international competitiveness of the knowledge-based European economic area.

Input demands from the perspective of policy analysis

To be sure, this new reform discourse is not blind toward issues of participation altogether. But its output-biased focus on the political process prevails even when it comes to advocate more participation: the inclusion of new actors does not derive its relevance from democratic reasoning at the level of meta-governing, but rather from the aim of reaching concrete reform goals at the level of first-order governing more effectively. When, with the fading belief in the autonomous steering capabilities of the state, the hierarchical idea of command-and-control lost its attractiveness to the more complex *governance* concept (see Mayntz 1996), the inclusion of civic and economic actors into the political process became a major reform target. However, the normative grounds on which new modes of horizontal (self)-governance have been advocated have little to do with concerns about self-determination or control of political power. The inclusion of private actors into the political process rather follows the output-oriented rationale of being instrumental for increasing the quality of political decisions and facilitating their implementation. Accordingly, the invitation does not address 'the people' in general, but aims at co-opting specific groups, such as professional experts who promise to bring in additional problem-solving resources, or potential veto players whose participation might increase their willingness to accept the decisions in which they were involved. When we talk about the new 'cooperative state', the same instrumental logic applies: inclusion – once a goal in its own right which needed no further justification but self-determination in the older reform discourse based on normative political theory – serves as an instrument to overcome state failure by activating citizens. In the language of new public management, where the economic standards for the evaluation of governance originated (see Mayntz 2006: 14), the same idea is mirrored in a more drastic way in the term 'customer integration' (see Priddat 2000: 153).

The Bologna reforms beyond policy analysis and first-order governing

How can these considerations about different criteria for the evaluation of reform be applied to the Bologna Process? Obviously the two reform discourses – one rooted in normative political theory, the other associated with policy analysis – do not only suggest very different evaluation criteria, they also focus their attention on different levels of reform. Rather than following the well-trodden path of evaluating the new educational policies associated with the Bologna Process by focusing on the quality of outcomes at the level of first-order governing, the original, but neglected perspective offered by normative political theory will be applied, which is primarily interested in reforms at the second and the meta-level of governing higher education in Europe.

The very beginning of the Bologna Process can serve to illustrate how much the two perspectives differ in their normative implications. Some of its major initiators, among them the German Federal Ministry of Education and Research, regarded the given distribution of competence in the field of higher education as an obstacle to reform. Consequently, they tried to make strategic use of the international level in order to outmaneuver institutional veto players in their domestic environments. Intergovernmentalization and informalization were complementary components of a strategic move to establish policy-making structures which allowed the inclusion of actors who supported the envisaged policy changes, and the exclusion of others who opposed them (see Toens 2008). Only 'a particular set of major stakeholders, that is, the groups representing heads and chief administrators of European universities, had been directly involved from the beginning' (Furlong 2005: 54).

From the output-oriented perspective of policy analysis, nothing is wrong about this European 'detour' as long as it is instrumental for opening the way to reform in the sense of producing 'better' policies in higher education. From the perspective of normative political theory, however, this strategic move and its effects are highly questionable because the desired policy change was brought about by establishing new institutional environments and informal modes of governance which shifted responsibilities to non-state actors, ignoring the democratically legitimated parliamentary policy-making procedures.

New visions: reform in higher education at the level of meta-governing

Educational reform at the level of meta-governing can be summarized as the implantation of economic principles into the system of higher education: the shift from the vision of a 'university in a democracy' (see Nitsch *et al.* 1965) to that of a 'university in an international education market'. Social democratic visions, such as 'democratic participation', 'equal opportunities' and 'political steering', which had provided the ideational guidelines for earlier reforms in higher education in the late 1960s, were replaced by those of neo-liberalism with 'market competitiveness' as the central idea. As a result of this fundamental ideological shift, education in Europe is now primarily framed – and legitimized – as an instrument to support the position of Europe as a competitive knowledge-based economic area.

Part of the explanation of this indeed revolutionary paradigm shift, which gradually transformed education into an economic issue, lies in the above-mentioned strategy of national governments to outmaneuver domestic reform obstacles. In order to employ the EU's (European Union) leverage, higher education had to be reframed as an issue of global competitiveness. According to Huisman and van der Wende (2004: 350), due to the incorporation of the Commission into the process, 'the economic rationale became more important than the political, educational and cultural rationales'. A chronological look at the different declarations issued during the Bologna Process reveals this gradual 'economic turn'. The original Sorbonne Declaration (1998) still lacks any mention of an economic rationale. In fact, the original motive behind it had precisely been the prevention of a commodification of the education sector during the GATS (General Agreement on Trade in Services) negotiations within the World Trade Organization. The declaration explicitly states that 'Europe is not only that of the Euro, of the banks and the economy'. The Bologna Declaration (1999) (now with the Commission as an observer) shows first economic considerations, recognizing that a common European education system is helpful 'in order to promote European citizens' employability'. The Prague Communiqué (2001), at which the Commission was a full member of the process, links its objectives directly to economic gains expected from a common education area. It explicitly claims that 'building the European Higher Education Area is a condition for enhancing the attractiveness and competitiveness' of Europe as an economic area. Originally a goal in itself, educational reform had by now gradually become a means to reach economic ends. This instrumental character is brought to light in ministerial statements emphasizing the necessity to accommodate the labor market's demands by introducing the new degree system, and the advantages of a universally accredited quality assurance system for students' access to the European labor market. The declaration also states that 'lifelong learning strategies are necessary to face the challenges of competitiveness' and that study programs need to be developed, 'combining academic quality with relevance to lasting employability' (Prague Communiqué 2001).

While in its initial stages the Bologna Process primarily contributed to strengthening the EU's role in the field of education, the causal chain gradually turned around, and the Bologna Process itself became increasingly affected by the activities of the EU in the field of education. In its Berlin Communiqué (2003) the Conference of Ministers responsible for Higher Education already quoted the proclamations of the European Council meetings in Lisbon (2000) and Barcelona (2002) to make Europe 'the most competitive and dynamic knowledge-based economy in the world, capable of sustainable economic growth with more and better jobs and greater social cohesion'. This condensed description may suffice to indicate that Bologna facilitated the spread of a normative belief system based on neo-liberal thinking. It resulted in an unprecedented reframing of the European discourse about higher education by reducing the value of education to its market value. The more firmly education policy became integrated into the EU context, the more it also became economized.

In Germany, market orientation has become the leading paradigm throughout almost all areas of reform in higher education today. It finds expression in such innovations as performance-related salaries for university teachers, or the introduction of tuition fees. The ideological infiltration of the educational system by the economic system has not only affected the normative standards but also the economic slang, most remarkably so in the almost satirical re-labeling of the social institution university as a 'service industry in the knowledge society which has to establish or defend a position on the market in competition with others' (Friedrich 2004: 4, author's translation).

Confronted with this economization of the criteria for distinguishing the direction and appropriateness of reform goals and measures in the field of higher education, political science does not seem to have decided yet whether it should reformulate its normative criteria in accord with the neo-liberal standards that have infiltrated the field of higher education in the political discourse, or whether it should re-establish its own original normative criteria for distinguishing between appropriate and less appropriate reform goals and measures; or, reformulated as a challenge to meta-governing: what should be the appropriate normative guidelines for deciding on opportunities *for whom* and on policies *to what end*?

So far, this makeover of the political discourse about reform in higher education has been met with remarkably little resistance from the perspective of normative political theory. Beyond occasional complaints about a further de-qualification of graduates it is overdue to link this ideational shift back to the civic foundations of democracy and to confront this neo-liberal vision of

reducing education to a commodity with the vision of educating politically
mature citizens.

Informalization and transnationalization: reform in higher education at the level of second-order governing

The economic re-framing of the normative guidelines for educational reform at
the meta-level was complemented by institutional reforms at the level of second-
order governing which took place as an informalization and transnationalization
of policy-making in higher education. These institutional reforms were logically
linked with those at the level of meta-governing because they translated the new
ideational frame into an institutional and procedural environment which was
deemed favorable for the implementation of concrete reform policies which followed the new course. Their joint focus is to reduce the role of the state and to
grant more autonomy to sub- or non-state institutions in higher education, such
as universities, rating agencies or quality assurance organizations. Accordingly,
a variety of institutional changes were initiated which aimed at less regulation,
more market competition and quality-raising diversification on the supply side of
higher education.

Taking all these innovations together, at the level of second-order governing
Bologna has created institutional opportunities for the participation of numerous
new political actors in the field of higher education, among them education consultants, thematic networks and university councils (*Hochschulräte* in the
German system). New organizational structures and patterns of public–private
interaction emerged, often involving transnational actors who owed their very
existence to the Bologna Process, such as the European Association of Quality
Assurance in Higher Education (ENQA). This shift of responsibilities from the
state to non-state actors was part of a complete restructuring of the existing education systems. In a general process of 'de-governmentalization' of higher education policy (Teichler 2004: 21), governments limited their role to coordinating
functions, and 'national regulators transfer[red] a substantial part of their norm-
setting power to university institutions which accepted their autonomy and made
use of it boldly' (Kohler 2004: 10).

However, even from an output-oriented goal-attainment perspective one may
raise doubts as to whether less regulation and more autonomy from the state
have really been achieved. Rather, a new trend to re-regulation seems to be
taking place (see Krücken 2004: 345). After non-state agencies have taken over
the recognition, accreditation and evaluation functions that had previously been
subject to state regulation, these functions are fulfilled within a confusing patchwork of new public–private governance arrangements. Even observers who, like
Peter J. Brenner (see Brenner 2007: 86–87), generally sympathize with the
Bologna reform goals, warn that one evil may have been replaced by another:
the relief expected from the removal of the bureaucratic constraints by the state
is neutralized by the new constraints of 'self-bureaucratization' within universities which are caused by the inflationary demands of peer reviewing, accredita-

tion, evaluation and documentation. These demands are formulated by accreditation and evaluation agencies which operate just like consulting firms: they take their professional expertise from those who pay them.

Normative political theory would paint an even darker picture of the institutional reforms in higher education brought about during the Bologna Process. Rather than as a reform project which has more or less successfully succeeded in creating institutional opportunities for more competition and self-regulation, the reforms of second-order governing would have to be evaluated in the light of the above-mentioned strategically motivated assault on the domestic distribution of institutional checks and balances. The legitimacy deficit resulting from such a move would only be justified if the new informal modes of policy-making were equipped with structures of participation of their own, such as mechanisms of direct participation, which could compensate the loss of parliamentary control. Obviously, one characteristic feature of the new patterns of public–private interaction is exactly the direct inclusion of non-state actors with increased responsibilities. As already mentioned, the convergence of the subjects and objects is supposed to improve the democratic legitimacy of a political reform process. Is this not exactly what we can observe?

In order to evaluate in how far the new inclusion mechanisms can compensate the loss of legitimacy caused by undermining the democratic decision-making procedures it is only fair that the legitimacy demands to be applied should be derived from an ideal-type of democracy which differs from the model of parliamentary democracy and is open to the idea that direct civic or stakeholder participation can be an alternative source of democratic legitimacy in contexts of functional self-regulation. In associative or deliberative theories of democracy the inclusion in horizontal modes of governance is conceived of as providing the opportunity for 'voice' in a consensus-oriented decision-making process, rather than 'vote' in a majoritarian decision-making process. From this perspective, the recognition as being 'an authority' on the basis of thematic expertise – rather than being 'in authority' on the grounds of democratic elections – may provide a sufficient alternative source for the legitimacy of private actors' claims to participation in the context of horizontal self-regulation (see Wolf 2002, 2008).

But even in associative or deliberative democracy, the involvement of non-state actors does not automatically improve the democratic legitimacy of the political process. Practices of inclusion and exclusion should still meet certain demands of transparency and should observe the principles of self-determination and congruence between those who make the rules and those who are supposed to follow them. This also means that a fair chance of participation should be granted to all kinds of stakeholders, not only those who are in support of the general philosophy of reform in higher education, but also those who oppose it.

Inclusion and exclusion at the European level

In a detailed account of the Bologna follow-up process, Katrin Toens (Toens 2009) shows that in the German case the different stakeholder groups did not profit in the same way from the autonomy gains which the informalization of policy-making in higher education offered them. Rather, the strong became stronger, and the weak became weaker with the emergence of informal practices. At the European level the emerging system of quality assurance and the work of the Bologna Follow-up Group are good examples of how the new institutional opportunities and the introduction of new modes of governance favored those interest groups who were capable of organizing themselves transnationally in comparison to others whose connections rested mainly with national parliaments. It also favored non-state actors who could offer important resources, such as thematic expertise, money or know-how, over those who could not. Therefore, mechanisms of inclusion *and* exclusion were activated simultaneously as equally important components of a strategy of 'controlled inclusion'. By outmaneuvering veto players in their domestic systems, the state – without sacrificing too much political control – delegated certain regulatory functions to carefully selected non-state organizations, such as the European Network of Quality Assurance, or the European University Association (EUA) in which the national rectors' conferences are organized at the European level.

Inclusion and exclusion at the university level

The fact that the university rectors have been involved in the Bologna Process from the very beginning, and more closely than any other group of professional stakeholders, has had a sustainable impact on the way in which the universities, in order to fulfill their new mission as firms, are dealing with the increased power they were given over their own programs. As declared in the Berlin Declaration (2003), 'ministers accept that institutions need to be empowered to take decisions on their internal organization and administration'. *Autonomy* is the keyword for describing the new external relationships of the universities with the state. But whose autonomy is this? And why 'autonomy', and not 'self-determination'?

The choice of the term 'autonomy' follows a certain logic. From the point of view of its initiators, i.e. the national executives and the university rectors who supported them, Bologna was all about gaining more autonomy (see Martens and Wolf 2009) in the sense of increasing their control over decision-making processes within the state or within the university, respectively. Therefore, for both the national governments and the representatives of the university administrations, 'autonomy' reflects the goal of strengthening their power rather than seeing it limited by more 'self-determination' of potential veto players. Like the national governments, the university rectors were also not interested in strengthening 'citizen participation' but in increasing 'system effectiveness', to take up Dahl's dualism once again.

Therefore, it comes as no surprise that, under the flag of autonomy, the decision-making architecture within European universities is currently fundamentally re-organized according to the vision of strengthening the executive. One of the paramount role models is the *Eidgenössische Technische Hochschule* (ETH) Zürich whose then acting President, Konrad Osterwalder, claimed that all over Europe no other public university is known to him in which the competencies of the executive, notably the president, are as strong as at the ETH (Osterwalder 2007: 84). This is by no means an isolated case. As Teichler (2004: 19–20) states, most university administrations have taken the chance to 'establish a managerial system characterized by stronger executive powers of the institutional leadership'.

With regard to the search for alternative sources of democratic legitimacy in the context of new modes of governance, and from the perspective of normative political theory, this kind of university autonomy cannot count as evidence for new practices of inclusion which are likely to strengthen self-determination and the control of power. Through the lens of policy analysis, however, the increasing autonomy enjoyed by the executive branch within universities could again be seen as an institutional reform in the right direction as long as it contributes to more competitiveness and efficiency. From this perspective, criticism would rather result from the concern that, although independent university councils have taken the place of former legal supervision by the state, the latter may still be lurking in the background and dig out again the regulatory torture instruments of the past command-and-control era. It is a fact that the decision-making competencies of a university council, which consists of economic, academic or administrative experts, may sometimes even exceed those formerly owned by the state, and certainly do exceed those of the different status groups, senates and assemblies within the universities. This would again cause considerable concern from the perspective of normative political theory, but not necessarily from that of policy analysis.

Conclusions

As the previous sections have shown, the Bologna Process is embedded in an overall neo-liberal reform discourse about the normative criteria of appropriateness of reforms in general. Within this new paradigm, the general goals of higher education were re-defined and new, informal institutional environments were created to facilitate the implementation of policy measures in accordance with the new ideational frame. The replacement of the concept of self-determination by the concept of autonomy reflects this paradigmatic shift in an illustrative way.

What are the normative implications of the competence shifts brought about by this reform process? In the neo-liberal logic taken on by mainstream policy analysis, if the choice is between system effectiveness and citizen participation, strengthening the executive branch is an acceptable price for breaking reform blockades. After all, from this point of view, the game is not about exerting power but about solving problems. In addition, the substitution of state control with supervising institutions, in which professional experts have the say, is welcomed because it is likely to remove the debates about educational reform from the battlefield of ideological politicization by political parties.

In this chapter, however, I have taken the opposite view. My main argument was that it is overdue to re-establish political science as the leading discipline for generating the normative foundations of the educational reform discourse, rather than leaving it to economists and their followers among policy analysts to define the criteria for the evaluation of educational reforms. The present preoccupation of our discipline with the outcomes of reform policies at the level of first-order governing should not make us blind to the normative implications of reforms in higher education at the levels of second-order and meta-governing. The success of educational reforms and the quality of the processes by which they are achieved should be evaluated by more comprehensive normative standards than effectiveness or efficiency. Political scientists should remember their original 'in-house' normative categories when they analyze reform, for example by applying democratic theory to the fundamental changes which are at present occurring in the field of higher education.

But can a discipline which is dominated by a 'governance' discourse, in which top-down and compliance-oriented thinking still prevails and output-criteria determine the appropriateness of claims for inclusion, still be a productive source from which normative visions for educational reforms can rise? Falling back on the famous slogans of the past, such as the 'democratic university' or 'education is a civil right', in order to challenge fashionable but one-sided visions like the one of the 'entrepreneurial university', is not an option any more. Today, a meaningful normative perspective on reform must be capable of reconciling demands of democratic participation on the one hand with equally legitimate demands concerning the quality of policy results on the other. The re-integration of the different demands into a consistent and comprehensive 'theory of democratic reform' will require an extended and somewhat more enlightened usage of the governance paradigm. To materialize this potential, the present pre-occupation with concerns about how to solve sectoral problems in the public interest most effectively and efficiently would have to be expanded to questions of democratic legitimacy. Rather than addressing new actors' constellations or new modes of governance in terms of their impact on problem-solving, they should also become thematic in terms of power redistribution in the normative horizon of self-determination instead of 'autonomy'. Or, as one colleague put it when the senate of his recently autonomous university had lost the competence to nominate the candidates to run for presidency to the newly established univer-sity council: 'There were times when universities were not autonomous but were still able to choose their presidents themselves.'

References

Berlin Communiqué (2003) *Realising the European Higher Education Area. Communiqué of the Conference of Ministers responsible for Higher Education*, Berlin, 19 September 2003.

Bologna Declaration (1999) *Joint Declaration of the European Ministers of Education*, Bologna, 19 June 1999.

Brenner, P.J. (2007) 'Die Bologna-Maschine. Die Universität im Strudel der Bürokratie', *Forschung & Lehre*, 14, 2: 86–88.

Dahl, R.A. (1994) 'A democratic dilemma: system effectiveness versus citizen participation', *Political Science Quarterly*, 109, 1: 23–34.

Friedrich, H.R. (2004) 'Nationale und internationale Grundlagen der Qualitätssicherung an Hochschulen', in W. Benz, J. Kohler and K. Landfried (eds) *Handbuch Qualität in Studium und Lehre – Evaluation nutzen – Akkreditierung sichern – Profil schärfen*, Stuttgart: Raabe, A 2.1, 1–18.

Furlong, P. (2005) 'British higher education and the Bologna Process: an interim assessment', *Politics*, 25, 1: 53–61.

Glotz, P. and Schultze, R.-O. (2005) 'Reform', in D. Nohlen and R.-O. Schultze (eds) *Lexikon der Politikwissenschaft*, Vol. 2, München: Beck, 836–842.

Greiffenhagen, M. (1978) 'Überlegungen zum Reformbegriff', in M. Greiffenhagen (ed.) *Zur Theorie der Reform. Entwürfe und Strategien*, Heidelberg: C.F. Müller, 7–34.

Huisman, J. and van der Wende, M. (2004) 'The EU and Bologna: are supra- and international initiatives threatening domestic agendas?', *European Journal of Education*, 39, 3: 349–357.

Kohler, J. (2004) 'Bologna und die Folgen', in W. Benz, J. Kohler and K. Landfried (eds) *Handbuch Qualität in Studium und Lehre – Evaluation nutzen – Akkreditierung sichern – Profil schärfen*, Stuttgart: Raabe, A 1.1, 1–20.

Kooiman, J. (ed.) (1993) *Modern Governance: New Government-Society Interactions*, London: Sage.

—— (2000) 'Societal governance: levels, modes, and orders of social-political interaction', in J. Pierre (ed.) *Debating Governance*, Oxford: Oxford University Press, 138–164.

Krockow, Ch. Graf von (1976) *Reform als politisches Prinzip*, München: Piper.

Krücken, G. (2004) 'Wettbewerb als Reformpolitik: De- oder Re-Regulierung des deutschen Hochschulsystems?', in P. Stükow and J. Beyer (eds) *Gesellschaft mit beschränkter Hoffnung. Reformfähigkeit und die Möglichkeit rationaler Politik*, Wiesbaden: VS Verlag, 339–356.

Martens, K. and Wolf, K.D. (2009) 'Boomerangs and Trojan horses: the unintended consequences of internationalizing education policy through in the EU and the OECD', in P. Massen, A. Gornitzka and Ch. Musselin (eds) *European Integration and the Governance of Higher Education and Research. The Challenge and Complexities of an Emerging Multi-level Governance System*, Berlin: Springer.

Mayntz, R. (1996) 'Politische Steuerung. Aufstieg, Niedergang und Transformation einer Theorie', in K. von Beyme and C. Offe (eds) *Politische Theorien in der Ära der Transformation*, Opladen: Leske and Budrich: 148–168.

—— (2006) 'Governance Theory als fortentwickelte Steuerungstheorie?', in G.F. Schuppert (ed.) *Governance-Forschung. Vergewisserung über Stand und Entwicklungslinien*, Baden-Baden: Nomos, 11–20.

Nitsch, W., Gerhard, U., Offe, C. and Preuß, U.K. (1965) *Hochschule in der Demokratie. Kritische Beiträge zur Erbschaft und Reform der deutschen Universität*, Berlin: Luchterhand.

Nullmeier, F. (2005) 'Umbau des Wohlfahrtsstaates – ein politikwissenschaftlicher Ansatz', in H. Vorländer (ed.) *Politische Reform in der Demokratie*, Baden-Baden: Nomos, 94–103.

Osterwalder, K. (2007) 'Ein spezielles Führungsgespann. Leitungsstrukturen an der ETH Zürich', *Forschung & Lehre*, 14, 2: 84–85.

Prague Communiqué (2001) *Towards a European Higher Education Area. Communiqué of the Meeting of the European Ministers in Charge of Higher Education*, Prague, 19 May 2001.

Priddat, B.P. (2000) 'reForm. Über den Wunsch nach Form in der Politik', in B.P. Priddat (ed.) *Der bewegte Staat*, Marburg: Metropolis, 119–165.

Sorbonne Joint Declaration (1998) *Joint Declaration on Harmonisation of the Architecture of the European Higher Education System, by the four Ministers in Charge for France, Germany, Italy and the United Kingdom*, Paris, 25 May 1998.

Teichler, U. (2004) 'The changing debate on internationalisation of higher education', *Higher Education*, 48, 1: 5–26.

Toens, K. (2009) 'Hochschulpolitische Interessenvermittlung im Bologna-Prozess. Akteure, Strategien und machtpolitische Auswirkungen auf nationale Verbände', in B. Rehder, Th. von Winter and U. Willems (eds) *Interessenvermittlung in Politikfeldern*, Wiesbaden: VS Verlag, 230–247.

Wolf, K.D. (2002) 'Contextualizing normative standards for legitimate governance beyond the state', in J.R. Grote and B. Gbikpi (eds) *Participatory Governance. Political and Social Implications*, Opladen: Leske and Budrich, 35–50.

—— (2008) 'Emerging patterns of global governance: the new interplay between the state, business and civil society', in A.G. Scherer and G. Palazzo (eds) *Handbook of Research on Global Corporate Citizenship*, Aldershot: Edward Elgar, 225–248.

12 Education policy and the harmonization of political science as a discipline

Erkki Berndtson

Introduction

Recent developments in the European Higher Education Area have raised questions about the future course of universities in Europe. There are studies which have tried to explain the current change and its impact on higher education (e.g. Chapter 5, this volume). Research on the outcomes of education policies on individual disciplines is, however, lacking. This chapter aims to fill the gap by looking at the discipline of political science, including a focus on its internationalization and harmonization.

The development of academic disciplines takes place in the context of structures of higher education. These are molded by educational ideologies, national laws, available resources and human interests. Through disciplines students are socialized into disciplinary practices, new researchers are recruited into the profession, research problems are legitimized and the use of available resources is decided. Relations between disciplines are also important, as the existing ones are able to control the birth of new ones. At the same time theoretical discussions within disciplines shape their practice (Berndtson 1991).

Disciplines

The analysis in this chapter is based on current documents, activities of key actors as well as historical evidence. The problem is approached from the perspective of historical institutionalism, which emphasizes theoretically informed empirical research (Mahoney and Rueschemeyer 2003). Historical contexts are reconstructed, however, through critical analysis of theoretical arguments. This way history is understood as a form of discursive practices (Gunnell 1990). The approach differs from traditional sociology of knowledge which focuses on external factors (social structure) in explaining the development of ideas. It also differs from the internalist histories of science (focus on scientific debates) by combining the external and internal factors.

The argument is that political science as an independent academic discipline emerged first in the United States in the late nineteenth century and coincided with the transformation of American higher education taking place at the time. This led to the professionalization and scientification of the discipline in the form of departments and professional associations. The American model of political science was later introduced in Europe (after World War II), but the

European study of politics has remained heterogeneous until today. As the European higher education system is changing in the course of Bologna reforms, this process contains factors which are strengthening the disciplinary and professional nature of the study of politics in Europe as well.

Political science and the structure of American higher education

In many narratives of American political science, the founding of the School of Political Science at Columbia in 1880 has been taken as a symbolic beginning of the discipline (e.g. Crick 1959; Somit and Tanenhaus 1982). Because of the early formation of the discipline in the United States, it has sometimes been argued that political science is a distinctly American science (see Gunnell 2002). The argument has to be modified, however. The American and European study of politics were actually quite similar at the end of the nineteenth century. The Columbia School was organized much the same way as the Ecole Libre des Sciences Politiques in Paris, which had been founded in 1871. At the time, similar institutions were established in other European countries (Facoltà di scienze politiche in Florence in 1874, the London School of Economics and Political Science in 1895). Columbia and European institutions were aimed to educate civil servants, diplomats and journalists, with curricula comprising of law, history, philosophy, economics and politics.

American and European paths began to diverge at the beginning of the twentieth century. The American Political Science Association was founded in 1903 to devote attention to problems of administration, legislation and constitutional and public law (Willoughby 1904: 27). With the founding of the Association the discipline began to gain its own identity. The launching of the *American Political Science Review* in 1906 became the final push in the disciplinary development, although it took until the 1920s before a distinctively American political science was solidified.

Important discussions about the nature of political science were carried out at a number of conferences, for instance, in the three influential national conferences on the science of politics, held in 1923, 1924 and 1925. A professional identity was formed and the discipline began to understand itself as a profession and a science (see Hall 1924; 1925; 1926). Political science defined its borders with other social sciences and separated itself from history and public law. The discipline focused on 'new aspects of politics' (Merriam 1925), as political scientists became interested in psychological explanations, experimented with statistics and tried to imitate natural sciences. They also substituted the old concepts of state and sovereignty with power, group dynamics and pluralism searching for a new theory of democracy (Gunnell 2007).

Political science became a discipline at the time when the structure of American higher education was changing. The Morrill Act (1862) started a new era, as the federal government acted for the first time in the field of education, providing aid to states which supported colleges with agricultural and mechanical instruction (Veysey 1965: 15). Private money was also used to establish new research universities, such as Cornell, Johns Hopkins, Stanford and the University of Chicago. The economic growth after the Civil War had created large business empires, whose owners channeled some of their wealth to science and philanthropy through foundations, which acted as intermediaries between business and universities (Friedman and McGarvie 2003).

Like so many other things in the United States, the new American system of higher education was a mixture of European and local traditions (Kerr 1982; Wittrock 1985). A German influence was noticeable especially in private research universities, as hundreds of American students had studied in Germany in the late nineteenth century and had become familiar with the 'Humboldtian' university.

American universities applied the Humboldtian idea of freedom and unity of teaching and learning to postgraduate education. At the same time many of them continued to rely on the old British liberal education, idealized by John Henry Newman in the mid-nineteenth century, at the undergraduate level. Universities were to cultivate the mind and to train good members for society, not to educate students for any specific profession. Universities were educational institutions, protecting scientific knowledge, not producing it (Kerr 1982: 2–3, 8).

Also the French higher education influenced the American system. In France the old universities had been abolished after the Revolution (and were not really restored until the late nineteenth century as loosely coordinated faculties; see Wittrock 1985: 18). Instead, 'the Napoleonic reforms' had created a system of elite professional education institutions (e.g. the Ecole Libre des Sciences Politiques). In the same manner, professional schools (medicine, law, business) were founded in the United States, the difference to France being that these schools were incorporated into the university structure. This 'Napoleonic model' matched well the practical orientation of American culture (Kerr 1982: 18).

European influences with indigenous factors created a new American university as a 'Modern University'. An important innovation was a system of departments, which contrasted with the German single-chair system. Departments stood between the individual professor and the university. This gave better possibilities for the recognition of new disciplines (Wittrock 1985: 25). Harvard introduced a new system of elective studies in 1869, which fostered precise study fields. Johns Hopkins was founded in 1876, concentrating on postgraduate research within departments (Veysey 1965: 320–322). And in 1892 the University of Chicago was opened as one of the first universities structured along departments (Goodspeed 1916). This internationally unique departmental structure, with political science as one of the new departments, became widespread between 1890 and 1910 (Abbott 2001: 122–123).

There were many reasons for the change, but the economic ones were the most prominent ones. In the late nineteenth century, there were no real standards for entering into most professions in America. Many state legislatures had even banned examinations or licensing as undemocratic (Sealander 2003: 230). At the same time there were hundreds of higher education institutions differing from each other, denominational colleges and secular liberal arts colleges, women's colleges and negro colleges, land-grant colleges and city universities, to name a few. In this situation the big foundations (Carnegie, Rockefeller) started to work with the federal government in order to create a coherent ideology and practice in higher education (Barrow 1990: 61). Industrialization, labor market and economic growth required common standards.

As education was a state right, it was impossible for the federal government to control different state systems in higher education. It was possible, however, to evaluate them (Barrow 1990: 111). From 1915 through 1928, the United States Bureau of Education participated (with funding from private foundations) in over 100 higher education surveys that embraced some 240 institutions (Barrow 1990: 119). These surveys helped to harmonize the American system by 1930. Direct funding from foundations also led to change in a second way: in order to receive grants, universities had to modernize their administrations and curricula and accept corporate accounting techniques (Sealander 2003: 230). It was no coincidence that many disciplines developed into professional enterprises in the 1920s.

American universities grew rapidly. In 1890 there were 173,000 students in higher education institutions, by 1939 the student enrolment had risen to 1,350,000 (Anderson 1939: 259–260). The development continued after World War II, as higher education became part of the post-war reconstruction and attracted large federal programs. The advancement of science and technology became national priorities after the 'Sputnik shock'. This guaranteed the continuous enlargement of academic faculty and student body. Clark Kerr (1982: 45–52, 163) has argued that these developments created a second great transformation in American higher education. Without any noticeable revolution the 'Modern University' was transformed into a 'Multiversity', universities becoming complex organizations with a wide array of tasks. This did not change the structure of American higher education, but strengthened its contacts with society. It also strengthened the position of disciplines, as the number of faculty members increased.

Changing European higher education

As the United States rose to a hegemonic power in world politics after World War II, its influence was felt also in academia. The image of the American university was introduced worldwide through American foreign policy and with financial help from American foundations (Berman 1980; Fisher 1980). Many foreign academics were also able to spend a year in the United States, especially through the Fulbright program. The American disciplinary system, with independent departments and scientific associations linking them together, started to gain ground in European higher education as well.

Contacts with American universities and scholars had their effect on European universities. The higher education system also changed because of an increasing number of students entering universities. This led to the establishment of new universities, which often broke away from old traditions. In spite of these changes, the three major higher education ideologies, the 'Humboldtian', the 'Newmanian' and the 'Napoleonic', still continued however to have their imprints on European higher education (see Chapter 3, this volume). The national systems have been, in fact, surprisingly different from each other, even to this day. This has diminished possibilities for creating a common European labor market as well as for building a strong European identity among citizens.

As the majority of European universities were public institutions, they were also an essential part of the post-Keynesian welfare state (Kwiek 2005). Until the 1970s higher education in Europe was understood as a national project and universities had an important role as instruments of political integration. Increasing criticism toward the welfare state, the European integration process and globalization pressures are now changing their role. Universities are increasingly expected to serve as part of the production process. Higher education is coming to be 'viewed as merely part of the public sector and its traditional claims to social uniqueness (and consequently economic and political uniqueness) are increasingly falling on deaf ears' (Kwiek 2005: 4).

The European Commission has been active in promoting the change. The Commission's communication on *The Role of the Universities in the Europe of Knowledge* (2003) is an example of how key European decision-makers look at higher education today. Universities are still essential institutions for the future of Europe, but they have not called into question what they are contributing to society (European Commission 2003: 22). Universities have a duty to their 'stakeholders' (students, public authorities funding universities, labor market, society-at-large) to 'maximise the social return of the investment' (European Commission 2003: 14). Universities have to change, because they 'are not at present globally competitive with those of our major partners' (European Commission 2003: 2).

The Commission has set three objectives for the European higher education. First, it is important *to ensure sufficient and sustainable resources for European universities*, but their funding should not be a sole duty of the public sector, as it cannot afford it. Universities have to find new sources of income by attracting private donations, selling services to the business sector and by introducing tuition fees. Universities also have to find ways to use resources more efficiently (European Commission 2003: 12–16).

Second, universities have to be restructured, as it is important to *consolidate the excellence of European universities* by identifying strengths of different institutions. As new knowledge is often produced in cooperation between 'producers' and 'consumers', academic disciplines also have to change, as there is an increasing need to develop interdisciplinary capability of scholars (European Commission 2003: 17). Furthermore, as universities have become complex organizations, they have to open their governance structures to professional experts from outside the academic world.

Third, *universities have to open up to a greater extent to society outside and increase their international attractiveness*. They have to become more involved in community life, acting as a forum of debate and dialogue between academics and citizens. At the same time they have to meet the challenge of increased global competition. The problem is that especially in comparison with American universities, European universities are less attractive, as financial, material and working conditions are not as good as in the United States (European Commission 2003: 7).

The views of the Commission reveal a vision for the future of European universities, which is shared by governments increasingly taking steps to privatize their systems of higher education. Applying the principles of New Public Management ideology, national authorities expect universities to find more resources from private sources and even founding of private universities is encouraged. Universities (and departments) have to compete against each other for funding. Salaries of teaching staff are increasingly based on the evaluation of teaching and research achievement. There are also pressures to elect members of university boards from outside academia (see Chapter 11, this volume).

At the same time governments are harmonizing the European higher education curriculum under the so-called Bologna Process (Reinalda and Kulesza 2006). Origins of the process lie in the Sorbonne Declaration (1998) by the British, French, German and Italian Ministers of Education. The process did not start officially, however, until 1999, when 29 European ministers responsible for education met in Bologna and made a joint declaration, committing their countries to restructure their systems of higher education and to create a European Higher Education Area (EHEA) by 2010. The process has developed through the so-called Follow-up Conferences (Prague 2001, Berlin 2003, Bergen 2005 and London 2007). At the moment 12 principles (action lines) have been set as common targets:

1 Readable and comparable degrees (Bologna Declaration 1999)
2 A system based on two main cycles (Bologna Declaration 1999)
3 A common system of credits (Bologna Declaration 1999)
4 Promotion of mobility (Bologna Declaration 1999)
5 Quality assurance (Bologna Declaration 1999)
6 European dimensions in teaching (Bologna Declaration 1999)
7 Lifelong learning (Prague Communiqué 2001)
8 Involvement of higher education institutions and students in the process (Prague Communiqué 2001)
9 Promoting the attractiveness of the EHEA worldwide (Prague Communiqué 2001)
10 Promoting closer links between the EHEA and the European Research Area (ERA) (Berlin Communiqué 2003)
11 The importance of social dimension (Bergen Communiqué 2005)
12 The employability of graduates (Bergen Communiqué 2005).

Although the process is a project of national governments, it cannot be separated from the policy of the European Commission. The Commission's funding facilitated the preparation of the Bologna meeting and many thematic interests of the Commission (mobility, lifelong learning, quality assurance etc.) have been included in the process from the beginning (Balzer and Martens 2004: 14–15). The Commission was also accepted as a full partner in the process during the Prague Follow-up Conference.

In Prague new consultative members, such as the National Unions of Students in Europe (ESIB), the European University Association (EUA), the European Association of Institutions in Higher Education (EURASHE) and the Council of Europe, were also brought into the process. Since then the number of consultative members has still risen, as the European Association for Quality Assurance in Higher Education (ENQA), the European Centre for Higher Education of the United Nations Educational, Scientific and Cultural Organization (UNESCO/ CEPES), the Education International (EI) Pan-European Structure, and the Union of Industrial and Employers' Confederations of Europe (UNICE), have been added to the group. The result has been a process of bureaucratic interest politics, where contents of the action lines are vague and reinterpreted from time to time (Berndtson 2007).

Reflections on the future of European higher education

From the perspective of interest politics, it is no wonder that the principles of the Bologna Process and New Public Management are sometimes in contradiction with each other. An interesting feature of the Bologna Process is that it seems to advocate a new kind of Network University. Universities would be nodal points in the system, where academic staff and students move from one institution to another. Degrees may be combined from studies in different universities and there will be a growing number of joint degrees (one indicator of European dimensions in teaching). A principle of lifelong learning also demands that universities acknowledge prior knowledge, which is consistent with designing more practically oriented degrees. As employability of graduates has been raised to one of the key targets of the Bologna Process at the moment, this also increases demands to teach practical skills to students.

The practical orientation of higher education does not function well with the goal of developing research universities and centers of excellence in Europe. Of course some European universities are already among the best in the world, but the problem is that the European higher education ideology advocates same strategies and goals to all universities. At the same time, European governments are reluctant to diminish the number of students in higher education. Nor are they willing to increase public funding of universities, as they 'cannot afford it'. This means that an attempt to develop universities capable of competing financially with American research universities at a large scale will fail. American universities have operated in a business culture from the beginning of the 'Modern University'. Europeans lack this experience and it is not easy to change these kinds of cultural and economic conditions in higher education rapidly. It is revealing that American top research universities have not increased their student bodies, although American higher education has faced many of the same problems that European higher education is having at the moment, such as overcrowded universities and deterioration of undergraduate teaching (on the earlier development, see Kerr 1982: 152).

On the other hand, if European governments changed their policy and increased the funding of few research universities, this would probably lead to decreasing funding for other universities. As this would raise much opposition, a more probable scenario is that pressures for a division of labor within existing universities will increase. Bachelor's degrees may develop into a degree 'for the masses' and the Master's degree will be 'for an elite' (Capano 2002: 87). This would have an effect on research opportunities of teaching staff at the undergraduate level, dividing the faculty into those who teach and those who do research. Teaching and research would grow apart, especially as the lack of public funding compels universities to look increasingly for outside research funds. In the end, research will suffer. Already now requirements for doctoral theses in many countries have been lowered (Goldsmith 2005).

Other goals are equally difficult to achieve. As the Commission would like to foster interdisciplinarity, many of the Bologna principles actually strengthen the disciplinary system. This can be seen by looking at the three key areas of the Bologna Declaration: degree structure, quality assurance and mobility. A 3-plus-2 model requires more planning than was the case in the 'old' system. Major subjects have become more important. A disciplinary structure is also strengthened by quality assurance mechanisms. Quality is measured as a quality of disciplines and departments. And finally, student exchange demands that studies taken in a foreign university must easily fit into the curriculum of one's home university and they must be easily measured. Departments and disciplines fulfill this requirement best.

This argument does not deny the fact that there are many interdisciplinary programs in higher education today. Universities have increasingly developed fields, such as gender studies, environmental studies, European studies, ethnic relations, politics of Central and Eastern Europe etc. But there is a limit for these. There are so many more social problems than there are existing departments that a university organized around them would be hopelessly fragmented. Social problems have their own life cycle and one cannot continuously develop new study fields. Problem-based knowledge is too abstract to be really able to compete with a problem-oriented knowledge of existing disciplines (Abbott 2001: 134–135).

Besides, it is difficult to change existing disciplines, as they fulfill key academic functions. It is not possible to be an expert on everything, so disciplines legitimate what there is to know about the subject (Abbott 2001: 130). Disciplines also constitute the macrostructure of the labor market. All faculties contain more or less the same departments. No university can challenge the system without depriving its PhD graduates of their academic future (Abbott 2001: 126).

In the end, the goal of interdisciplinarity will lose to disciplinary pressures. Interdisciplinarity is an old idea which has never worked well. When the disciplinary structure was created in American universities, one of its problems in the social sciences was that it separated different social phenomena from each other. Foundations tried to correct this by emphasizing the need for interdisciplinarity. This was one of the policies of the Social Science Research Council (founded in 1923), as well as a key element in behavioralism of the 1950s (Berndtson 1997). The problem has been that after the disciplinary structure came into existence, disciplines have developed into bureaucratic institutions, competing against each other.

The future of political science as a discipline in Europe

How do these changes affect European political science? To answer this question, it is important to put the study of politics in Europe in its historical context. Before World War II political science in Europe was understood as political sciences. The study of politics remained closely linked to history, law and other social sciences. Especially in continental Europe it was part of law faculties, and public law was the codified language to talk about the state (Wagner 2001: 26) and, 'academic disciplines in the American sense – groups of professors with exchangeable credentials collected in strong associations – did not really appear outside the United States until well into the post-war period' (Abbott 2001: 122–123). Although there were a few individual professors in political science before the war, the first European departments were not established until the 1940s and the real growth of the discipline did not begin until the 1960s (see Klingemann 2007b). It is also revealing that all European national political science associations, except one, have been founded after the war.

The example of American political science with its structured programs, journals and associations (Cairns 1975: 203) was important for the discipline in Europe (see UNESCO 1950). Europeans also had a sincere interest in the American way of studying politics, as new kind of information was needed in post-war Europe. In Germany the discipline was introduced by American occupation forces as the science of political re-education (Rupp 1996), in Italy it was used by reform-minded social scientists to advance social change (Graziano 1987) and for social scientists in other countries, it offered an alternative to the old legalistic political culture.

There was, however, no European political science community, as political scientists worked within their own countries. If European scholars met with each other, it was usually in the United States (see Daalder 1997). It was not until 1970 when the European Consortium for Political Research (ECPR) was launched that European political scientists began to cooperate at the European level (Berg-Schlosser 2006).

However, this 'Americanization' of the European study of politics has never been complete. The influence of American political science has varied between different countries and over time. When American political science is *science*, British scholars prefer to use the concept of political studies, and the French still talk about political sciences. A recent book on the state of political science in

Western Europe (Klingemann 2007b) illustrates well differences among European political science communities. There are communities which are oriented toward empirical Anglo-American political science (mainly in Northern Europe and in some Central and Eastern European countries), there are policy-oriented communities (the Netherlands, Germany, Sweden), sociologically oriented ones (France, Spain) and those with a strong connection to political philosophy (Italy).

As the Bologna Process is now strengthening the disciplinary system in higher education, it is also harmonizing disciplines. A good example is a document on undergraduate courses in political science which European political scientists prepared for the Berlin Follow-up Conference (European Conference of National Political Science Associations 2003). It was proposed that the amount of political science studies in a BA degree should be at least half of all credits and that these should consist of the core subject areas of:

1   political theory/history of political ideas;
2   methodology (including statistics);
3   political system of one's own country and of the European Union;
4   comparative politics;
5   international relations;
6   public administration and policy analysis; and
7   political economy/political sociology.

Although one should not overemphasize the importance of this document, it represents a large number of European political scientists and promotes political science as a discipline. As Paul Furlong (2007: 402) stated:

> We have ... to some extent to defend ourselves against potential and real threats resulting from the radical changes in Higher Education now sweeping across Europe ... in this process of reform we have the opportunity to promote political science as a discipline, indeed I would say as one of the three core social science disciplines.

One of the consequences of strengthening and harmonizing the discipline as a profession and trying to develop a core curriculum for it is that European political scientists will increasingly become isolated from society. This is already the case with American political scientists, as many of them are disciplinary intellectuals without contacts to the world of politics outside academia (Abbott 2001: 130). Because of its historical background and traditions, European political science is still more heterogeneous, open and politically relevant than its older companion. As Philippe C. Schmitter has noted, 'I do not think it is exaggerated to claim that, while American political scientists see their task as exclusively "professional", their European counterparts see it as equally "intellectual"' (2002: 29).

One of the manifestations of American professionalism is a strong emphasis on the scientific study of politics. American political scientists have been keen to identify themselves with research traditions imitating natural science. Although from time to time protests, such as the post-behavioral revolution (Easton 1969) and the Perestroika movement (Monroe 2005), have arisen against the scientification of politics, the quantitative orientation and formal modeling have been in a hegemonic position in American political science from the early 1960s on. This has often been seen as contributing to increasing political irrelevancy of American political science (Sartori 2004: 786). But this is only a part of the story. Political irrelevancy can also arise from abstract theorizing prevalent in some philosophically oriented research traditions. The real problem is professionalism, which cuts itself off from politics and tries to legitimize its position using the 'right' ontological, epistemological and methodological arguments.

The European study of politics now seems to be heading in the same direction. Although many European political scientists may still prefer qualitative research over quantitative research (Klingemann 2007a: 30) and although European political science may still be more historically oriented, more comparative and more macro-sociological than its American counterpart (Berg-Schlosser 2007: 415), professionalism and harmonization of the discipline are becoming facts of life in Europe as well. The Bologna Process and the New Public Management reforms are clearly speeding up this development.

One of the consequences of reforms has been the increasing competition among scholars in the world of diminishing resources. This has led political scientists to accept common standards in research. Practices used in American academia, that are norms on how disciplines should be organized and the fetish attached to peer-reviewed articles in journals (Schmitter 2002: 31), have come widely in use. Furthermore, scholars, especially in small European countries, have to write increasingly in English, as their careers depend on international evaluation. Language is one mechanism contributing to political irrelevancy, as the use of English language (in non-English speaking countries) will diminish the impact of political scientists in their own political context.

It is difficult to fight against this development. Political scientists should ask, however, whether the development is good or bad for the study of politics. If the discipline wants to be politically relevant and intellectually heterogeneous and exciting, how should it be organized? There are at least three important issues to consider. First, how can European political science at the same time be both local and global in its orientation? It would be important to preserve national varieties in the study of politics, as political conditions vary country by country. Second, how can political science keep its borders open to other social sciences? Politics does not operate in a vacuum, but is integrated with economic and social spheres of society. A strong professionalism leads too often to attempts to make politics an autonomous field of study. Third, how is it possible to keep political science methodologically heterogeneous? Strong convictions are bound to make methodological issues more important than problems themselves. These are no easy questions, but maybe it is time to discuss them.

Toward a conclusion...

The history of American and European education policies shows that changes in the structures of education have an impact on the nature of academic disciplines. Although one should bear in mind the differences between the early twentieth-century United States and the early twenty-first-century Europe, it is interesting that the two cases have similarities concerning the harmonization of higher education (states versus federal state/European Union, survey movement versus open method of coordination). The Bologna Process is not only a technical project restructuring the European higher education area. It is an example of new modes of governance in higher education, which will produce a profound effect on the nature of existing academic disciplines as well. If the Bologna Process changes the way we study politics, it may well also change what we know about politics.

References

Abbott, A. (2001) *Chaos of Disciplines*, Chicago: University of Chicago Press.

Anderson, W. (1939) 'Political science enters the twentieth century', in A. Haddow, *Political Science in American Colleges and Universities 1636–1900*, New York and London: D. Appleton-Century Company, 257–266.

Balzer, C. and Martens, K. (2004) 'International higher education and the Bologna Process. What part does the European Commission play?', paper presented at the epsNet Plenary Conference, Prague, June 2004.

Barrow, C.W. (1990) *Universities and the Capitalist State*, Madison: University of Wisconsin Press.

Bergen Communiqué (2005) 'The European higher education area – achieving the goals', *Communiqué of the Conference of European Ministers Responsible for Higher Education*, Bergen, 19–20 May 2005.

Berg-Schlosser, D. (2006) 'Political science in Europe: diversity, excellence, relevance', *European Political Science*, 5, 2: 163–170.

—— (2007) 'European political science – the role of the European Consortium for Political Research (ECPR)', in H.-D. Klingemann (ed.) *The State of Political Science in Western Europe*, Opladen and Farmington Hills: Barbara Budrich Publishers, 409–415.

Berlin Communiqué (2003) 'Realising the European higher education area', *Communiqué of the Conference of Ministers responsible for Higher Education*, Berlin, 19 September 2003.

Berman, E. (1980) 'The foundations' role in American foreign policy: the case of Africa, post 1945', in R.F. Arnove (ed.) *Philanthropy and Cultural Imperialism*, Boston: G.K. Hall & Co., 203–232.

Berndtson, E. (1991) 'The development of political science. Methodological problems of comparative research', in D. Easton, J.G. Gunnell and L. Graziano (eds) *The Development of Political Science*, London and New York: Routledge, 34–58.

—— (1997) 'Behavioralism. Origins of the concept', paper presented at the XVIIth IPSA World Congress, XVIIth IPSA World Congress, Seoul, August 1997.

—— (2007) 'The state of the Bologna Process: the emerging European quality assurance bureaucracy', *epsNet Kiosk Plus*, 5: 39–46.

Bologna Declaration (1999) 'The European higher education area', *Joint Declaration of the European Ministers of Education*, Bologna, 19 June 1999.

Cairns, A.C. (1975) 'Political science in Canada and the Americanization issue', *Canadian Journal of Political Science*, 8, 2: 191–234.

Capano, G. (2002) 'Implementing the Bologna declaration in Italian universities', *European Political Science*, 1, 3: 81–91.

Crick, B. (1959) *The American Science of Politics*, London: Routledge and Kegan Paul.

Daalder, H. (ed.) (1997) *Comparative European Politics*, London and New York: Pinter.

Easton, D. (1969) 'The new revolution in political science', *American Political Science Review*, 63, 4: 1051–1061.

European Commission (2003) *The Role of the Universities in the Europe of Knowledge*, *COM (2003) 58 Final*, Brussels, 5 May 2003.

European Conference of National Political Science Associations (2003) 'The Bologna declaration and the basic requirements of a Bachelor of Arts (BA) in political science in Europe', in B. Reinalda and E. Kulesza (2006) *The Bologna Process – Harmonizing Europe's Higher Education*, Opladen and Farmington Hills: Barbara Budrich Publishers, 223–225.

Fisher, D. (1980) 'American philanthropy and the social sciences: the reproduction of a conservative ideology', in R.F. Arnove (ed.) *Philanthropy and Cultural Imperialism*, Boston: G.K. Hall & Co., 233–268.

Friedman, L.J. and McGarvie, M.D. (eds) (2003) *Charity, Philanthropy, and Civility in American History*, Cambridge: Cambridge University Press.

Furlong, P. (2007) 'The European Conference of National Political Science Associations: problems and possibilities of co-operation', in H.-D. Klingemann (ed.) *The State of Political Science in Western Europe*, Opladen and Farmington Hills: Barbara Budrich Publishers, 401–407.

Goldsmith, M. (ed.) (2005) *Doctoral Studies in Political Science – A European Comparison*, Paris: epsNet Reports #10.

Goodspeed, T.W. (1916) *A History of the University of Chicago*, Chicago: University of Chicago Press.

Graziano, L. (1987) 'The development and institutionalization of political science in Italy', *International Political Science Review*, 8, 1: 41–57.

Gunnell, J.G. (1990) 'The historiography of American political science', in D. Easton, J.G. Gunnell and L. Graziano (eds) *The Development of Political Science*, London and New York: Routledge, 13–33.

—— (2002) 'Handbooks and history: is it still the *American* science of politics?', *International Political Science Review*, 23, 4: 339–354.

—— (2007) 'Making democracy safe for the world: political science between the wars', in R. Adcock, M. Bevir and S.C. Stimson (eds) *Modern Political Science*, Princeton and Oxford: Princeton University Press, 137–157.

Hall, A.B. [*et al.*] (1924) 'Reports of the national conference on the science of politics', *American Political Science Review*, 18, 1: 119–166.

—— (1925) 'Reports of the Second National Conference on the Science of Politics', *American Political Science Review*, 19, 1: 104–162.

—— (1926) 'Report of the Third National Conference on the Science of Politics', *American Political Science Review*, 20, 1: 124–170.

Kerr, C. (1982) *The Uses of the University*, Cambridge: Harvard University Press.

Klingemann, H.-D. (2007a) 'A comparative perspective on political science in Western Europe around the year 2005', in H.-D. Klingemann (ed.) *The State of Political Science in Western Europe*, Opladen and Farmington Hills: Barbara Budrich Publishers, 13–40.

—— (ed.) (2007b) *The State of Political Science in Western Europe*, Opladen and Farmington Hills: Barbara Budrich Publishers.

Kwiek, M. (2005) 'Renegotiating the traditional social contract? The university and the state in a global age', ECER keynote address, Dublin, September 2005.

Mahoney, J. and Rueschemeyer, D. (eds) (2003) *Comparative Historical Analysis in the Social Sciences*, Cambridge: Cambridge University Press.

Merriam, C.E. (1925) *New Aspects of Politics*, Chicago: University of Chicago Press.

Monroe, K.R. (ed.) (2005) *Perestroika!*, New Haven and London: Yale University Press.

Prague Communiqué (2001) 'Towards the European higher education area', *Communiqué of the meeting of European Ministers in charge of Higher Education*, Prague, 19 May 2001.

Reinalda, B. and Kulesza, E. (2006) *The Bologna Process – Harmonizing Europe's Higher Education*, Opladen and Farmington Hills: Barbara Budrich Publishers.

Rupp, H.K. (1996) 'Democratizing a country and a discipline. The (re-)establishment of political science as political education in West Germany after 1945', in R. Eisfeld, M.T. Greven and H.K. Rupp (eds) *Political Science and Regime Change in 20th Century Germany*, Commack: Nova Science Publishers, 55–108.

Sartori, G. (2004) 'Where is political science going?', *PS: Political Science and Politics*, 37, 4: 785–786.

Schmitter, P.C. (2002) 'Seven (disputable) theses concerning the future of "transatlanticised" or "globalised" political science', *European Political Science*, 1, 2: 23–40.

Sealander, J. (2003) 'Curing evils at their source: the arrival of scientific giving', in L.J. Friedman and M.D. McGarvie (eds) *Charity, Philanthropy, and Civility in American History*, Cambridge: Cambridge University Press, 217–239.

Somit, A. and Tanenhaus, J. (1982) *The Development of American Political Science*, New York: Irvington Publishers.

Sorbonne Declaration (1998) *Joint Declaration on Harmonisation of the Architecture of the European Higher Education System*, Paris, 25 May 1998.

UNESCO (1950) *Contemporary Political Science*, Paris: UNESCO.

Veysey, L.R. (1965) *The Emergence of the American University*, Chicago: University of Chicago Press.

Wagner, P. (2001) *A History and Theory of the Social Sciences*, London: Sage.

Willoughby, W.W. (1904) 'Report of the secretary for the year 1904', *Proceedings of the American Political Science Association*, 1: 27–32.

Wittrock, B. (1985) 'Before the dawn .. humanism and technocracy in university research policy', in B. Wittrock and A. Elzinga (eds) *The University Research System*, Stockholm: Almqvist and Wiksell International, 1–37.

13 Political science and educational research

Windows of opportunity for a neglected relationship

Jürgen Enders

Traditionally, education was not in the centre of political science while political science was not in the centre of education research. This is surprising given the important role of education for the making and transformation of modern nation-states. It is even more surprising given the manifold perspectives recent political reform of education as a field of real-life experiment has to offer for the study of shifts in governance and the transformation of the nation-state. New windows of opportunity for a more fruitful relationship between political science and educational research have emerged. It is thus more than timely to overcome what the editors of this volume call 'the neglected relationship between education and political science'.

In this chapter, I will first address this basic assumption of the volume and raise the question: how come? I will hypothesize that various reasons are likely to be considered in order to explore the relative neglect of education in political science in the past: the low esteem of education in society and in policy-making as well as the low esteem of educational research in the academic pecking order, the problems of disciplines with multi-disciplinary field-based research, the assumption that education as a societal sub-sector has little new or exciting to offer to the core of political science, and the specific problems of self-objectification of political scientists (while not only of political scientists) who are themselves affected and involved in political reform in education. In doing so, I do not neglect that political science has made important contributions to the study of education in the past. The emergence of specialized journals such as the *Journal of Education Policy*, the *International Journal of Education Policy and Leadership*, *Comparative Education*, or *Higher Education Policy* also indicates a certain degree of institutionalization of political studies on education. Moreover, from time to time education turned out to be at the forefront of the study of the changing relationship between the state and society. Analyses and differentiation between state control models and state supervising models (Neave and van Vught 1991; Goedegebuure *et al.* 1994) as well as the shift from '*ex ante* control' to '*ex post* control' leading to the rise of the evaluative state (Neave 1989, 1998) were, for example, established relatively early in the field of educational policy studies. They exemplify that the field of education has to offer manifold perspectives to the study of governance reforms in sectors previously under tight control by the nation-state.

I will move on to show how recent developments in the field of education provide manifold windows of opportunity for the study of shifts in governance and statehood in transition. The 'publicness' of education, including the important role of governmental responsibility, oversight and financing, the legal status of the organizational providers and their staff, is currently challenged in many ways. There are many indications that education has become a field of major social transformations and political experimentation: international and transnational organizations are gaining in importance in the field of education, certain powers are being transferred as well to sub-national levels, political actors are increasingly inclined to experiment with quasi-market mechanisms in the governance and financing of education, and the inclusion of civil society, stakeholders and private actors is shaping the governance of the system. Finally, I will briefly point to some further challenges for the study of education from the perspective of political science, namely the important contribution political science has to make in order to understand the impact of ongoing political reform for the democratic legitimacy and effectiveness of education.

About a neglected relationship

Assuming that the editors of this volume have a point in claiming that 'education has basically remained a "homeless" and underestimated topic' in political science during the last decades, I would like to put forward a number of working hypotheses that might contribute to a further understanding of this situation. In doing so, I fully acknowledge that such considerations must have a speculative character given the lack of a conceptual framework and empirical information on the determinants of problem choice in political scientists' research.

Conventional wisdom suggests, however, that problem choice in research is not only driven by academic curiosity, intellectual path dependency and innovativeness but also by the academic prestige or social esteem of a given topic or field. In this respect, education as a societal sub-system and as a field of research faced for quite a while some problems in becoming a fashionable subject. National opinion polls tended to show that education did not rank among the most important national issues or that education was among the most important issues due to the perception of manifold problems within institutionalized education. Results of prestige rankings of occupations usually showed the teaching profession in the upper ranks overall but in the lower ranks of the highly qualified professions (Hoyle 2001; UNESCO 2004). The university and the academic profession may be regarded as an exception of this because they provide *higher* education and because of the prestige added by the social esteem of science and research. Massification of higher education has to some extent undermined the exceptionalism of universities in this respect as well. From time to time education has been important in political programmes or in pre-election campaigns but until recently it mainly formed part of, or stood in the shadow of, issues of welfare policy or social policy.

Further, we can assume that educational research does not hold the highest esteem within the academic pecking order even within the social sciences

(Becher 1989). 'Soft science', 'pre-paradigmatic research', 'a-theoretical', 'merely practice oriented', 'idiographic' are frequently heard concepts in this context. We may also assume certain problems of political science as a discipline – however fragmented it may be – with a multi-disciplinary field of research. Parts of educational science can be characterized as multi-disciplinary fields or as fields to which researchers from various disciplinary backgrounds contribute. Contributions from many disciplinary backgrounds have long been welcome, such as the psychology of teaching and learning, the history of educational systems and institutions, the economics and financing of education, the sociological study of education and social inequality, studies on the policies and politics of education, to name just a few examples. Such a disciplinary range of perspective is by no means surprising given the range and character of questions that research on education as a societal sub-system has to address:

> Who gets taught what, how and under which circumstances? How, by whom and through what structures, institutions and processes are these things defined, governed, organized and managed? What are the relations between education and other social institutions, especially the family and the labor market? In whose interest are these arrangements and what are their social and individual consequences?
>
> (Dale 2000: 92)

The merit of multi-disciplinary perspectives on education that has a potential to cut across disciplines and their favoured thematic areas is, however, not universally appreciated. It is certainly consoling to see how the concept of 'mode 2' research (Gibbons *et al.* 1994), superseding the traditional, discipline-based 'mode 1', has gained in popularity in the political discourse. Up to now, however, research into education as a multi-disciplinary and field-based study is often criticized for lacking desirable disciplinary characteristics such as distinct theoretical traditions, relatively codified knowledge and institutionalized channels and styles of communication. The obvious response to these and related criticism is to call for strongly discipline-based contributions of political science, sociology or economics to the field of educational research. The obvious problem of this approach is that many important cross-cutting questions will remain underserved.

We may further hypothesize that educational policy has not been perceived as a 'hot topic' for quite a while. Indeed, a very good case can be made for arguing that education has been regarded as one of the most national and state-protected of activities. The 'leitmotiv' of the development of national systems of education, especially in mainland Europe, is characterized by assumptions about national unity and homogeneity as regards nationally standardized arrangements; uniformity in the services provided; and the legal enactment of educational providers as public institutions set around a series of laws, circulars and decrees. In this context, education policy was, among other things, designed to emphasize its role as a national entity shielded from external interests by the state. To a large extent education became heavily subsidized, publicly provided by employees of the state, and closely regulated with regard to curriculum, teaching and staff, infrastructural facilities, and achievement standards. Even the modern university – supposed to be the most international part of the educational system – formed 'part and parcel of the very same process which manifests itself in the emergence of an industrial economic order and the nation-state as the most typical and most important form of political organization' (Wittrock 1993: 305). This is a recent phenomenon from a historical perspective and it is an interesting question why the development of a public mandate in education took the form of establishing publicly controlled, state-funded and state-owned institutions, rather than a system of granting operating subsidies and contracts to non-public organizations. In any case, until recently political science could live under the assumption that no major paradigm shifts have taken place in educational policy that would be worth major investigations into this realm.

Finally, the study of political reform in education confronts most researchers with a specific problem of self-objectification. As academic professionals they form themselves part-and-parcel of the educational system, which may imply that they are object as well as subject of the very reform under study. This provides a specific challenge to the capacity of research to take a disinterested and objective perspective on political reform and to contribute to the self-objectivation of the academic field (Bourdieu 1988). Many recent reforms in education have, for example, an impact on the status, power, identity and practices of the academic profession. Employment relations and salary scales are changing, organizational leadership and management takes over certain powers that have traditionally been assumed by the academics themselves, increasing measures of evaluation and accountability eat up academic time and put the academic teacher under public scrutiny. Study reforms in the wake of the Bologna Process mean for many academics a wholesale redistribution of the content and organization of their teaching practices, fields of study – including political science – come under pressure of international standardization (see Chapters 11 and 12, this volume). Further examples could be given to show that educational reforms are by no means neutral to those who wish to study them while being themselves objects of these very reforms. It is thus neither surprising nor illegitimate that academics, their professional organizations and informal networks try to influence such political reforms with a careful eye on their own professional interests at stake. Moreover, educational policy analysts are increasingly interwoven with policy-making itself that is in search of further expertise and legitimacy for political reform. Such a minefield of object–subject relationships between education, educational reform and policy analysis is not very likely to put the study of political reform in (higher) education upfront on the agenda of political analysis.

Windows of opportunity

Recent developments in the field of education provide, however, manifold new windows of opportunity for the study of shifts in governance and statehood in transition. There are many indications that education has, first, been re-discovered as an important field for the political agenda, and, second, has become a field of major social transformations and political experimentation.

The re-discovery of the role of education for economic and social welfare is certainly crucial in both respects. The phenomenon as such is not all new since it was already in the 1950s and 1960s that a certain boom in the economics of education could be observed. In those days, the belief that substantial educational investment is needed in order to ensure economic growth was usually accompanied by a readiness to reduce inequality of opportunities in education. Nowadays, the contribution of education to economic growth and social cohesion has returned to the political agenda but is accompanied by a new grand narrative about the centrality of education in the knowledge society and the role of education for the innovation capacities of a country or region in global competition (Jakobi 2007). Policy-makers, funders and users of education are all expressing their interest in learning more about the changing role of education in the knowledge society, the educational effectiveness in schools and universities, 'best practices', and ways to improve their own national, regional and local systems and institutions. Increasing evaluation and monitoring of education policies and educational achievements is often motivated by interest or concern for system differentials in performance and their potential impact on the labour force and labour productivity. National and international league tables and rankings for schools and universities have grown enormously in popularity and have become a growing market of consumer information. This re-discovery of the socio-economic role of education – even though nowadays addressed by new labels such as knowledge society, innovation capacities or global competition – is accompanied by quite breathtaking shifts in governance in education.

Internationalization, Europeanization and globalization have certainly contributed to the revitalization of comparative and international education and their study within the perspective of political science. While globalization has typically been portrayed as an economic phenomenon, there is also much evidence that demonstrates its fundamental political and cultural dimensions and implications, including the field of education (Crossley and Watson 2004). Education is one example of the inter-relationship between the economic, political and cultural dimensions of globalization. A new grand narrative of the role of education has emerged on a truly global level. This goes together with 'the emergence of a set of generic education policies, the globalization of policy if you like' (Ball 1998: 117), along with the translation and implementation of such policies into the national and local context. The relationship between transnational, national and local politics and policies, their impact on educational systems, institutions and practices, has thus gained in importance and has helped to stimulate further interest in policy studies in the field of education (Martens *et al.* 2007). The export and import, the transfer and borrowing of educational policies has also intensified and is actively encouraged by international organizations as well as government bodies and agencies (Enders and Fulton 2002; Martens 2007). Clearly there is much that can be learned from the experience of others as well as from emerging international trends for political reform agendas in education. But awareness is also growing that uncritical international transfer may lead to unexpected consequences in different contexts, that reforms that seemed promising at a first glance turned out to produce mixed performance in the long run, and that common political agendas do by no means necessarily lead to common implementation practices and policy outputs. The more recent history of the Bologna Process may serve as one illustrative example for the growing complexity of educational policies (Witte 2006; Chapter 10, this volume) that are certainly worthwhile to be furthermore addressed by political scientists interested in multi-level and multi-actor governance studies.

At the most fundamental level, even the dominance of the nation-state as an exclusive framework for the study of educational policy is increasingly questionable (Enders 2004). This is not to suggest that the nation-state is no longer an important player in the field, or that it could be neglected in the political analyses of education. Nation-states actively use global narratives and international reform agendas to support their own political agendas and increasingly claim the role of education for their own national innovation capacities and national competitive advantage. In this sense, globalization also implies a political agenda for re-nationalization.

Certain resources, competences, tasks and political processes are also transferred to sub-national levels. Such de-centralization may take different forms. Institutional paths for sub-nationalization are well known in federal states where responsibility for education may shift to the regional level. In unitary states as well as in federal states further authority may also be delegated to local governments who may already have been in charge of certain aspects and parts of the education system (see Chapters 6 and 7, this volume). Other forms of de-centralization may be called inter-mediarization when certain dimensions of statehood move to intermediary bodies and organizations, for example in the areas of funding, accreditation, evaluation and oversight of educational providers. Further, schools and universities as the organizational providers of education have become important foci of attention in the system's coordination. EURYDICE, the information network on education in Europe, has recently reported on 'School autonomy in Europe. Policies and measures':

> Over the past twenty years, schools have been the subject of much deliberation and have undergone many reforms, in particular as regards their autonomy. There has been a strong focus on the need to improve democratic participation, the management of public funding invested in education and, especially in recent years, the quality of teaching. The approaches taken differ in terms of the rhythm of reforms, the scale of the transfers of authority and the areas they apply to, the stakeholders who benefit from them and

the control or accountability mechanisms in place ... Although reforms have been going on for several decades, school autonomy remains a key issue on the political agenda of many if not most European countries.

(EURYDICE 2007: 4)

Government attempts to enhance the autonomy and self-steering capacities of universities as corporate actors (de Boer *et al.* 2007) provide another example of partly enforced self-regulation within the education system. Such processes of devolving authorities to the organizational level relate in different ways to the overall shifts in governance in the education system. Top-down regulation and control have lost acceptance and legitimacy in public sectors. Guidance by the government, its intermediate bodies and other stakeholders is seen as more effective, efficient and democratic. But the provision of guidance assumes that there is an addressee – the organization – who is enabled to receive advice and to act on it. Second, devolving authorities to the organizational level forms an integral part of new public management approaches that stimulated educational reform to a certain extent. Third, a related factor that supported the rise of the organization concept in education is due to the idea of introducing market-like mechanisms and conditions (as in some other public sectors). A side effect of this was to stimulate the rise of the educational providers as organizational actors because markets need actors, individuals and organizations that can buy and sell, produce and consume.

Education is becoming a genuine field for multi-level governance in which political power and legitimacy are shared between different levels and may shift between them. Attention thus needs to be focused on the complex ways in which the place and role of the nation-state is transforming in education under the influence of globalization and sub-nationalization that may operate in a contradictory or oppositional direction. Theoretically-informed research on policy diffusion, reception and implementation would hypothesize an increasing universalism of transnationally disseminated models whose reception and implementation interact with different politico-administrative institutions as well as context bound social meanings and beliefs. Institutionalized schooling and educational expansion may then be regarded as a universal trend deeply embedded into the development of modernity (Meyer and Ramirez 2000) while it becomes particular when it is contextualized within the different inter-relationships between schooling, labour-market structures and professional careers; between selection and certification in education and social stratification in society; between the organizational structure of education and the system of public administration (Schriewer 2000).

The introduction of market-type coordination mechanisms in education provides another important element of recent shifts in governance in education (Enders and Jongbloed 2007; see also Chapters 3 and 8, this volume). In many countries important ingredients of markets are still not in place in education, while quasi-market elements are becoming increasingly popular in education policy-making. Teixeira *et al.* (2004) have shown that experimentation with market mechanisms takes mainly three forms: the first is the promotion of competition between education providers. The second is the privatization of education – either by the emergence or growth of a private education sector or by means of privatization of certain aspects of public institutions. And the third is the promotion of economic autonomy of education institutions, enhancing their responsiveness and articulation to the supply and demand of factors and products. In terms of financing, increasing costs and fiscal stringencies generate discussion and action as regards new forms of external non-governmental funding of education. Revenues from non-state resources play a growing role or are expected to do so in the future. A worldwide trend is visible towards increasing cost-sharing; that is the shift of some of the costs-per-student from government and taxpayers towards students and their parents. This trend can be detected in increasing tuition fees in countries that are already used to such cost-sharing as well as in the implementation of tuition fees in countries where fees were unknown. Fees paid by students and their families are accompanied by other income-generating activities such as commercial cross-boarder education and courses, commercial e-learning, external funding from private sponsors, and sometimes even direct ties with business. Marketization in education thus is a complex and multi-faceted process.

Other forms of self-regulation are also increasingly stimulated by governmental actors that have a potential for collective action to compensate for market and government failures. The use of policy networks that include public actors and private actors, such as business, consumer groups and other stakeholders (Raab 1992) in setting political priorities or in smoothing the implementation of new policies for education has certainly gained in importance. Policy nowadays postulates the efficiency and effectiveness of steering in and by such networks as a means to stimulate cooperation between heterogeneous partners as well as a means for neo-corporatist policy-making (Börzel 1998; Thatcher 1998). Programmes such as the Education Action Zones in England and the new Community Schools in Scotland have, for example, been stimulated to draw students and families into wider social networks through which markets may be disciplined and tamed and where local government is assumed to take network capacity (Jones and Bird 2000). Developing countries establish policy networks in order to enhance schooling overall or to implement specific programmes, e.g. for the introduction of information and communication technology in education. Transnational initiatives, such as the Bologna Process, create their own multi-level and multi-actor networks that considerably change over time in terms of membership and institutionalization. Networks are also becoming more formalized such as the European Network of Policy Makers for the Evaluation of Education Systems.

Obviously, governance arrangements and instruments are becoming more complex and mixed between hierarchies, markets and networks while we still know very little about their effects and thus their efficiency and legitimacy in coordinating education. Faith in the market is based on the fundamental tenet that competition creates efficiencies, cost savings and productivity gains. In summing up the findings of their book on markets in higher education Dill *et al.* (2004: 345) point, for example, to 'the strong indications that the pressure on universities for more market-like behavior has had a positive impact in terms of cost per graduate and scientific productivity'. Obviously, higher education is hosting nowadays more students and research is delivering more outputs with overall funding that has not followed this growth. Dill *et al.* (2004) also point to the contribution of market mechanisms to the transparency in the system and the operation of universities, their growing flexibility, resilience and responsiveness. At the same time, serious concerns about the costs of an increasingly fierce and globalizing 'academic arms race' (Dill 2005) are raised. In such a race institutions and scholars rather invest in their standing in the positional market for reputation than responding to genuine market needs. Facing competition in markets and quasi-markets for customers and funding, the competition in informal and formal ranking systems for academic reputation can become an end in itself. Public money may increasingly be used to reproduce or enhance the reputation of institutions and scholars, rather than as a means of serving the private and the public good.

Faith in networks is based on the tenet that cooperation and trust will create efficiencies, productivity gains and legitimacy. Enhancing further linkages between actors from different social systems, such as politics, schools and universities, industry, and representatives of civil society, is part-and-parcel of the increasingly visible move from top-down steering and hierarchical forms of governance to interactive processes and policy networks. The basic assumption apparently is that the social relationships between these systems are limited and thus have to be increased by governmental incentives and that public policies will gain in legitimacy by integrating other groups of society into the policy process. Both assumptions can, however, be contested. Geuna *et al.* (2003) have, for example, argued that many networks between universities and other stakeholders have been created top-down by governmental policies rather than by the bottom-up demand of the organizations and partners involved. It seems unlikely to these authors that such top-down initiated networks will develop strong capacities for sub-sectoral linkages and cooperation. Political networks in education (like in other sectors) furthermore raise questions about the inclusion and exclusion of stakeholders and interest groups, their power relationships within the networks, and the political legitimacy of and responsibility for such forms of horizontal governance.

Following the analyses presented above, it becomes clear that new ideas and practices emerge not only on how to organize an education system and its institutions, but also on how to organize its relationship with society and economy. Schools and universities are driven by this transformation while they are also expected to be drivers of the knowledge-based society. The old regime of a more or less strict separation between the national, transnational and sub-national, between the public and the private is diminishing. The blurring of boundaries brings about entirely new institutional settings in relation to the cooperation and interface of educational providers with governments, other stakeholders, allies and competitors. Governance, financing and ownership are not given institutional characteristics but form dynamic relationships that undergo change and reform as well. The ongoing and multi-faceted dynamics in the field thus form part-and-parcel of a broader transformation towards a new social contract for education in the knowledge-based society.

Outlook

This chapter has argued that recent developments in the field of education have created new windows of opportunity for the study of this societal sub-system from the perspective of political science. The relationship between the nation-state and education is continuously changing and education has become a field of major social transformations and political experimentation. What was once assumed to be a rather stable and exclusive domain of national political statehood has become a sub-system in constant flux, including changing relationships between education and the nation-state. International and transnational organizations and institutions are gaining in importance in the field of education. Certain resources, competences, tasks and political processes are being transferred to sub-national levels, for example to federal states, to intermediary organizations or to the schools and universities as the organizational providers of education. Education is becoming a genuine field for multi-level governance in which political power and legitimacy are shared between different levels and may shift between them. Such processes of vertical transformation are accompanied by horizontal transformations. Political actors are increasingly inclined to experiment with quasi-market mechanisms in the governance and financing of education in order to strengthen private funding, competition and self-regulation in the field. Equally important, civil society, stakeholders and private actors are incorporated into the governance of education, leading to the emergence of new political arenas and public–private policy networks.

These trends are by no means all new and may be regarded quite differently in different national settings. What may be thought of as quite innovative ways of governing education in one context may be seen as quite traditional in another context. Processes of transnationalization, sub-nationalization, marketization and socialization may be nested but may also occur independently from each other. These trends also do not necessarily lead to a weakening of the nation-state in the field of education. The role of the nation-state in education is certainly contested while there is potential and evidence for a revitalization of the nation-state in education as well. In any case, the transformation of the nation-state is taking place in a field – education – that was historically assumed to be at the core of the modern nation-state as we know it and assumed to be strongly bound to national traditions. Overall, education has thus become an increasingly fascinating case for the study of policy changes and political reform, changing actor constellations and policy instruments, the circumstances under which they emerge and the policy output they deliver. The different chapters in this volume clearly show the rich contribution of political science to the study of education as a policy field as well as their contribution to the overall study of the causes, processes and consequences of statehood in transition.

Certainly, much work still needs to be done to increase our analytical capacity and empirical insights into the ongoing political dynamics in education as a policy field in its own right. There is, for example, good reason to extend our scholarly interest to still more comparative studies addressing different levels of the educational system as well as to cross-sectoral research comparing the field of education with other societal sub-sectors. Finally, political science also has to make a unique contribution to the classical question of the effects of political reform in terms of democracy and effectiveness (Scharpf 1999) in education and beyond.

Like in other sectors of society, education has become a field where political reform revitalizes questions regarding the democratic legitimacy of ongoing change (see Chapter 11, this volume). Many recent reforms in education have a built-in tendency to stress the improvement of the technical efficiency of the system. They shift attention from input legitimacy to output legitimacy with certain de-politicizing effects, especially when they are accompanied by a rhetoric that claims that 'There is no alternative' to the reforms at stake (Dale and Robertson 2007). Participation, transparency and accountability then become mere instrumental means to the need of the policy process to achieve its envisaged policy output. Obviously, this should challenge political science to bring back issues of power and interest, of political control and responsibility, and of the rights of citizenship in a more fundamental way.

Finally, the study of political reform in education has to offer major contributions to the crucial question 'Does reform matter?'. Many reforms in education carry with them explicit or implicit expectations about the quality of the system and more or less elaborate theories about the ways to improve this quality in a more substantial way than the current focus on technical efficiency seems to suggest. But does reform work? What are, for example, the consequences of the introduction of quasi-market instruments for access and equity in education? Do they lead to new forms of social exclusion and, if so, under which circumstances can such an effect be avoided? Does the introduction of competence measurements lead to political action that leads to a measurable increase in competence for students, or does it turn out to be without substantial consequences for school performance? Does the Bologna Process lead to increasing mutual recognition of degrees, international mobility of students and highly qualified professionals on the labour market? Or does it lead to a mere streamlining of educational processes in terms of cost efficiency? Findings on such questions about the substantial implications of political reform will also be of relevance for political practice and policy learning.

References

Ball, S. (ed.) (1998) 'Comparative perspectives in education policy', *Comparative Education*, 34, 2 (special issue).

216 *J. Enders*

Becher, T. (1989) *Academic Tribes and Territories: Intellectual Enquiry and the Cultures of Disciplines*, Milton Keynes: Open University Press.

Börzel, T.A. (1998) 'Organizing Babylon – on the different conceptions of policy networks', *Public Administration*, 76, 2: 253–273.

Bourdieu, P. (1988) *Homo Academicus*, Stanford: Stanford University Press.

Crossley, M. and Watson, K. (2004) *Comparative and International Research in Education: Globalization, Context and Difference*, London: Routledge/Falmer.

Dale, R. (2000) 'Globalization: a new world for comparative education?', in J. Schriewer (ed.) *Discourse Formation in Comparative Education*, Frankfurt a.M.: Peter Lang, 87–110.

Dale, R. and Robertson, S. (2007) 'New arenas of education governance – reflections and directions', in K. Martens, A. Rusconi and K. Leuze (eds) *New Arenas of Educational Governance. The Impact of International Organizations and Markets on Educational Policy Making*, Houndmills: Palgrave, 217–228.

de Boer, H., Enders, J. and Leisyte, l. (2007) 'Public sector reform in dutch higher education: the organizational transformation of the university', in *Public Administration*, 85, 1: 27–46.

Dill, D.D. (2005) 'The public good, the public interest, and public higher education', paper prepared for the conference 'Recapturing the "Public" in Public and Private Higher Education', City University of New York, 22 April 2005.

Dill, D.D., Teixeira, P., Jongbloed, B. and Amaral, A. (2004) 'Conclusion', in P. Texeira, B. Jongbloed, D.D. Dill and A. Amaral (eds) *Markets in Higher Education: Rhetoric or Reality?*, Dordrecht: Kluwer, 327–352.

Enders, J. (2004) 'Higher education, internationalisation, and the nation-state: recent developments and challenges for governance theory', *Higher Education*, 47, 3: 361–382.

Enders, J. and Fulton, O. (eds) (2002) *Higher Education in a Globalising World. International Trends and Mutual Observations*, Dordrecht: Kluwer.

Enders, J. and Jongbloed, B. (2007) 'The public, the private and the good in higher education and research: an introduction', in J. Enders and B. Jongbloed (eds) *Public-Private Dynamics in Higher Education. Expectations, Developments and Outcomes*, Bielefeld: Transcript, 9–38.

EURYDICE (2007) *School Autonomy in Europe. Policies and Measures*. Online, available at: www.eurydice.org/ressources/eurydice/pdf/0_integral/090EN.pdf.

Geuna, A., Salter, A.J. and Steinmueller, W.E. (eds) (2003) *Science and Innovation, Rethinking the Rationales for Funding and Governance*, Cheltenham: Edward Elgar.

Gibbons, M., Limoges, C., Nowotny, H., Schwartzman, S., Scott, P. and Trow, M. (1994) *The New Production of Knowledge*, London: Sage.

Goedegebuure, L.C.J., Kaiser, F., Maassen, P.A.M., Meek, V.L., van Vught, F.A. and de Weert, E. (eds) (1994) *Higher Education Policy: An International Comparative Perspective*, Oxford: Pergamon Press.

Hoyle, E. (2001) 'Teaching: status, prestige, and esteem', in *Educational Management, Administration and Leadership*, 29, 2: 139–152.

Jakobi, A.P. (2007) 'The knowledge society and global dynamics in education policy', *European Educational Research Journal*, 6, 1: 39–51.

Jones, K. and Bird, K. (2000) 'Partnership as strategy: public-private relations in education action zones', *British Educational Research Journal*, 26, 4: 491–505.

Martens, K. (2007) 'How to become an influential actor – the "Comparative Turn" in OECD education policy', in K. Martens, A. Rusconi and K. Leuze (eds) *New Arenas of*

Educational Governance. The Impact of International Organizations and Markets on Educational Policy Making, Houndmills: Palgrave Macmillan, 40–56.

Martens, K., Rusconi, A. and Leuze, K. (eds) (2007) *New Arenas of Educational Governance. The Impact of International Organizations and Markets on Educational Policy Making*, Houndmills: Palgrave Macmillan.

Meyer, J.W. and Ramirez, F.O. (2000) 'The world institutionalization of education', in J. Schriewer (ed.) *Discourse Formation in Comparative Education*, Frankfurt a.M.: Peter Lang, 111–132.

Neave, G. (1989) 'On the cultivation of quality, efficiency and enterprise: an overview of recent trends in higher education in Western Europe, 1968–1988', *European Journal of Education*, 23, 1/2: 7–23.

—— (1998) 'The evaluative state reconsidered', *European Journal of Education*, 33, 3: 265–284.

Neave, G. and van Vught, F. (eds) (1991) *Prometheus Bound: The Changing Relationship Between Government and Higher Education in Western Europe*, Oxford: Pergamon.

Raab, C.D. (1992) 'Taking networks seriously: education policy in Britain', *European Journal of Political Research*, 21, 1–2: 69–90.

Scharpf, F. (1999) *Governing in Europe: Effective and Democratic?*, Oxford: Oxford University Press.

Schriewer, J. (ed.) (2000) *Discourse Formation in Comparative Education*, Frankfurt a.M.: Peter Lang.

Teixeira, P., Jongbloed, B., Dill, D.D. and Amaral, A. (eds) (2004) *Markets in Higher Education: Rhetoric or Reality?*, Dordrecht: Kluwer.

Thatcher, M. (1998) 'The development of policy network analysis. From modest origins to overarching frameworks', *Journal of Theoretical Politics*, 10, 4: 389–416.

UNESCO (2004) 'Education Ministers speak out'. Online, available at: http://portal. unesco.org/education/en/ev.php-URL_ID=27722&URL_DO=DO_TOPIC&URL_SECTION=201.html.

Witte, J. (2006) *Change of Degrees and Degrees of Change. Comparing Adaptations of European Higher Education Systems in the Context of the Bologna Process*, Enschede: CHEPS.

Wittrock, B. (1993) 'The modern university: the three transformations', in S. Rothblatt and B. Wittrock (eds) *The European and American University since 1800*, Cambridge: Cambridge University Press, 298–314.

14 Conclusion

Education policy, political science and the state in transition

Anja P. Jakobi, Kerstin Martens and
Klaus Dieter Wolf

'Education, education, education' has been Tony Blair's mantra during his time as British Prime Minister (Wolf 2002). As the different contributions in this volume show, he was by far not the only leading politician determined to reform the education system for more effective spending, more equal access, for improving outcomes or for other reasons. In recent years, education has moved centre-stage in politics, being conceived as means for individual and collective development, employability and the transition to the knowledge society. In particular the latter has been a vision that triggered educational reform across the world, unifying industrialized as well as developing countries in striving to improve educational outcomes (Jakobi 2007).

Whether or not the political turn to education will ultimately fulfil the promises made by its proponents is an important empirical question for future research. As we pointed out in Chapter 1, education policy as a field of political science has been under-researched despite its growing significance on the political agendas worldwide. Our intention with this book is to raise the awareness for education policy among political scientists and to demonstrate that the discipline as a whole, as well as its different sub-disciplines, has much to offer and that we can gain a lot by analysing this field. The results contained in the different chapters of this volume encourage the continuation of these efforts.

The governance perspective chosen in this study with its focus on political change in the field of education made the recent emergence of new actors and instruments particularly visible. Identifying trends towards privatization and changed state governance, the chapters on comparative education policy by Klitgaard, Dobbins and Hudson (Chapters 2, 3 and 4) show that the implementation of market-based elements in schools or higher education is a widespread phenomenon. But their studies also indicate that these processes neither follow a uniform pattern of adapting to new political and economic conditions nor do they imply a general retreat of the state. Klitgaard's analysis of reform developments in the United States and Sweden illustrates the important impact of political institutions and the leverage they give to veto players when the adoption of specific education policies is at stake. As Dobbins shows in his analysis of the reforms of formerly state-centred education systems, policy convergence is not an automatic reflex. Education reforms come about in different shapes and sizes depending on country-specific differences, such as historical legacies, the influence of policy entrepreneurship and executive leadership. Hudson's analysis of the changes in the education systems of some northern European states proves that the state has still not given up control or responsibility for education. Overall, even in times of new governance instruments and manifold political change, the state in general and public actors' choices in particular are still an important factor for shaping the education policy agendas and outcomes of education reform processes.

The contributions of Toens and Ahonen, as well as Grimaldi and Serpieri on public policy and administration (Chapters 5, 6 and 7), shed light on the processes and causal mechanisms that accompany political change towards new forms of governance. In particular, their studies demonstrate how reforms of existing structures may lead to unintended consequences for the state and its role in education policy. Toens, in Chapter 5, shows that the process of internationalizing higher education offered a window of opportunity. The German system originally did not enable private actors to enter higher education policy, but the reforms provided them with a new playing field in which the role of the state as only one among other players was consolidated. The introduction of new administrative forms of government, as presented by Grimaldi and Serpieri in their case study of an Italian region, demonstrates how the establishment of such structures actually provides space for leadership and policy entrepreneurs in this process. The attempts at different retrenchment processes as described by Ahonen (Chapter 7) reflect how bounded rationality may be at work in education policy-making, even in the highly esteemed Finnish education system that is famous for its school policies.

A new set of actors in policy-making has also been established in the course of political internationalization processes, of which education policy has become an important and integral part in recent years. As the chapters of Verger, de Ruiter and Nagel (Chapters 8, 9 and 10) have shown, national education politics cannot be adequately examined anymore without taking into account their embeddedness in multi-level policy-making settings. Verger exemplifies this interplay between actors and institutions at the national and the international level of policy-making by showing how national preferences also shape actor participation in generating positions towards the international sphere, in his case the GATS agreement. De Ruiter demonstrates that national governments opt for the European level, despite strong incentives for keeping education within national responsibility. Nagel's analysis shows how the changing role of the state as only one among other actors in newly emerging educational governance arrangements finds its manifestation in new transnational governance networks.

Finally, the governance perspective does not only facilitate new studies in the field of education that support assumptions about general trends towards changing modes of governance; these observations also underline the need to extend our approach to the study of normative reflections about their impact and desirability. If education policy is increasingly shaped and implemented by a new interplay among a new set of actors, what do these new constellations mean for the role of the state in this policy field (and beyond) in normative terms? This extension to normative considerations must by necessity also imply a critical self-reflection about the often reductionist preoccupation of governance studies which seem to be primarily interested in policy outcomes in terms of effectiveness. Employing the perspective of normative political theory in his study of changing modes of governance in higher education, Wolf's contribution (Chapter 11) reminds the discipline not to neglect this valuable tool when moving within the governance paradigm. His account of how the new forms of governance – although often justified as means to increase autonomy and self-determination – have in fact restricted stakeholder participation as well as the influence of democratically legitimated institutions within and beyond the universities underlines the general usefulness of such a critical perspective for the analysis of processes of changing modes of governance. Driven by similar concerns about the present state and the perspectives of political science, Berndtson's study of the academic discipline (Chapter 12) shows how education reforms shaped the development of political science as an academic discipline. His analysis raises some concern as to what extent its richness and breadth can be maintained under the streamlining pressures which are exerted on it, notably by the trend towards reforming higher education according to international standard curricula. As he outlines, this may have important consequences for scholars' overall notion of the political, and may thus lead to an impoverishment rather than progressive enhancement of the discipline.

In brief, education has been a regular subject of reform across the world, but research on education policy from a political science perspective is still in its infancy. To show the potential insights to be gained from the combination of political science and education policy, this concluding chapter will first focus on what political science can contribute to the analysis of education policy – more specifically: 'What do we know more about education policy when we analyse it from a governance perspective?' Second, we will focus on how the subject can enrich the discipline by reversing the first question to 'What do we know more about politics after having analysed education policy?' Finally, based on these findings, as well as from a general perspective on research on education policy, we will outline future areas of research that seem to be in particular fruitful for further inquiry.

Education policy from a political science perspective

What are the discipline's contributions to the knowledge about education? In this volume, we applied the different sub-disciplines of political science to clarify various aspects of current education policy development, in the same manner they usually structure political science research.

Comparative politics shed light on the different settings that are realized within the states, how they differ and what the effects of such differences are. As the contributions from this perspective show, existing institutions and historical paths play a major role in the implementation of new governance instruments.

So even in times of worldwide talk about globalization, global policy-making and trends towards convergence, the state and its specific history remain important and decisive.

Public policy and administration examined how governance changes, such as new settings or actors, are incorporated into the existing political system. New modes of governance, as these contributions illustrate, can cause severe implementation problems. They touch upon the relation of the state to surrounding stakeholders. New governance instruments that include additional stakeholders can facilitate the emergence of new sets of powerful actors, turning formerly excluded or marginalized groups to very central players. However, success is by no means guaranteed, since powerful coalitions can create effective obstacles to policy change. There is thus no inherent logic to a governance instrument with regard to successful implementation.

The undiminished relevance of domestic factors is also underlined by examining the emerging multi-level game in education policy from the perspective of *International Relations*. Although the growing importance of educational policies generated and agreed upon at the international level cannot be denied, educational programmes agreed upon at this level may follow very different paths when entering the domestic realm. In any case, they do not automatically trigger changes at the level of the nation state. Even when confronted with rather uniform goals, as in the case of GATS or the OMC, states have a variety of options, according to specific political ideologies but also depending on domestic actors' strategic choices. The contributions to this volume clearly show how these differences at the domestic level can operate: bounded rationality may hamper decisions on educational reforms and the choice of specific governance instruments strongly depends on the political system, such as veto-points or the actors interests in a multi-level setting, to name just some examples.

Finally, *normative political theory* makes visible deficits of new modes of educational governance which are usually overlooked by practitioners who are primarily interested in the output side of governance processes. This reminds us of the fact that the state is – and should be – responsible for more than effective problem-solving in the field of education. Even if the scene may be enriched by additional and increasingly important non-state actors, the state remains the only institution which can effectively guarantee that the formulation and implementation of goals in education policy remain in accordance with the demands of the self-determination of all addressees.

Moreover, a reflection on the discipline of political science in the context of education reforms, as well as on its relation to the neighbouring disciplines, sheds light on possible blindspots: As political scientists, we are often directly concerned by reforms in education policy in what we teach, whom we teach and what we need to consider important. Since the basis of democracy is an informed citizen, the task for political science in informing citizens is far from easy, and education policy reforms may have an important impact on the younger generation and the future political system.

In sum, unlike other disciplines dealing with education, such as education science, sociology and economics, political science is obviously the discipline that is mainly and primarily focused on 'the political' in education policy, comprehensively understood as the analysis of policy, politics and polity. Compared to education science this means that our interest in the governance of education should not primarily be policy oriented with only practical aims such as creating better educational conditions, to enable teacher involvement or the like. It should also reflect on educational policy changes at the concrete institutional and ideological level in terms of the more general trends and patterns of politics and policy-making and their impact on the political system. Thus our research interests are complementary with those of educational sociology which is mainly interested in the effects of educational institutions over the life-course and the consequences of lower or higher educational achievements for the coherence or polarization of a society. Obviously, we also do not want to interfere with economists who mainly analyse the expected outcomes of educational reform and regard educational reforms as a function of expected public revenue. Nonetheless, describing these complementarities and adding the contributions of political science to the existing body of research on education carried out by other disciplines definitely does not mean that all research problems will automatically be tackled. Compared to other disciplines, political science is a 'latecomer' which still has to establish a research agenda of its own in the field of education, a neglect that – as we see it – can also be taken as a chance and may influence the progress of the discipline itself.

Political science, governance and education policy

We used the governance paradigm as the substantial focus and common starting point for all contributors to this volume. It was intentionally chosen to link the findings of the different chapters to current debates in political science, in particular about the future of the state. By applying a governance perspective we wanted to examine the extent to which political steering in the field of education is actually shifting away from the traditional national constellation in which the state is regarded as the main actor in education policy. Thus, we wanted to examine how education policy-making has moved from public to private governance and from local or national to international, transnational and supranational governance. Researching education policy from the different perspectives has provided us with a broad and detailed picture of current trends in the making of public policy: new forms of decision-making are being introduced, as in the case of German curricular reform (Chapter 5, this volume) or Italian regional education conferences (Chapter 6, this volume). International actors and institutional settings – such as the EU or the WTO – are becoming more important as a new level of education regulation (Chapter 8, this volume). Further, market instruments – like vouchers or calculations of school capacities (Chapter 7, this volume) – are being introduced. Goals such as the autonomy of institutions or the international compatibility of curricula have moved centre-stage in education policy. But even given these exemplary changes, government is far from becoming unimportant, and a retreat of the state is not in sight.

From a broader perspective, the findings in this volume show that politics play a major part in educational reform and that outcomes certainly cannot be sufficiently explained by the demands created by the problems to be solved. Nor can long-term policy traditions tell us much about the actual treatment of education in a given political system: a liberal welfare regime does not necessarily lead to the implementation of market-oriented approaches, while a social-democratic regime does not necessarily avoid instruments of individual choice when veto players enter the game (Chapter 2, this volume). Actors' choices have also been relevant for the development of education in transition countries: although Central and Eastern European countries share a history of strong state control, they only partially moved in the same direction after being exposed to Western European models and policy goals. Important causes for the different directions of change were administrative and political leadership, as well as incentives given to the groups concerned (Chapter 3, this volume). All these findings indeed leave little room for functionalist explanations that contend that education reforms are mainly triggered by 'objective' necessities.

The political component is visible, traceable and important for the outcome of education reforms: Conditions such as globalization and economic competition may deliver a good rationale for education policy reform, but whether economic reasoning ultimately succeeds depends on the advocacy groups that draw attention to such arguments and on whether and how they are preferred over others. One may welcome or regret this process, but the success of any ideational framework for policy reforms is dependent on political processes. The same is true for the choice of instruments applied, for example whether or not a state decides to switch from process control to output based modes of governance. It is the task of political science to identify such elements of the current wave of educational reform not only as being politically shaped, but also as being shaped in a manner that is typical of other policy fields: agenda-setting procedures, bounded rationality, important veto players and non-state actors, multi-level games, the intention to reduce costs and much more.

Education is a field where governance studies seem particularly promising, given the traditionally strong governmental interest and instruments applied, as well as the number of reforms currently carried out in this policy field. As the contributions of this volume clearly show, the governance perspective can be linked to international issues, for instance whether or not specific problems should be dealt with at the European level (Chapter 9, this volume); but it can also relate to the national level (Chapter 4, this volume), the regional level (Chapter 6, this volume) or even the level of sub-systems like the university system (Chapter 3, this volume). Because of its openness – which could also be subject of criticism – this concept offers new perspectives for broader analysis: The changing role of the state may not only be reflected in changing instruments at the domestic level, but also in the switch from one level to the other. Comparing governance activities at the national level with those at the international or sub-national level could reveal more closely where the state actually still comes in and where it does not, and whether or not a retreat at one level follows intensified engagement at others, comparable to a zero-sum game. Moreover, new networks and new ways of decision-making can also supplement formerly purely national policy processes, so that a change in the modes of governance does not necessarily signify a zero-sum game in terms of influence (Chapter 10, this volume).

Moreover, studying education policy also shows that even if an issue is salient and broadly discussed, intended changes do not necessarily follow. Wolf's example of a newly autonomous university that is not capable of selecting its rector anymore is only one example where the consequences of reforms did not meet the expectations raised in the beginning. Education is a central cultural institution in modern society (Meyer and Ramirez 2003; Meyer *et al.* 1997), and the political debate reflects this by giving it high priority. Policy outcomes may be unexpected or even contradictory to original intentions. Comparing these dynamics to policy fields that are different in their saliency could shed more light on whether the importance of a political issue can – under some conditions – have adverse effects on its implementation.

Bringing together the findings of this volume with regard to the supposed shift from government to governance, we can confirm the general trend of statehood in transition. The new, but still important role of the state is a finding that becomes particularly obvious when analysing education policy from a governance perspective. The state is transforming, neither completely retreating, nor remaining what it was. All contributions have shown that the transformation from hierarchical control-and-command steering by the state to new modes of governance is indeed particularly striking in the case of education, precisely because this field has previously been so strongly linked to the state. Nonetheless, the state is not rendered unimportant, but is changing its role and instruments, leaving space for other actors, but also conquering new political arenas.

Perspectives for further research

As an issue of worldwide political interest – although often not of political expenditure – education proves to be a particular enlightening field of studies on contemporary statehood. The volume has shown how the role of the state is being supplemented by private and international actors, but also how basic rules of politics, such as implementation difficulties, negotiations of interests and the like, are still in place. In this volume, we have chosen the governance perspective among the different possible approaches that political scientists could use as a starting point for the study of education as a policy field. However, this choice does not mean that political science is bound to this approach of analysing education policy and could not solve puzzles by using other perspectives than ours. It is an interesting question for comparative research, why and how a topic such as education either becomes a 'hot' issue or is neglected. What are the factors that influence the perception of policy-makers, and how far do countries differ in that respect? Does the public debate on education actually influence public investment, or is it stimulating increased private contribution? Based on the concepts we deal with in this volume and elaborating on observations made in the different chapters, we expect the following fields to be particularly fruitful for further research: while exploring them, we put an emphasis both on issues that are closely linked to a state in transition, as well as on those that deal with other subjects.

The internationalization of education

Education is not only facing the challenges of marketization but also of internationalization. This volume has already sketched the role of GATS, the EU and other international forums. Research on these aspects, however, has only recently begun (see Jakobi 2009; Hartmann 2006; Martens and Wolf 2006), and there are still many questions to be solved, for example, why and how far countries open or close the educational sector in the GATS, or whether, why and how the EU is expanding its authority in education. Linked to these developments is a range of questions concerning how international or transnational networks form, which rules are applied therein, and how decisions are made. The new multi-level setting of education is thus also expanding the polity of educational policy-making beyond the nation state. Moreover, given the increasing number of foreign students in countries across the world – constituting the internationalization of education on a micro-level – research on education policy could also be linked to migration issues.

Path-dependence and changes of paths

Given the current wave of reforms, education policy can serve as a fruitful field for studying path dependencies and changes of paths: with the emphasis on educational outcomes, the United States has witnessed a strong increase of political activities in education at the federal level (Davies 2007; McGuinn 2006), while Germany, whose outcomes are not much better, has decided to keep the political responsibility for education at the level of the states. Facing the same goals and critiques, one country increasingly is centralizing education policy while the other is decentralizing. Why and how could that happen, and what is the more promising strategy? Historical institutionalism, for example, could contribute to an enhanced understanding of such development.

New actors and actors' networks

Given the fact that the state is redefining its role in education policy, other players are now of increasing interest. This pertains, in particular, to non-state actors who are shaping and implementing education policies. As shown in this volume, their activities can affect policy outcomes. The role of non-state actors thus needs to be studied more closely, including not only unions or traditional non-governmental organizations, but also the education industry, professional experts, business and employers. Additionally, since education policy faces many comparable changes across the world, the field also provides a good starting point for research on policy networks and their role in diffusing education reforms. While the role of networks in education politics and the importance of policy entrepreneurs has been analysed, the role of networks in diffusing political aims has attracted little research so far.

Administrative changes due to reforms

The political attention on reforming education tends to focus on educational outcomes, thus: learning results. By doing so, the question of how these outcomes are produced institutionally is likely to be neglected. It is not only the teacher that determines learning, but also a series of administrative entities from the national, to the regional, local and institutional level. If governance changes, these administrative entities have to change, too, and it would be worth looking closely at what happens inside these administrations – or what does not. Grimaldi and Serpieri have shown intended and unintended consequences of educational reform in the regional and local administration. Further areas for the evaluation of administrative changes could be ministries, schools, universities or the like. This area of research also cuts across the dimension of internationalization in education: when policy-making takes place beyond the nation state, this may well influence the national administration which used to be the main actor, and the question arises how the administration develops in this context. Does it open up to this sphere easily and can it work with international counterparts immediately? How do administrations of specific ministries that used to be focused on domestic activities adapt to an international environment? Whether at the international, national or sub-national level, it is only reasonable to guess that the changed politics of education also result in changed practices in administrative institutions. These questions are not only interesting for researchers of education policy administration, but also those concerned with effective policy implementation and those who are interested in intended and unintended consequences of reforms. Moreover, specific techniques to administer education may prove to be a forerunner for other policy areas: the method of evaluating education publicly and internationally can also be applied to evaluating healthcare, pension systems and the like, so that these developments in education policy may also signify an upcoming trend in other policy fields.

Normative questions

Wolf (Chapter 11, this volume) has reminded us that analyses of governance tend to ignore normative issues, a somewhat disturbing fact given the obvious necessity to link governmental activity – or non-activity – to questions of legitimacy. Obviously, while political science has increasingly turned to positivist theorizing, a more normative approach to governance questions needs to be strengthened. It could be based, for example, on criteria of legitimate state intervention, and as such it could enrich not only research but also policy-making. It should, however, also find solutions to conceptual challenges, such as developing normative criteria for the evaluation of the new public–private or private–private governance arrangements to which the existing state-oriented categories cannot be applied. It could offer a basis for the debate about standards of appropriateness from which institutional solutions that guarantee equal participation, or concrete educational reform policies could be derived. For example which groups of pupils should policy-makers focus on – those with difficulties in keeping pace in school or those who are considered to have high potential? Given the fact that even the wealthiest states will not spend sufficient resources to take care of both groups (not to mention the mass of pupils between these poles), this is not a trivial question, and political science could profit from addressing it.

Economization and education

The book outlined some, but not all, trends towards privatization in education. Education faces not only new governance forms in schools or higher education institutions. There is also an increasing global market of education in which not only individual clients select individual companies, but also countries position themselves as part of a global business and initiate policies which support this development (compare Martens and Starke 2008). But it is still largely unclear whether countries will react to this and, if so, in what manner. The shift in education towards a commodity not only has an impact on the emerging market itself, but also raises the question how far the state can or should maintain some responsibility for the content and quality of education. More specifically, one could also address the role that private providers actually play and how far they can substitute or complement state activities.

Relation of education to other policy fields

Since education policy has only rarely been researched in political science, its linkage to other fields is still underdeveloped. Resulting from the central importance of education in modern society (Meyer and Ramirez 2003; Jakobi 2009), we can expect it to be frequently used as an instrument for achieving different political aims. We know about the links between education and the labour market, the economy, social policy and other areas, but it is not yet clear how the linkages between these fields have changed over the years, and what the driving forces for this development are. Labour-market policies, for example, have increasingly drawn on education as a means for qualifying a de-skilled labour force (OECD 1995), and the enhancement of qualifications is often seen as the more intelligent strategy compared to the redistribution of income towards the unemployed, as the discussions on workfare show. Researching education policy and its links to other fields could also imply that the spectrum of social policy research is broadening. Education policy has not been included in Esping-Anderson's (1990) typology of welfare states, in which the process of de-commodification was the indicator to determine regime types. Current education policy, in particular when focusing on active labour-market policies, seem to 're-commodify', and could therefore reveal much about social policy development in general. Moreover, education has always been a means for realizing specific social policy goals, such as health, children rights and so forth (see Kaufmann 2002). State activity in education has shifted from processes to outcomes (see Chapters 3 and 4, this volume). 'Product evaluation' and quality control have become standard procedures in education. A systematic comparative assessment of this trend across policy fields would be interesting: can the same shift also be observed in other areas? As Klitgaard (Chapter 2) shows, healthcare and education underwent similar developments in the United States and Sweden, which support his argument on veto-players. Yet whether this holds true for other areas of social policies – such as pensions – has still to be examined. The systematic linkages and possible changes over time, however, still remain a subject of further research.

In sum, a more systematic inclusion of education policy in mainstream political science thus bears much potential for creating new research questions, new linkages among the different research fields and for new insights. Looking back and looking ahead, political science has still much to do to enlighten us about education policy. This volume is only one step forward.

References

Davies, G. (2007) *See Government Grow*, Lawrence: University Press of Kansas.
Esping-Andersen, G. (1990) *The Three Worlds of Welfare Capitalism*, Princeton: Princeton University Press.
Hartmann, E. (2006) *Konturen postnationaler Staatlichkeit. Interdependenz zwischen GATS und UNESCO beim Aufbau eines globalen Arbeitsmarktregimes*, Dissertation, University of Kassel.
Jakobi, A.P. (2007) 'The knowledge society and global dynamics in education policy', *European Educational Research Journal*, 6: 39–51.
Jakobi, A.P. (2009) *International Organizations and Lifelong Learning. From Agenda-Setting to Policy Diffusion*, Houndmills: Palgrave (in press).
Kaufmann, F.-X. (2002) *Sozialpolitik und Sozialstaat: Soziologische Analysen*, Opladen: Leske and Budrich.
McGuinn, P. (2006) *No Child Left Behind and the Transformation of Federal Education Policy, 1965–2005*, Lawrence: University Press of Kansas.
Martens, K. and Starke, P. (2008) 'Small country, big business? New Zealand as an education exporter', *Comparative Education*, 44, 1: S.3–19.
Martens, K. and Wolf, K.D. (2006) 'Paradoxien der Neuen Staatsräson – Die Internationalisierung der Bildungspolitik in der EU und der OECD,' *Zeitschrift für Internationale Beziehungen*, 13, 2: S.145–176.
Meyer, J.W. and Ramirez, F.O. (2003) 'The world institutionalization of education', in J. Schriever (ed.) *Discourse Formation in Comparative Education*, 2nd edn, Frankfurt/Main: Peter Lang, 111–132.

Meyer, J.W., Boli, J., Thomas, G.M. and Ramirez, F.O. (1997) 'World society and the nation-state', *American Journal of Sociology*, 103: 144–181.

OECD (1995) *The OECD Jobs Study. Implementing the Strategy*, Paris: OECD.

Wolf, A. (2002) *Does Education really matter? Myths about Education and Economic Growth*, London: Penguin.

Index